PICTURING
THE BORDER

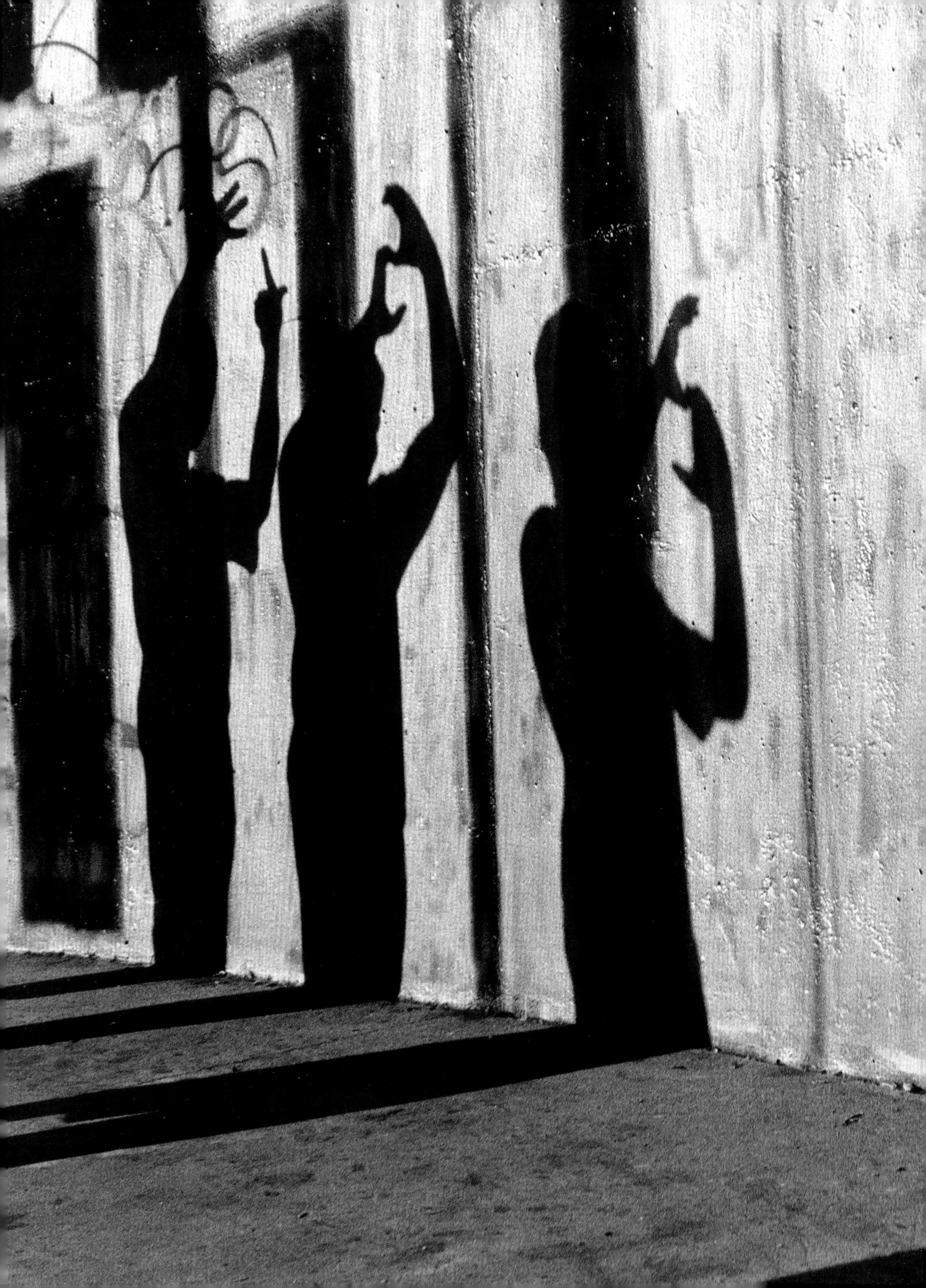

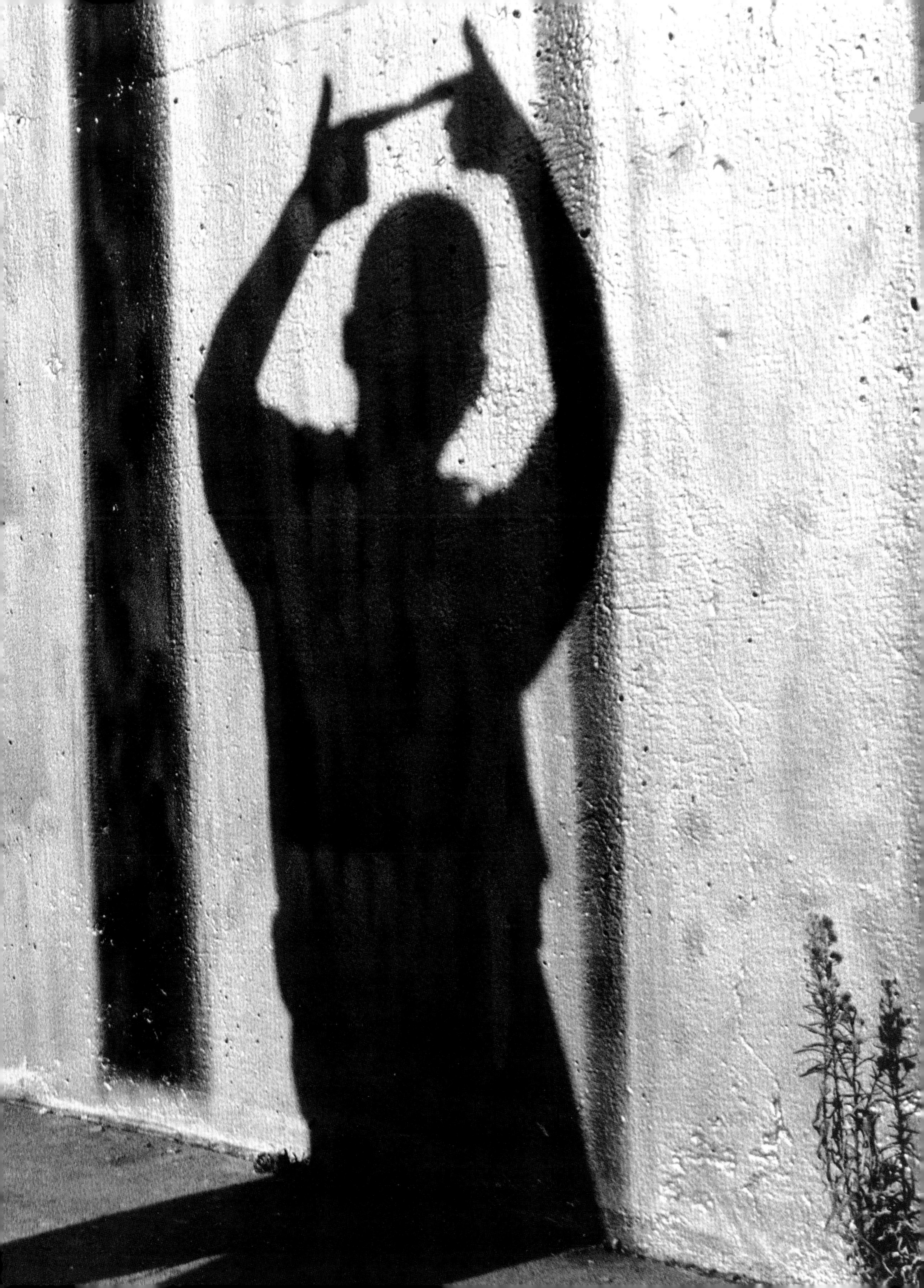

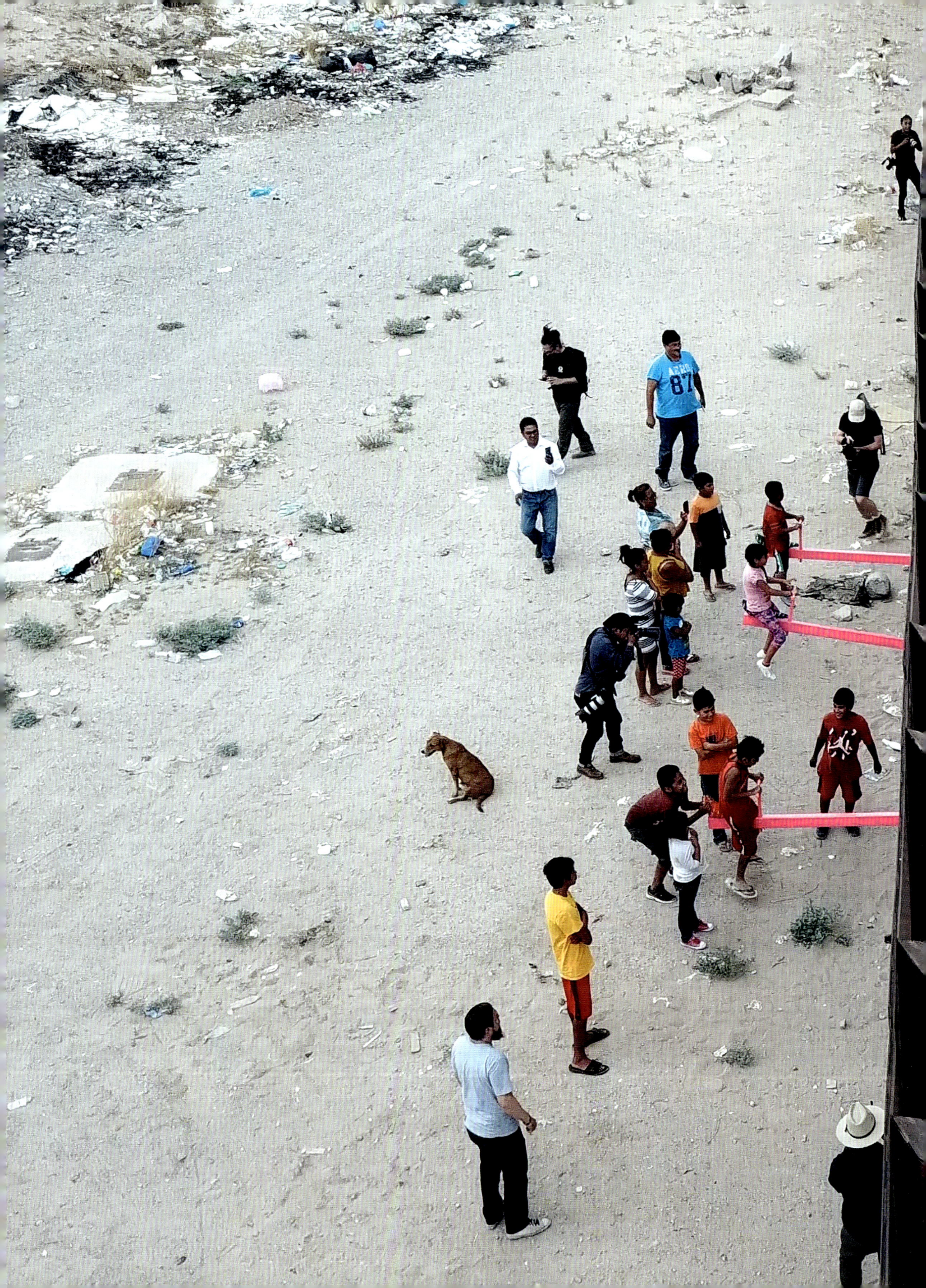

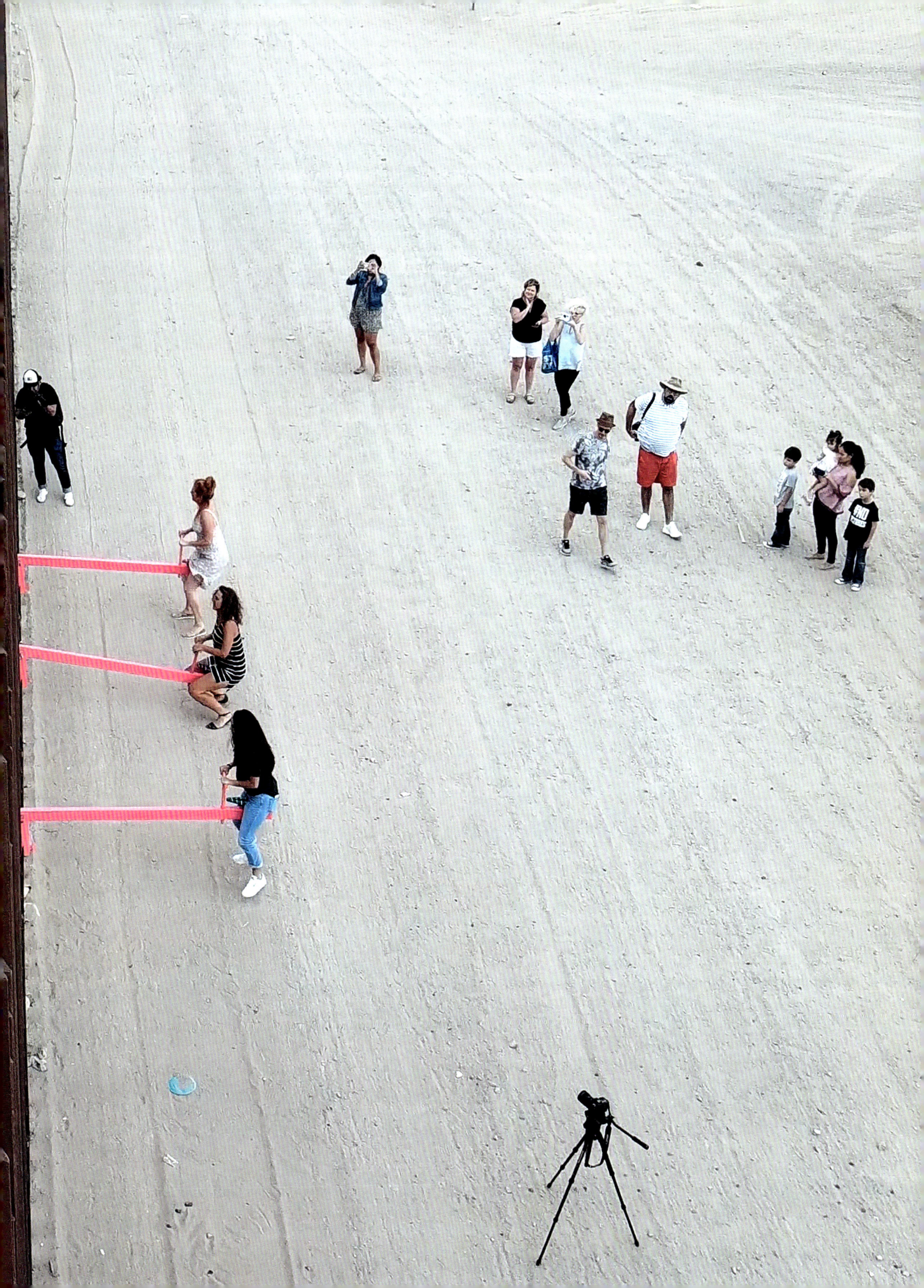

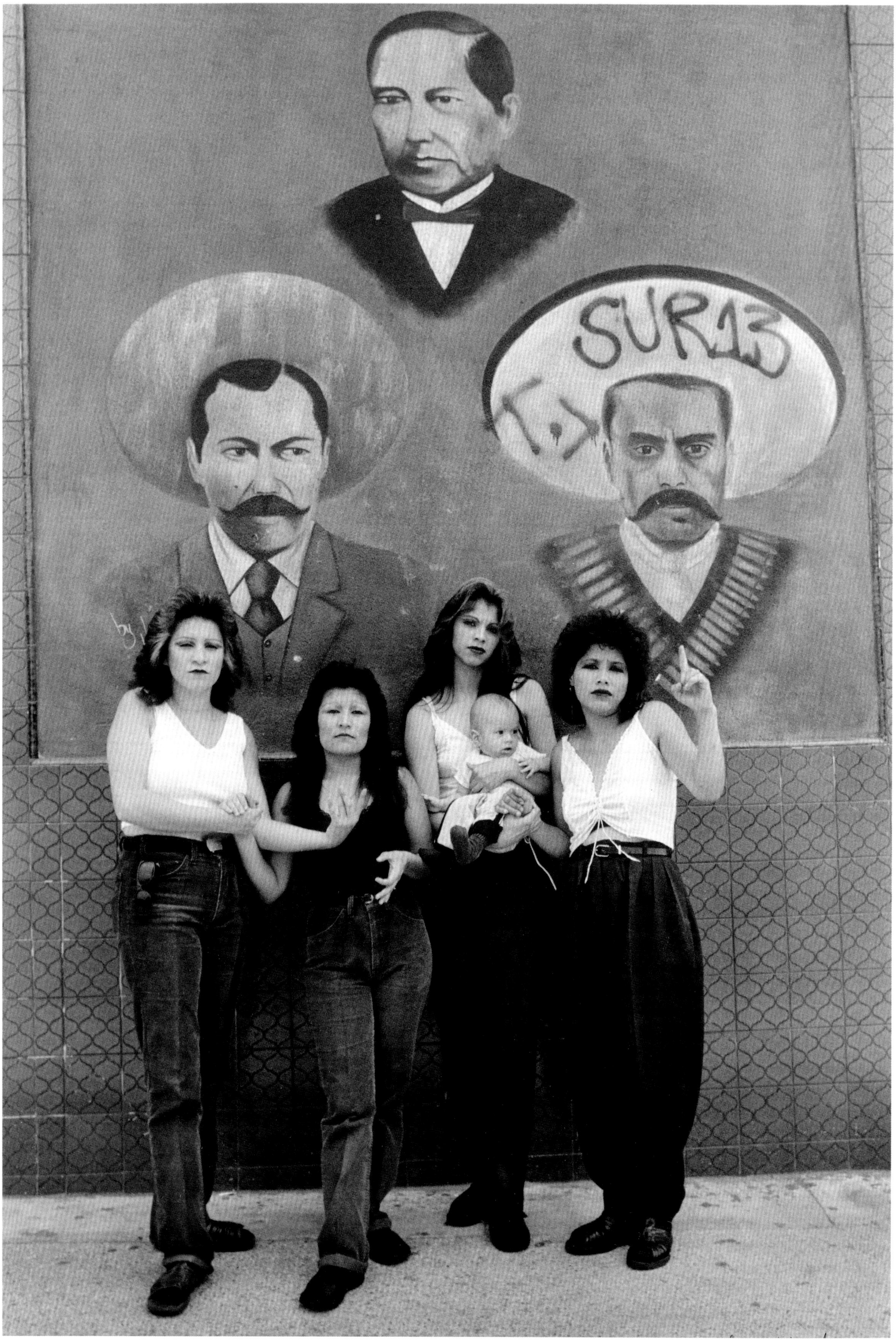
SUR13

Nadiah Rivera Fellah

PICTURING THE BORDER

The Cleveland Museum of Art

Distributed by Yale University Press, New Haven and London

THIS PUBLICATION IS MADE POSSIBLE IN PART BY THE ANDREW W. MELLON FOUNDATION

Published on the occasion of the exhibition *Picturing the Border*, on view at the Cleveland Museum of Art from July 21, 2024, to January 5, 2025.

Principal annual support is provided by Michael Frank and the late Pat Snyder, the Kelvin and Eleanor Smith Foundation, the John and Jeanette Walton Exhibition Fund, and Margaret and Loyal Wilson. Generous annual support is provided by an anonymous supporter, the late Dick Blum and Harriet Warm, Gary and Katy Brahler, Cynthia and Dale Brogan, Dr. Ben and Julia Brouhard, Brenda and Marshall Brown, Richard and Dian Disantis, the Jeffery Wallace Ellis Trust in memory of Lloyd H. Ellis Jr., Leigh and Andy Fabens, the Frankino-Dodero Family Fund for Exhibitions Endowment, Florence Kahane Goodman, Janice Hammond and Edward Hemmelgarn, Marta Jack and the late Donald M. Jack Jr., Carl T. Jagatich, Eva and Rudolf Linnebach, William S. and Margaret F. Lipscomb, Bill and Joyce Litzler, the Roy Minoff Family Fund, Lu Anne and the late Carl Morrison, Jeffrey Mostade and Eric Nilson and Varun Shetty, Tim O'Brien and Breck Platner, William J. and Katherine T. O'Neill, Michael and Cindy Resch, Betty T. and David M. Schneider, Paula and Eugene Stevens, the Womens Council of the Cleveland Museum of Art, and Claudia Woods and David Osage.

The Cleveland Museum of Art is funded in part by residents of Cuyahoga County through a public grant from Cuyahoga Arts & Culture.

This exhibition was supported in part by the Ohio Arts Council, which receives support from the State of Ohio and the National Endowment for the Arts.

Images of the works of art in the exhibition were provided by the lenders, unless otherwise noted.

Objects in the collection of the Cleveland Museum of Art were photographed by museum photographers Howard Agriesti, David Brichford, and Gary Kirchenbauer. James Kohler prepared the digital files. The museum holds copyright to its images. When known, other copyright holders and photographers are acknowledged in the credits.

Designed by Tom Barnard, Director of Publications

Rachel Beamer, Publication Project Manager

Sarah Peroli, Exhibition Project Manager

Edited and indexed by Jane Friedman

Proofread by Kathleen Mills

Map designed by Diana Peraita

Color management by Maurizio Brivio

Printed and bound by SYL L'Art Gràfic Premium, S.L. in Barcelona, Spain

Library of Congress Control Number: 2024932764

ISBN: 978-0-300-27876-7

NOTES TO THE READER

All measurements are in centimeters; height precedes width precedes depth. Catalogue numbers appear in [brackets].

The Cleveland Museum of Art
11150 East Boulevard
Cleveland, OH 44106-1797
www.clevelandart.org

Distributed by
Yale University Press
302 Temple Street
P.O. Box 209040
New Haven, CT 06520-9040
www.yalebooks.com/art

Cover: *La Reina—16 de Septiembre* [17]. Ricardo Valverde. Collection of Esperanza Valverde and Christopher J. Valverde, Ricardo Valverde Estate. © Esperanza Valverde and Christopher Jude Valverde

pages 2–3: *Cholos, Harpys, East L.A.* [detail, 37]. Graciela Iturbide. The J. Paul Getty Museum, Los Angeles, 2007.65.4. © Graciela Iturbide

pages 4–5: *Teeter-Totter Wall* [6]. Ronald Rael and Virginia San Fratello with Colectivo Chopeke. Photo: Ronald Rael

page 6: *Cholos, White Fence, East Los Angeles* [35]. Graciela Iturbide. The J. Paul Getty Museum, Los Angeles, 2017.41. © Graciela Iturbide

page 10: *Grammar of Gates / Gramática de las puertas* [4] . Miguel Fernández de Castro. Courtesy of the artist. © Miguel Fernández de Castro

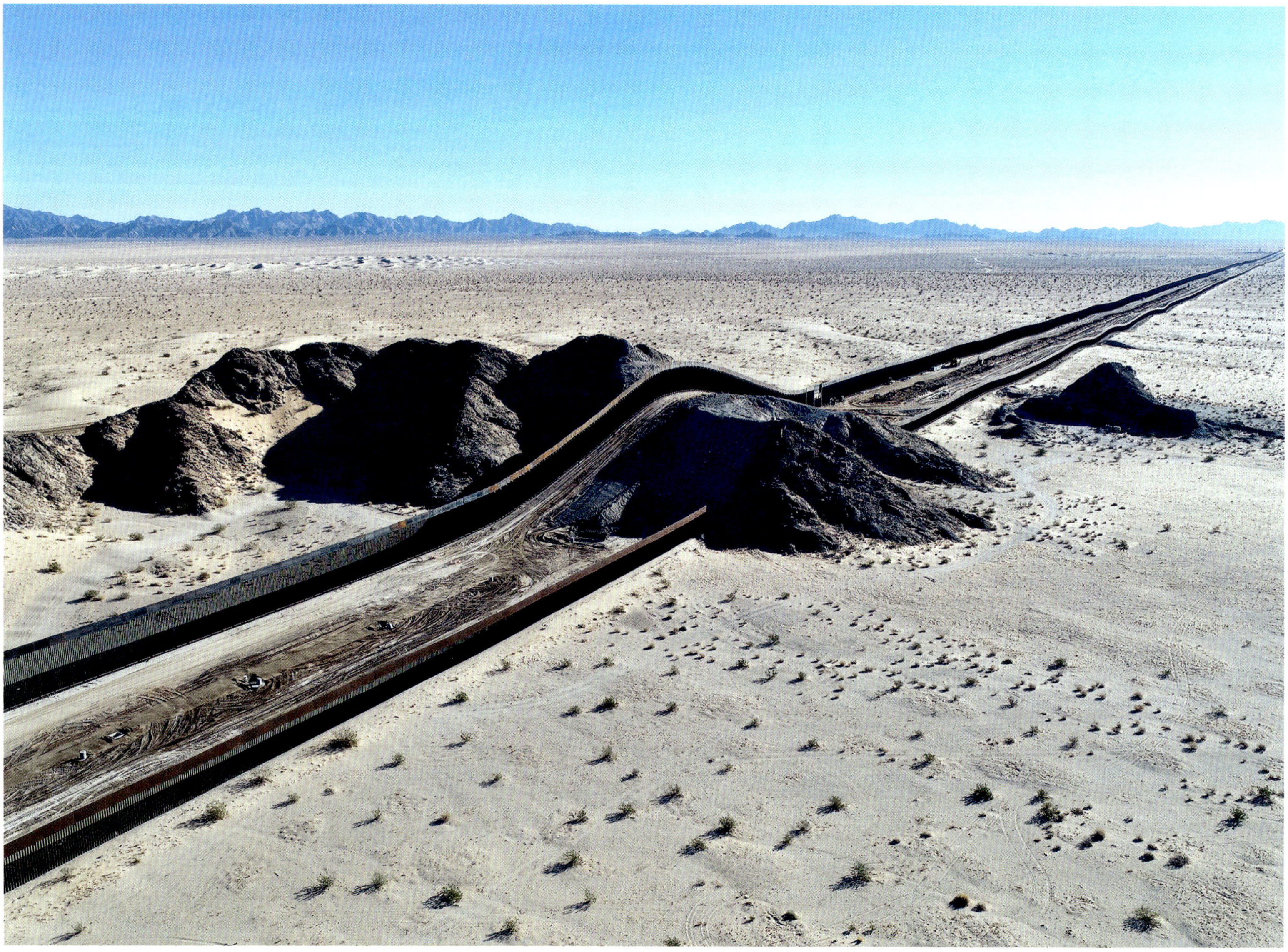

DIRECTOR'S FOREWORD

Picturing the Border features photographs of the US-Mexico borderlands from the 1970s to the present taken by border residents as well as by outsiders. The earliest images in the exhibition form an origin story for the topicality of the US-Mexico border at the present moment and demonstrate that issues related to the border have been a critical point of inquiry for artists since the 1970s.

Although Cleveland is far from the country's southern border, stories of global migration are woven into the very fabric of the encyclopedic collection at the Cleveland Museum of Art as well as its community and members throughout Northeast Ohio. *Picturing the Border* gives a human face to these stories and brings to life the various threads that stitch together an ever-growing understanding of, and empathy for, the migrant experience.

Nadiah Rivera Fellah, curator of contemporary art, has brought to light a range of migration narratives, presenting the work of photographers from both sides of the border and, notably, those who themselves call the borderlands home. We are proud that the exhibition is accompanied by an important scholarly publication that features new insights on the subject of Latinx photography and on the history of the US-Mexico border. *Picturing the Border* has also prompted the opportunity to expand our permanent collection in this area, precipitating recent acquisitions by artist Laura Aguilar and the donation of an important work by Ada Trillo, who witnessed firsthand the perilous and extensive journey migrants have undertaken from Central America to the United States.

I offer my heartfelt thanks to the artists in this show and the visions of the border they have shared with all of us. In addition, I want to acknowledge the generosity of the various lenders: the Laura Aguilar Trust; the Center for Creative Photography, University of Arizona; Teddy Cruz and Fonna Forman; Miguel Fernández de Castro; the J. Paul Getty Museum, Los Angeles; Susan Meiselas; Rael San Fratello; Guadalupe Rosales; the Ricardo Valverde Estate; and Alex Webb.

We value our museum as a place where a range of diverse perspectives—sometimes joyful, sometimes painful—are equally welcome.

William M. Griswold
Director
Sarah S. and Alexander M. Cutler Chair
The Cleveland Museum of Art

ACKNOWLEDGMENTS

A photograph from my own family's photo album records a moment in Shallowater, Texas, in 1967. A woman and two girls are sitting on and leaning against the front of a Pontiac on a sunny day. My maternal grandmother, Augustina, the family member I am often told I physically resemble, has inscribed the photograph at the top, "Our 2 cars." At the bottom edge of the photograph she's written, "Diana, Sylvia, and ME." As a curator and museum worker, it has always troubled me to see handwriting on the face of a photograph. Here, however, the unorthodox act of writing on a photo, compounded by the all-caps "ME," further enriches the photograph: an insistence to be recorded, remembered; an adamant pride of place that at once gives subjectivity to the image and the archive it occupies. Within the larger project of researching photography in the US-Mexico borderlands and the importance of bringing visibility to the Latinx communities within these territories, I recognize the significance of not only the personal family moment this photograph documents but also the conceptual declaration of existence within those spaces with the transgressive inscription, "ME."

Picturing the Border originated as my doctoral dissertation at the City University of New York's Graduate Center. The topic was approved by the Art History Department in November 2016, the week after Donald Trump was elected. Moments after it was officially approved, my primary advisor, Dr. Anna Indych-López, took me aside and urged, "You better finish this thing." I understood the gravity of her statement. With an entire family history of borderlands residents and immigrants behind me, and with the future of that demographic in this country suddenly more uncertain and tenuous, I embarked on this study. Thank you, Dr. Indych-López, for pushing me from the inception of this project and advising me on the finer points of my writing and research, as well as the big-picture importance of this work. I am thankful as well to the members of my dissertation committee, Dr. Antonella Pelizzari, Dr. Katherine Manthorne, and Dr. Adam Goodman, for their mentorship and thoughtful feedback. I am especially grateful to Sean Abbott-Klafter, who has been a supportive and critical interlocutor. I am also indebted to the Latinx-photography scholars who have laid the groundwork for this field of study: Elizabeth Ferrer, E. Carmen Ramos, C. Ondine Chavoya, Deborah Cullen, Roberto Tejada, and Pilar Tompkins Rivas.

This exhibition and the accompanying catalogue would not be possible without the support, talent, and dedication of my exceptional colleagues at the Cleveland Museum of Art. I heartily thank Director William M. Griswold and Virginia N. and Randall L. Barbato Deputy Director and Chief Curator Heather Lemonedes Brown for encouraging the development of *Picturing the Border.* In supporting this undertaking, they have welcomed a diverse range of artists to complement the narratives found elsewhere in the museum.

My generous and talented colleagues in the curatorial division were also vital to the realization of *Picturing the Border.* I especially thank Mark Cole, Barbara Tannenbaum, and Emily Liebert for serving as interlocutors throughout the development of the exhibition, and Deirdre Vodanoff for helping with the many details of the show. My sincere thanks also to Heidi Strean, the Margaret and Loyal Wilson Chief

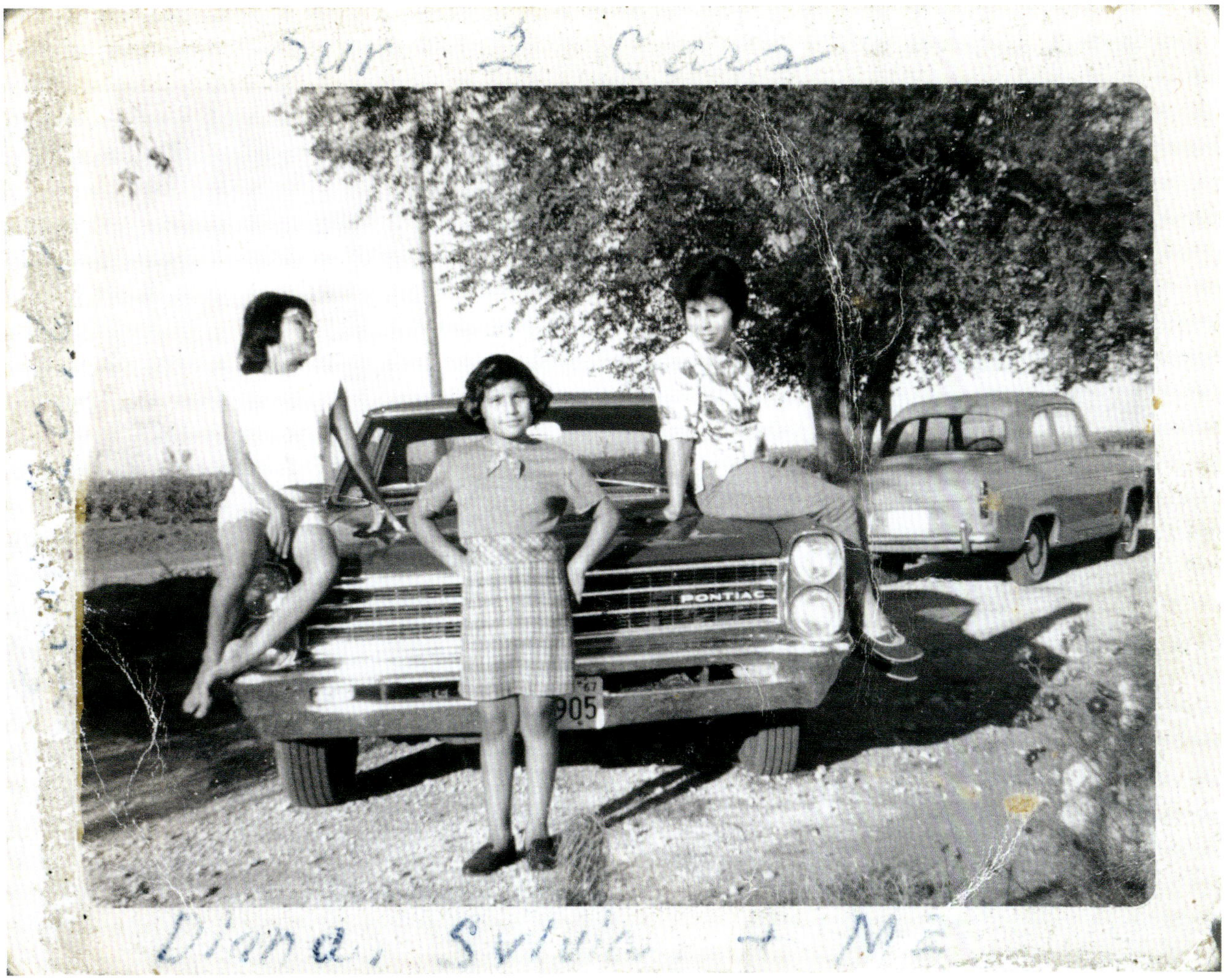

Diana Sanchez, Sylvia Sanchez, and Augustina Rivera Sanchez, Shallowater, Texas, 1967.
Courtesy of Sylvia Rivera Fellah

Exhibition, Design, and Publications Officer. In particular, Emily Mears's and Sarah Peroli's skillful management and coordination played a crucial role. The CMA's design team, led by Andrew Gutierrez, animated the narratives of *Picturing the Border* in real space. Peter Kratcoski translated the ideas at the core of the exhibition into a graphic identity, and Amy Sparks edited the exhibition materials. In the Department of Collections Management, Laura Ziewitz ensured that the works constituting the exhibition traveled safely to and from the CMA. Our Department of Conservation, led by Sarah Scaturro, helped safeguard the works with precision and expertise; thank you to Moyna Stanton, Mark Spisak, and Ivey Barker.

For bringing this book to life, I thank Tom Barnard, Rachel Beamer, and Jane Friedman. I especially want to recognize Natalie Scenters-Zapico. A poet whose poignant work I have often returned to for impressions of her borderlands home, Natalie has contributed an essay that brings yet another dimension to the border and its spaces in ways I could not have imagined. I am eternally grateful to her for rounding out the perspectives included here.

Translating the main ideas and interpretive approaches underpinning *Picturing the Border* into robust programming was a key goal from the outset. For their help in realizing this goal, I thank my colleagues in the Division of Programming and Public Engagement. This project greatly benefited from collaboration with Rachel Arzuaga, Stephanie Foster, Cameron McConnell, Erin Fletcher, and Ryanaustin Dennis. A sincere thanks to the staff at the CMA's Ingalls Library, especially Matthew Gengler and Marsha Morrow, for sourcing hard-to-find photo books for this project and lending them to the exhibition.

I thank the Department of Communications and External Relations, led by Todd Mesek, for helping to spread the word about the exhibition, as well as Howard Agriesti and David Brichford in Photographic and Digital Imaging Services for the wonderful images of this show to share with our audiences.

Chief Philanthropy Officer Bruce Loessin and his team helped make *Picturing the Border* a reality by securing financial backing for the project. All exhibitions at the Cleveland Museum of Art are underwritten by the CMA Fund for Exhibitions. Principal annual support is provided by Michael Frank and the late Pat Snyder and the John and Jeanette Walton Exhibition Fund. The exhibition was supported in part by the Ohio Arts Council, which receives support from the State of Ohio and the National Endowment for the Arts. The Andrew W. Mellon Foundation supported the publication of this catalogue.

I am also indebted to the artists and their family members who opened their homes and archives to me, and generously spent hours answering my questions about their photographs and time spent in the borderlands: the Laura Aguilar Trust, William Camargo, Teddy Cruz and Fonna Forman, Miguel Fernández de Castro, Thalía Gochez, Lourdes Grobet, Muriel Hasbun, Graciela Iturbide, Eniac Martínez, Susan Meiselas, Ronald Rael and Virgina San Fratello, Guadalupe Rosales, Ada Trillo, Esperanza Valverde, and Alex Webb. In the course of researching this topic, two of the photographers with whom I worked closely, Lourdes Grobet (1940–2022) and Eniac Martínez (1959–2019), passed away. I feel immense gratitude to be publishing their work and their words in this volume.

For their invaluable assistance throughout my research, I would also like to recognize the staffs at the Center for Creative Photography, University of Arizona; Centro de la Imagen; the Magnum Photos Archive; and the UCLA Chicano Studies Research Center.

Before my time at the Cleveland Museum of Art, this project was supported by a fellowship from the Inter-University Program for Latino Research/Mellon Foundation, as well as by grants from the Center for Creative Photography, the Mellon Foundation, and the Social Science Research Council.

This project has been inspired by stories of migration in my own family: By my mother Sylvia's family, who migrated from Mexico to the borderlands of Texas at the turn of the twentieth century, and by those in our family who lived in the region prior to 1845 and had the border cross *them*. By my maternal grandmother, Augustina, and her siblings, who worked as farm laborers picking cotton in El Valle (the Rio Grande Valley). By my father, Adnan, who emigrated from Tripoli, Libya, in 1975. Above all, this book is dedicated to my daughters, Ava and Zayna. They have many generations of strong migrant women to guide their paths.

Picturing the Border is for migrants everywhere, those in our own families, and those whose stories are represented throughout the permanent collections of this museum.

Nadiah Rivera Fellah
Curator of Contemporary Art

Map of the border between the United States and Mexico

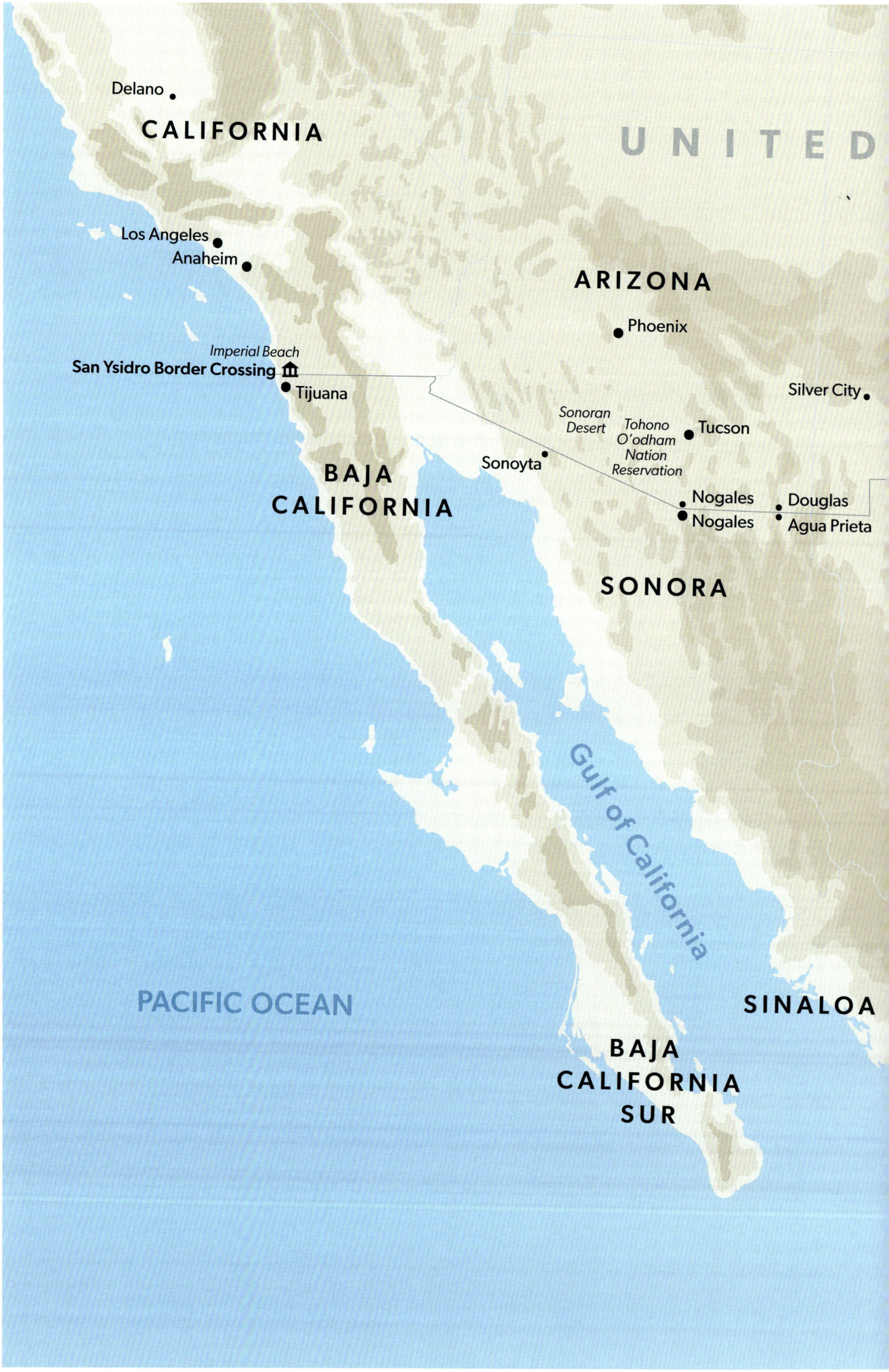

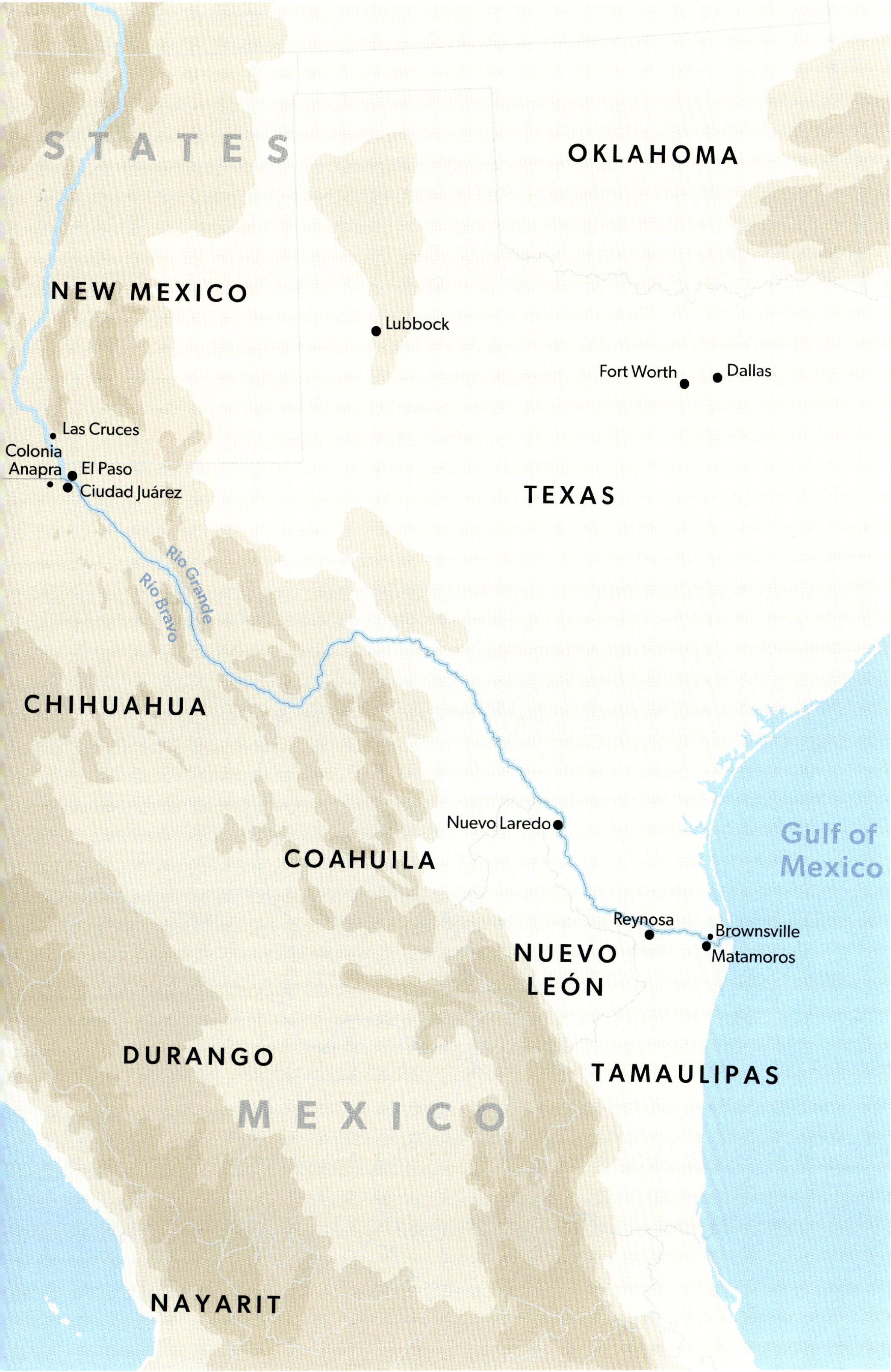
STATES
OKLAHOMA
NEW MEXICO
Lubbock
Fort Worth
Dallas
Las Cruces
Colonia
Anapra
El Paso
Ciudad Juárez
TEXAS
Río Grande
Río Bravo
CHIHUAHUA
Nuevo Laredo
Gulf of
Mexico
COAHUILA
Reynosa
Brownsville
Matamoros
NUEVO
LEÓN
DURANGO
TAMAULIPAS
MEXICO
NAYARIT

INTRODUCTION

For the last five decades, the US-Mexico border has been a highly contentious site for artists, human rights activists, environmental activists, and migrants rights activists alike. The border's physical makeup has undergone dramatic changes during these years, becoming increasingly industrialized, urbanized, and militarized. These developments, which escalated in the aftermath of 9/11, have fueled xenophobic, incendiary rhetoric directed toward migrants and the Latinx population. In their reporting on the subject, mainstream and conservative news outlets have described migrants in hostile terms accusing them of posing threats to the American economy and to national security, and often characterizing the situation at the border as an "invasion" by "floods of illegal aliens."

A news photograph that quickly became a lightning rod for border developments in 2018 speaks to the dangerous intersection of human rights concerns and media interests (fig. 1). The photograph documents the conflict between the US Border Patrol, the Mexican Federal Police, and the Migrant Caravan, a group of Central American migrants primarily from Honduras, who, seeking asylum in the United States, migrated to the San Ysidro border crossing in Tijuana, Mexico. In November of that year, the members of the caravan were met with a police blockade on the Mexican side of the border fence and tear-gas canisters fired by Border Patrol from the US side. Taken by South Korean photographer Kim Kyung-Hoon (born 1974), a photojournalist for the international news agency Reuters, the image records the moment when dozens of migrants scattered as a canister hit the ground, and tear gas rose into the air in clouds of smoke. In the foreground Maria Lila Meza Castro, a migrant woman from Honduras, runs with her five-year-old twin daughters, both dressed only in a T-shirt and diapers, one wearing flip-flops, the other shoeless, and with no visible possessions. Gripping each daughter by the forearm, Castro is captured midstride as she runs from the tear gas, their three figures frozen in a precarious moment before they threaten to tumble to the ground in her rush to get the family to safety. Castro's face at the center of the photograph is particularly arresting. Brow furrowed in concentration, tongue pursed at the side of her mouth, she is in survival mode as she pulls her daughters out of harm's way. In the background the triple layers of the border fence—concrete, steel, and barbed wire—can be clearly seen, and the American flag is evident just beyond its top edge.

Castro's T-shirt strikes a particularly ironic note, featuring the faces of two princesses from the Disney children's movie *Frozen* (2013). The shirt's tight fit and lace sleeves indicate it is meant for a child, perhaps a garment salvaged from a donations bin, becoming a material symbol of the mother's sacrifices on her journey northward. The Disney figures strike another note as well—that of a multi-billion-dollar media conglomerate whose products are exported to nations south of the US border for consumption and dissemination, following a path well-trodden by American corporations for generations. It is a reminder that while corporate entities are freely allowed to cross borders in the interest of realizing profits, people such as Maria Lila Meza Castro and her daughters are not.[1] The shirt underscores the fact that, in the same space where material and natural borders dangerously collide, via the fence and the Tijuana riverbed, so too do corporate and personal interests.

The image went viral on social media and across the internet, becoming a flashpoint for activists to pinpoint the inhumane use of force against migrant refugee families and the illegal

Figure 1. *Maria Lila Meza Castro, center, a 39-year-old migrant woman from Honduras, runs away from tear gas with her 5-year-old twin daughters, Saira Nalleli Mejia Meza, left, and Cheili Nalleli Mejia Meza, near the border between the US and Mexico, in Tijuana, Mexico, November 25, 2018*, 2018. Kim Kyung-Hoon (Korean, born 1974). Photo: Reuters / Kim Kyung-Hoon

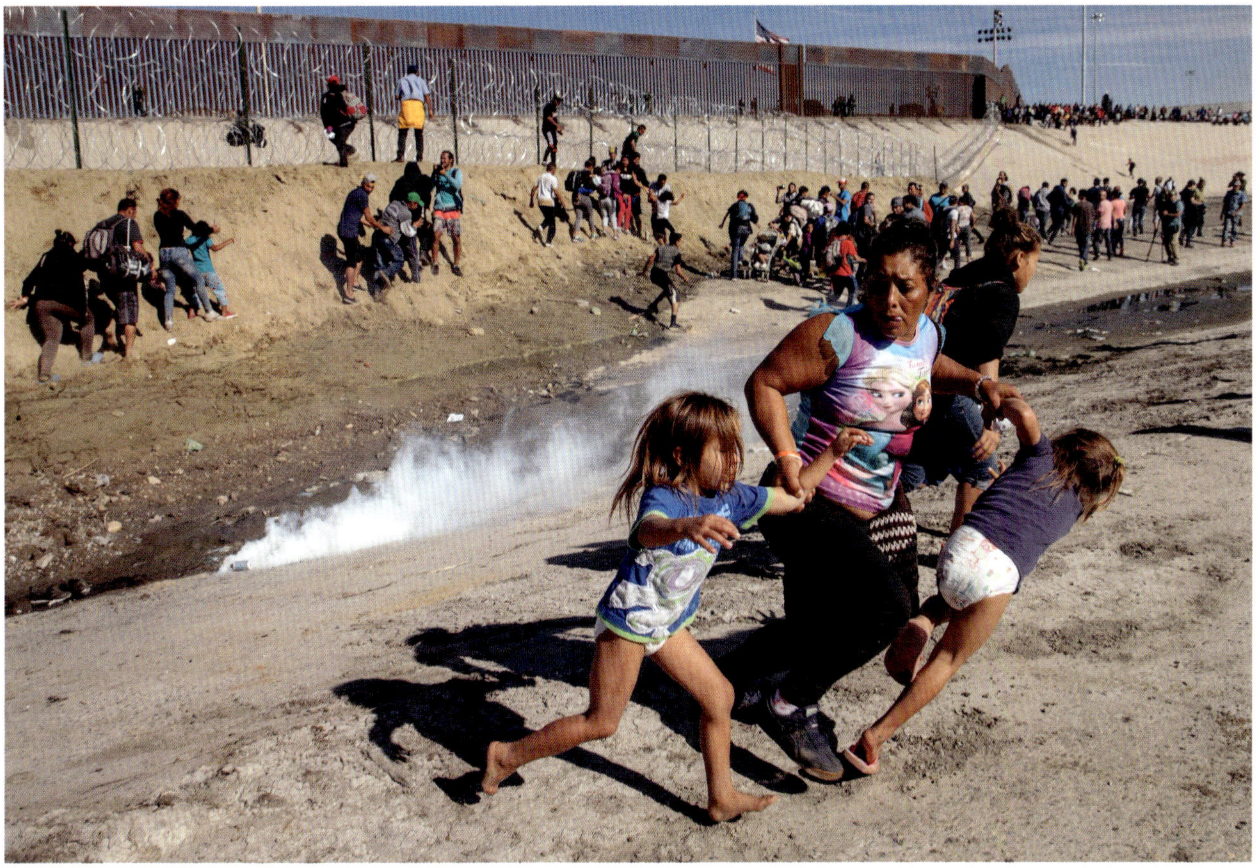

denial of asylum brought to bear on those seeking it. The tear-gas canister—seen at the base of the rising cloud of smoke rolling into the shallow ditch of the Tijuana riverbed—is a punctuating element in the composition. Its presence recalls similar uses of militarized tear gas against unarmed citizens, including its use against Black Lives Matter protesters in Ferguson, Missouri, in 2014, and against Indigenous participants in the Dakota Access Pipeline Protests, begun in 2016. Almost immediately after it was taken, the photograph became a powerful vehicle to counter negative perceptions of immigrants at that moment in the US political climate, perceptions the Trump administration continued to perpetuate.

While images like Kim Kyung-Hoon's can serve as effective rallying cries against the inhumane treatment of migrants and asylum seekers, they can also feed into problematic narratives. In particular, they help sustain the trope of "border as battlefield" that circulates prominently in the media, characterizing the border and immigration as out of control and meriting a warlike, militarized response. Moreover, such media images of intense conflict seldom humanize or confer agency upon their migrant subjects.

In contrast, the photographs in *Picturing the Border* offer a more nuanced portrayal of life in the borderlands. The exhibition positions the US-Mexico border as a cultural framework and highlights how Latinx photographers—many of whom are border residents themselves—resist being defined by the border and its conflicts, and have instead formulated alternative photographic vocabularies with regard to place, identity, and race. Indeed, some of the most compelling imagery of the borderlands region attests to generations-long cross-border familial relationships, personal identities that carry markers of both countries, and hybrid cultures that toggle between influences from the United States, Mexico, and farther south in Latin America [1]. *Picturing the Border* shows that artists working on the US-Mexico border have been remarkably ahead of their time in deterritorializing issues surrounding *home*, in the process creating images that sensitively interrogate notions of family, national identity, and gender politics.

Whereas news stories often make little attempt to convey migrants' viewpoints or the realities of their lives, the photographic works discussed in chapter 1, "Border Stories," center migrant experiences and moments of resistance. This section examines published photo books and photo essays by artists from both sides of the border, among them Lourdes Grobet, Zoe Leonard, Eniac Martínez, Susan Meiselas, Ada Trillo, and Alex Webb. Their series picture migrants in tandem with social movements supporting political change, human rights, and racial and socioeconomic equality. Unconstrained by the demands of daily news outlets, these artists retain full control over the production of their images and accompanying texts to tell stories of Indigenous migration, border cityscapes, and the precarious activities of undocumented border crossers: counternarratives to the denigrating, one-dimensional portrayal of immigrants in the mass media.

Chapter 2, "The Urban Border," considers photographs documenting the built environments of border cities and addresses the demographics of their Latinx populations. Artists including Ricardo Valverde, Harry Gamboa Jr., George Rodriguez, Laura Aguilar, and William Camargo are deeply aware of the psychological effects of these cities on their inhabitants. Their exploration of the urban environment manifests in spatial investigations that parallel real-life displacements and deterritorializations. Many artworks capture the claustrophobic aspect of these urban spaces via the overwhelming presence of freeway overpasses and concrete barriers in inner-city neighborhoods.

These visual narratives also address the labor movement's presence in border cities [2]. The 1960s witnessed the start of worker protests at maquiladoras, or foreign-owned factories, in Ciudad Juárez, Tijuana, and other Mexican border cities. Women workers were at the forefront of these struggles for unionization, pay equity, and improved working conditions, struggles supported by African American activists as well, countering the often-circulated images of Mexican American male labor leaders like Cesar Chavez [3].[2]

Chapter 3, "Familial Spaces on the Border," focuses on photographs of domestic and familial spaces in the US-Mexico borderlands. An important element of Chicano cultural nationalism in the 1960s and 1970s was the concept of *la familia de la raza* (the family of the race). A metaphor fusing familial cultural values with the Chicano Civil Rights Movement, *la familia de la raza* reinforced heteronormative familial structures such as the male-headed household. In the decades following the Chicano movement's peak in 1968–69, artists such as Louis Carlos Bernal, Amalia Mesa-Bains, Laura Aguilar, and Christina Fernandez have challenged and troubled the concept's patriarchal basis, creating portraits of maternal domestic governance that reflect the social realities of working-class families in the US-Mexico borderlands as well as affirm LGBTQ+ presence within Latinx communities. Envisioning cultural empowerment through the matriarchal and queer domestic spaces in their photographs, these artists have played a vital role in generating new familial tropes and collective memories while providing a richer reflection of their borderland homes.

Chapter 4, "Images of Cross-Border Identities," explores photographs of cholo/as, the Chicanos associated with

[**1**] *Albert y Lynn Morales, Silver City, N.M.*, 1978.
Louis Carlos Bernal (American, 1941–1993).
Chromogenic print; 23 x 23 cm.
Collection of the Center for Creative
Photography, University of Arizona,
Gift of the artist, 80.45.1. © Lisa Bernal Brethour
and Katrina Ann Bernal

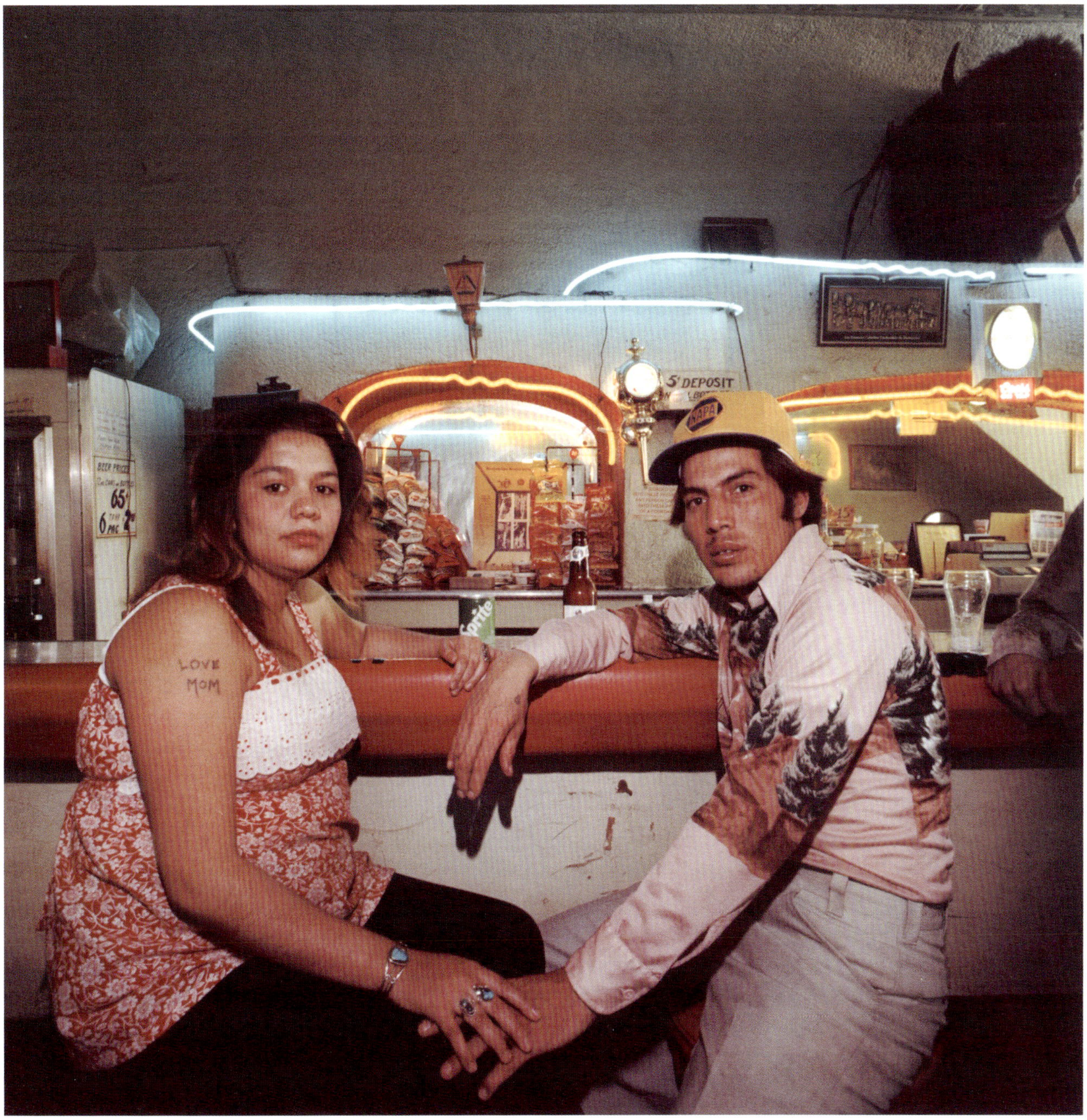

[**2**] *Untitled [Undocumented worker holding Huelga flag at United Farm Workers Demonstration, El Mirage, Arizona]*, negative 1978, printed 2016. Louis Carlos Bernal. Digital Inkjet Print; 40.6 x 40.6 cm. Collection of the Center for Creative Photography, University of Arizona, Louis Carlos Bernal Archive. © Lisa Bernal Brethour and Katrina Bernal

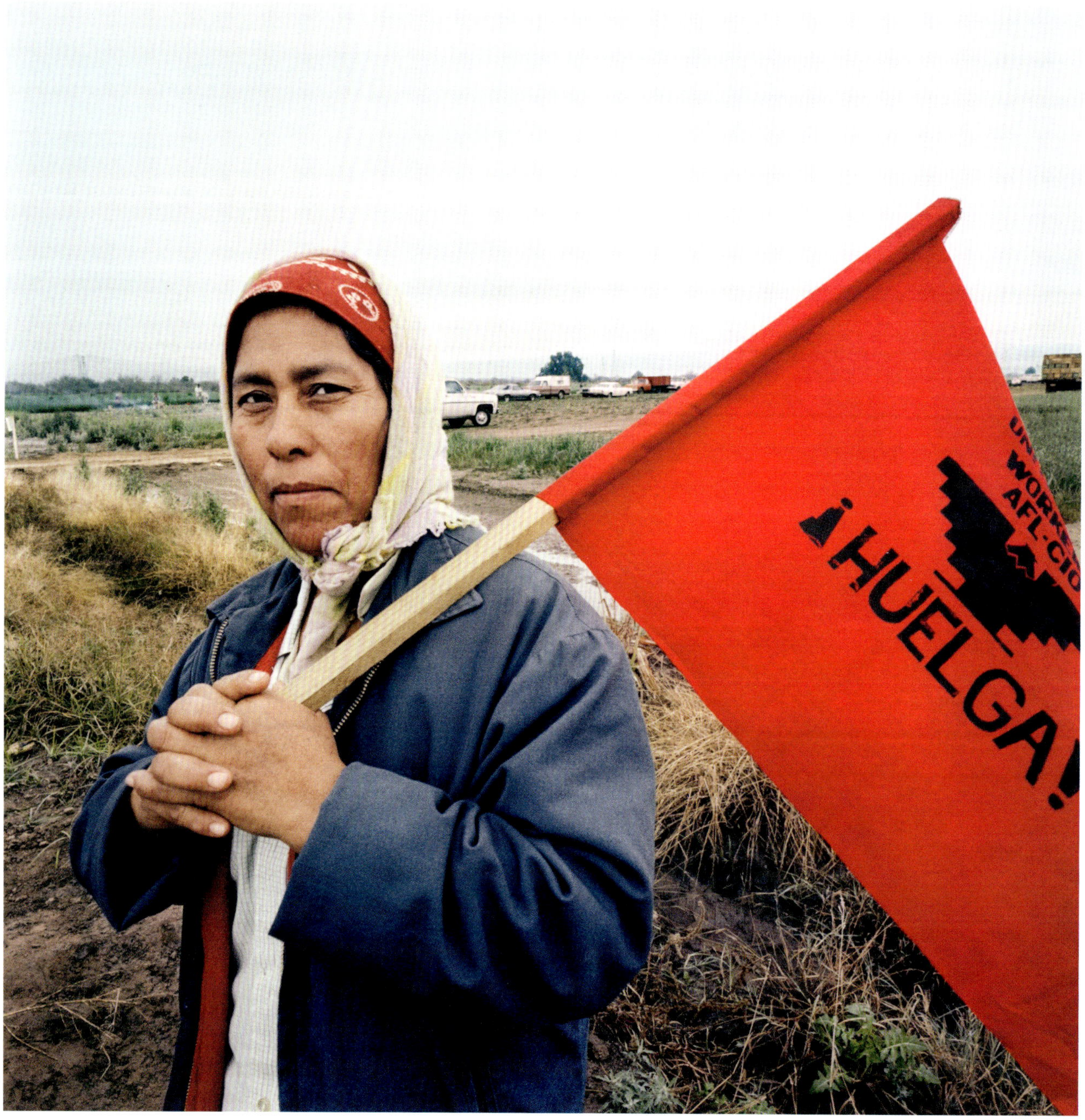

[**3**] *Delano*, negative 1969, printed 2021.
George Rodriguez (American, born 1937).
Gelatin silver print; 22.9 x 33.9 cm.
The J. Paul Getty Museum, Los Angeles,
2021.31.4. © George Rodriguez

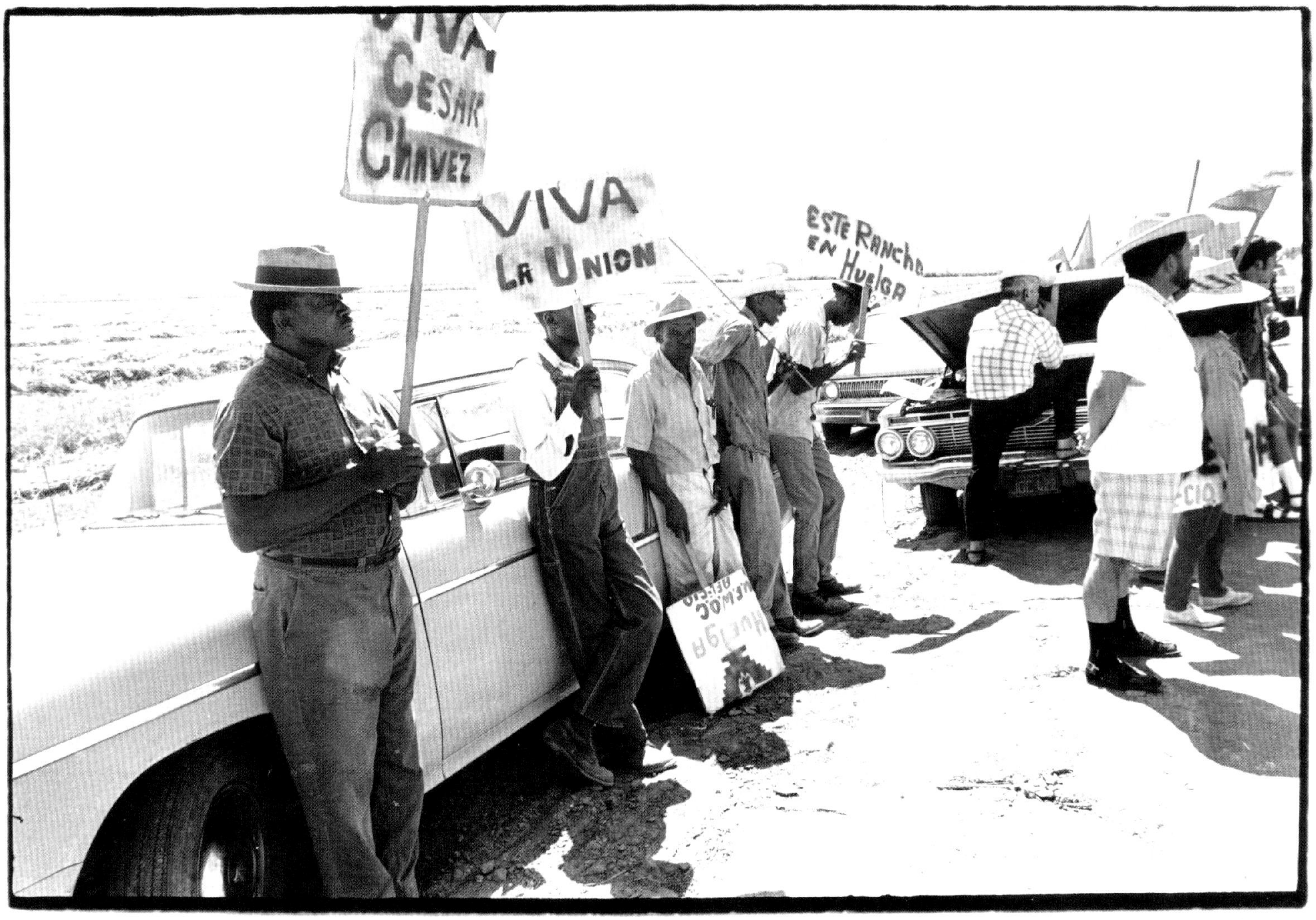

lowrider subculture known for their ritual of cruising the boulevards in their neighborhoods. Cholo/as' appropriation of symbols of Mexican identity in the United States becomes a tool for the performance of "cross-border identities" that complicate the notion of citizenship or fixed national or political identity, and signify border residents' complex relationship to their Mexican heritage. Photographers on both sides of the border have taken a particular interest in cholo/as' transnational lifestyle. Graciela Iturbide made a series of photographs on the subject in Los Angeles in 1986, while other artists who have documented cholo/as and their precursors, pachuco/as, include Louis Carlos Bernal, John Valadez, Max Yavno, and, more recently, Thalía Gochez and Guadalupe Rosales.

Since the initial creation of what we recognize as the modern-day boundary between Mexico and the United States with the signing of the Treaty of Guadalupe Hidalgo (1848) and the Gadsden Purchase (1854), the physical makeup of the borderlands has undergone dramatic shifts, leading to its becoming a fixture in mainstream news cycles.[3] Factors that contributed to these shifts include the Border Industrialization Program, introduced in 1965, and the North American Free Trade Agreement (NAFTA), signed in 1994; both made the border a site of foreign capital investment and led to or stimulated its industrialization. These policies spurred northward migration, whereby laborers, drawn by the promise of factory employment, began arriving at the border in significant numbers. Beginning in the 1960s, economic crises in Mexico, compounded by what Mexican officials deemed "surplus workers," prompted northward migration, leading to the rise of the borderlands' populations and the growth of once-small towns in the border region.[4] The immigration policies of the Carter, Reagan, and George H. W. Bush administrations contributed to the increased militarization of the border and to the extent of resources allocated toward border security. These developments escalated in the aftermath of 9/11 during the George W. Bush administration's so-called "War on Terror," which led to the expansion of homeland security and intensified efforts to secure US borders. It was largely during these decades that derogatory portrayals of migrants, especially from Mexico and Central America, began to circulate throughout conservative and mainstream news outlets, alongside a general rise in xenophobic rhetoric.

In addition to these major historical developments, there are also lesser-known histories surrounding the occupation and surveillance of the borderlands, among them the displacement of various Indigenous groups. In his film *Grammar of Gates / Gramática de las puertas* (2019), Miguel Fernández de Castro (born 1986) explores how the border slices through the ancestral lands of the Tohono O'odham Nation, an Indigenous people living in the Sonoran desert.[5] Using footage from the movie *Geronimo Jones* (1970) and combining it with drone footage and landscape views of the Sonora-Arizona borderlands, where Fernández de Castro lives and works, the film evokes prior popular-cultural portrayals of Native inhabitants of the borderlands while also addressing the issue of surveillance, a phenomenon that involves actors on both sides of the border [4]. Fernández de Castro explains, "Nowadays, the military and expansionist gaze is not exclusive to the US Border Patrol, but is shared by the powerful and heavily-armed Mexican mafia groups who control access to the border in Sonora. Organizations on both sides of the border, either governmental or criminal, rely on similar vision technologies and through them exert brutal violence

[**4**] *Grammar of Gates / Gramática de las puertas*, 2019. Miguel Fernández de Castro (Mexican, born 1986). Single-channel video with sound; 20:31 minutes. © Miguel Fernández de Castro

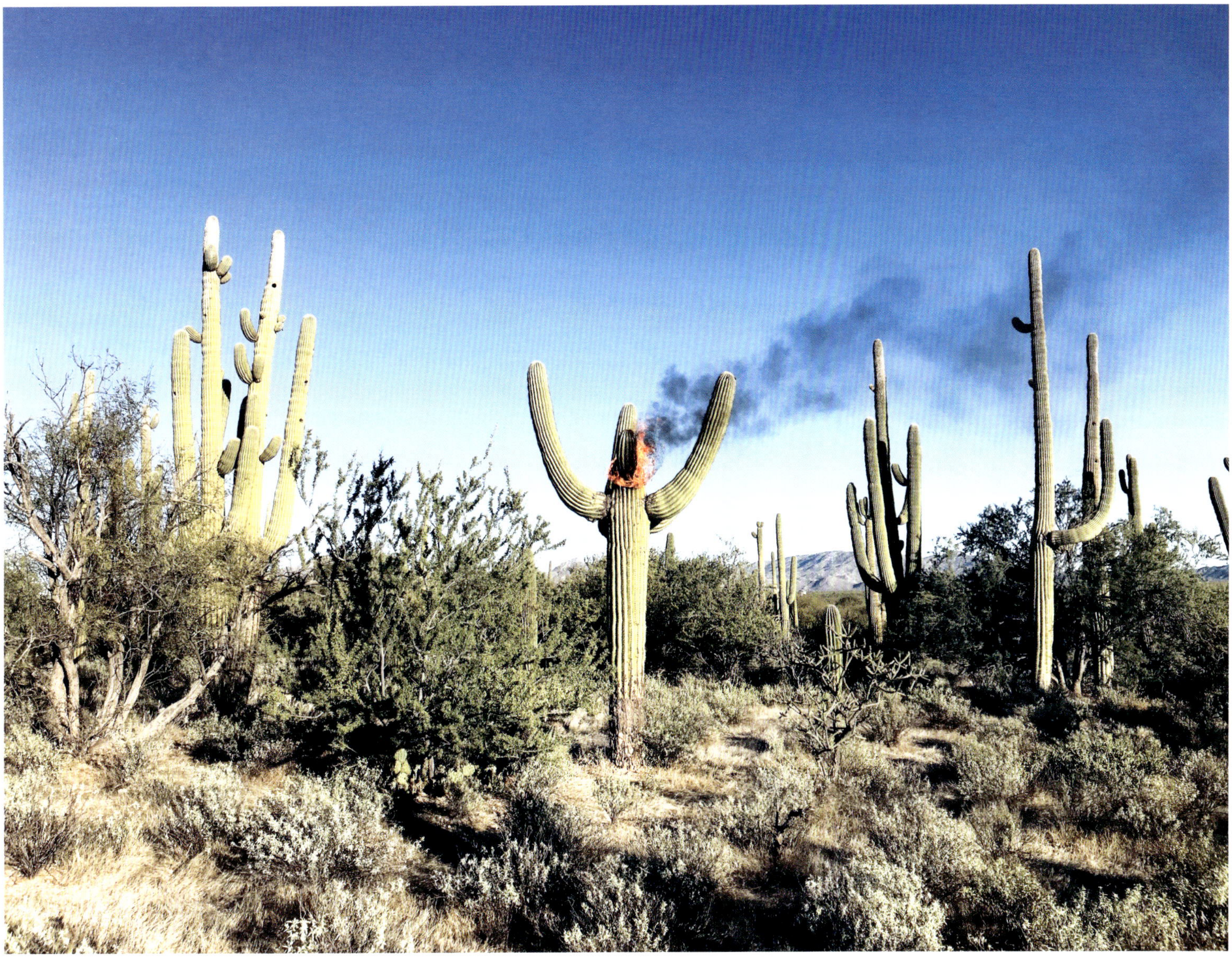

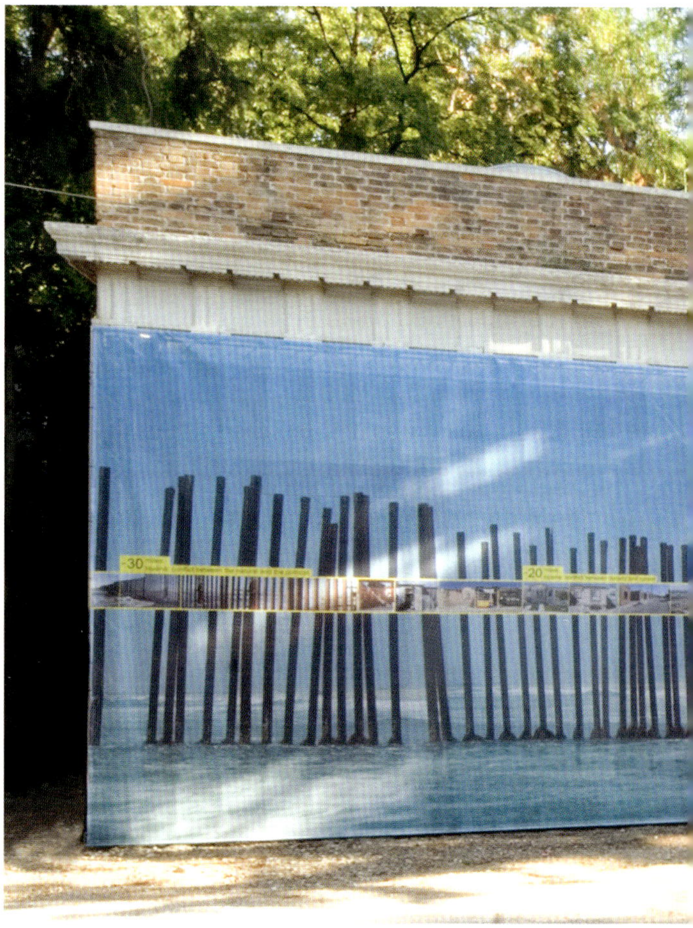

[**5**] Installation view of Estudio Teddy Cruz + Fonna Forman's *Radicalizing the Local: 60 Miles of Trans-Border Urban Conflict* (2008), commissioned by the US Pavilion for the Venice Architecture Biennale of 2008. Teddy Cruz (American, born Guatemala, 1962). Fonna Forman (American, born 1968). Print from a digital file; dimensions variable.
© Teddy Cruz + Fonna Forman

over the bodies that inhabit these lands."[6] The soundtrack to *Grammar of Gates* consists of the artist reciting passages from *A Practical Spanish Grammar for Border Patrol Officers* (1968), a book he came across when researching documents issued by the US Department of Justice. He discovered that colonial legacies of occupation were overtly embedded in the book's phrasing and grammar exercises, thus becoming "violent blueprints for interactions" between the Border Patrol and migrants, as well as Native inhabitants.[7]

The borderlands' ecological history has increasingly become a focal point in works addressing the region. In 2008, Teddy Cruz (born 1962) and Fonna Forman (born 1968) collaborated on *Radicalizing the Local: 60 Miles of Trans-Border Urban Conflict*. The project follows a path through two border cities—San Diego and Tijuana—from thirty miles north of the border to thirty miles south of the border, charting its trajectory through "natural and artificial ecologies." Documenting the scope of the border's built environment, ranging from private homes and subdivisions to military infrastructure, to a colliding network of waterways, *Radicalizing the Local* takes the form of a large-scale, panoramic photocollage with text, enabling viewers to "walk" the miles perpendicularly across the border themselves and bear witness to its topographies [5].[8]

I will conclude this discussion with another viral image of the border, taken nine months after the previously discussed Migrant Caravan photograph (see fig. 1). Rather than documenting conflict, this image features an unexpected moment of joy, evoking the full range of imagery associated with this fraught site. It is a photograph of an architectural intervention, *Teeter-Totter Wall* (2019), custom-designed seesaws temporarily straddling the border near El Paso, Texas, and Ciudad Juárez, Mexico, based on a concept developed by California-based designers Ronald Rael (born 1971) and Virginia San Fratello (born 1971) [6].[9] The pair also produced a video documenting the installation and telling the story behind the project, which is included in *Picturing the Border*.[10] Rael recounts that initially, he and San Fratello requested permission to install the teeter-totters but did not receive a response from US government officials. As a result, working with the community on the other side of the wall, in Colonia Anapra, Mexico, whom the pair knew well, Rael's team staged a guerilla-style intervention. "Immediately," he says, "all the kids jumped on these teeter-totters." Mothers with children and other community members can be seen riding the bright-pink structures, waving at one another through the slatted border fence.

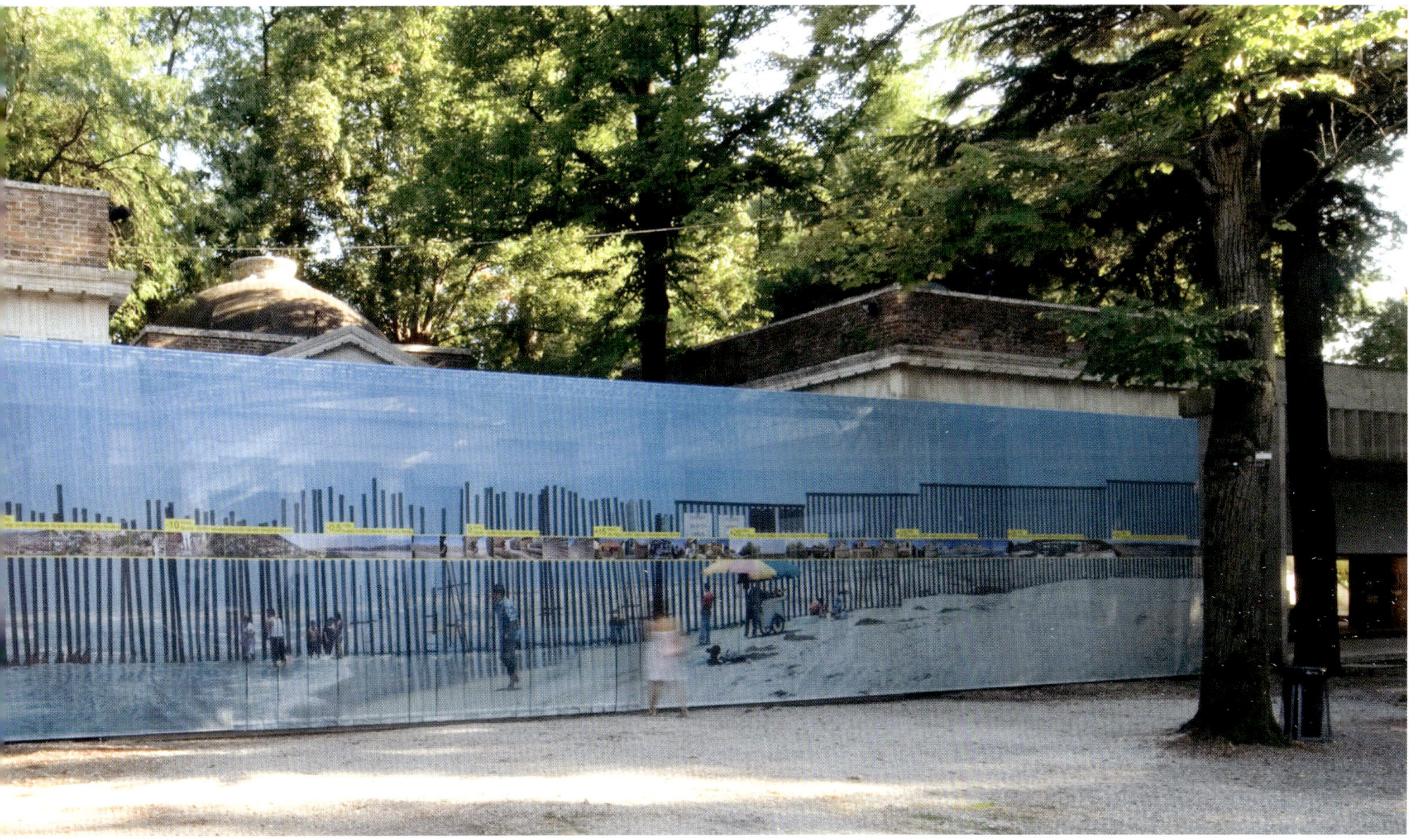

[**5a**] Installation view of Estudio Teddy Cruz + Fonna Forman's *Radicalizing the Local: 60 Miles of Trans-Border Urban Conflict* (2008), commissioned by the US Pavilion for the Venice Architecture Biennale of 2008. © Teddy Cruz + Fonna Forman

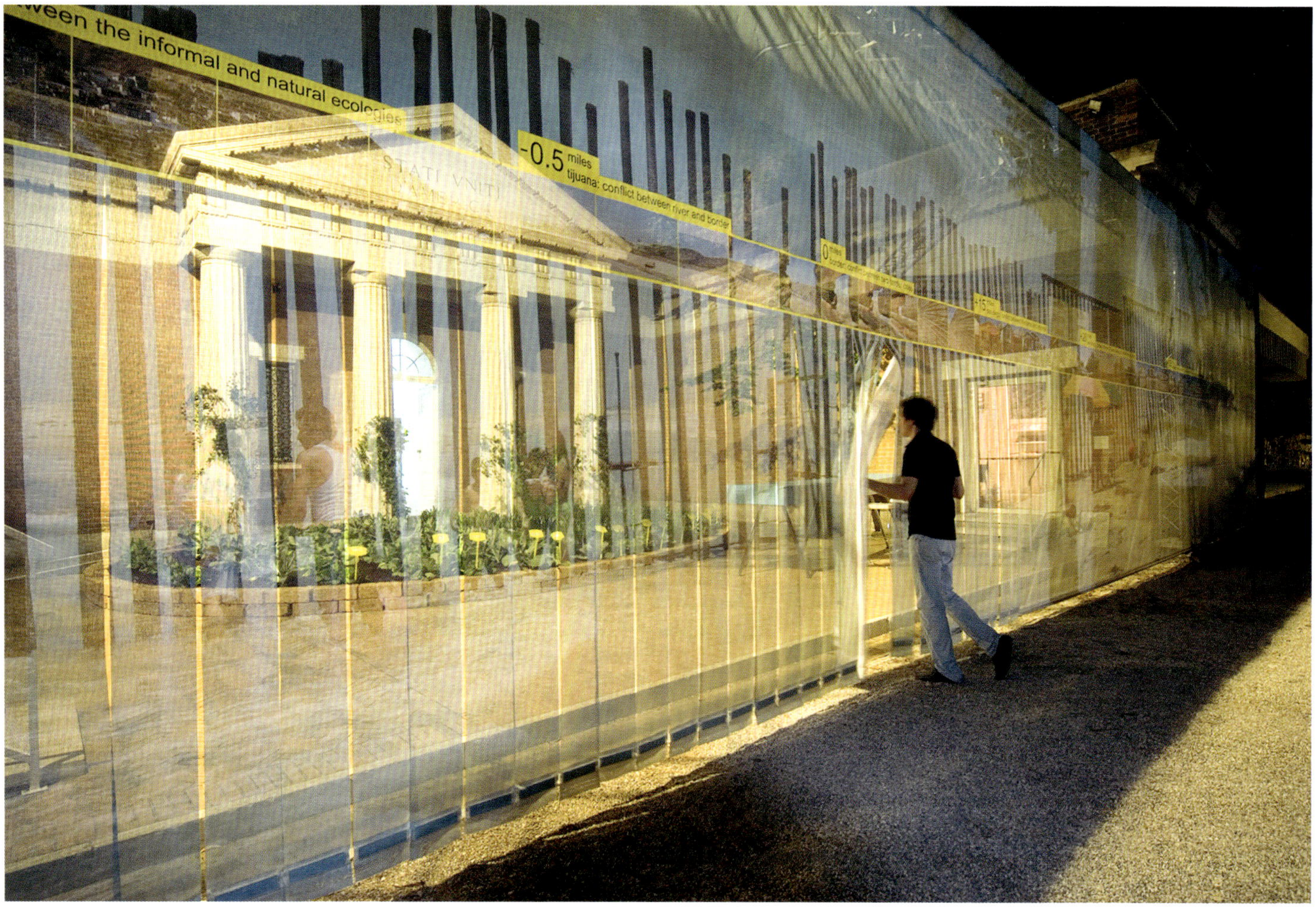

[**5b**] Installation view of Estudio Teddy Cruz + Fonna Forman's *Radicalizing the Local: 60 Miles of Trans-Border Urban Conflict* (2008), commissioned by the US Pavilion for the Venice Architecture Biennale of 2008.
© Teddy Cruz + Fonna Forman

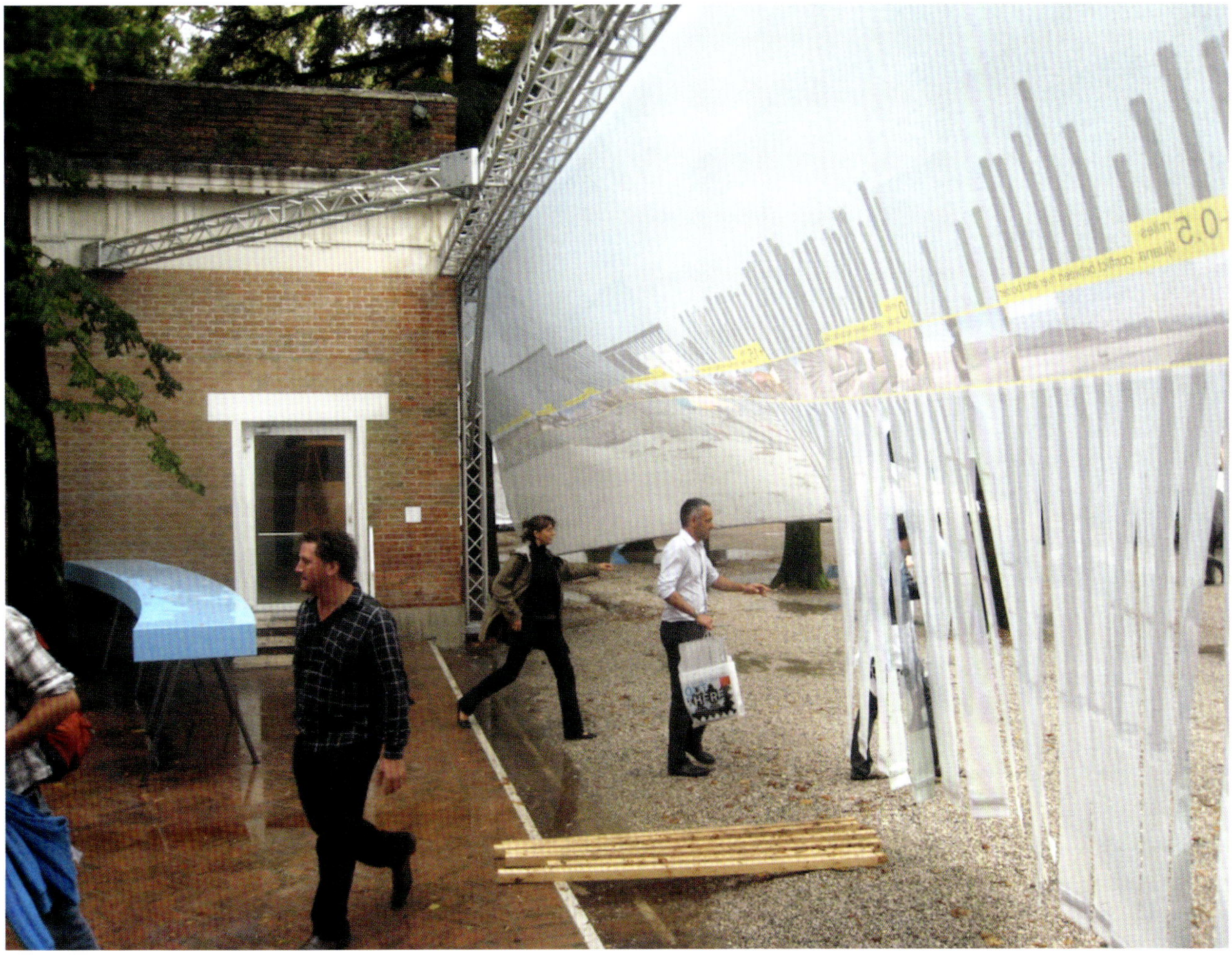

On his social media, Rael wrote, "The wall became a literal fulcrum for U.S.-Mexico relations and children and adults were connected in meaningful ways on both sides with the recognition that the actions that take place on one side have a direct consequence on the other side." Images of *Teeter-Totter Wall* quickly spread across the internet, and the Rael San Fratello studio later received international accolades for their design.[11] This subversive act transformed the Trump administration's expensive border-wall undertaking from a spatial divide meant to impose intimidation, control, and fear to whimsical playground equipment and a source of joyful connections, thereby undermining all it had been constructed to represent.[12] As Rael comments in the video, "Within those spaces of violence, life must continue. And what is life without joy?"

[**6**] *Teeter-Totter Wall*, 2019. Ronald Rael (American, born 1971) and Virginia San Fratello (American, born 1971) with Colectivo Chopeke. Single-channel video with sound; 4:13 minutes. Photo: Ronald Rael

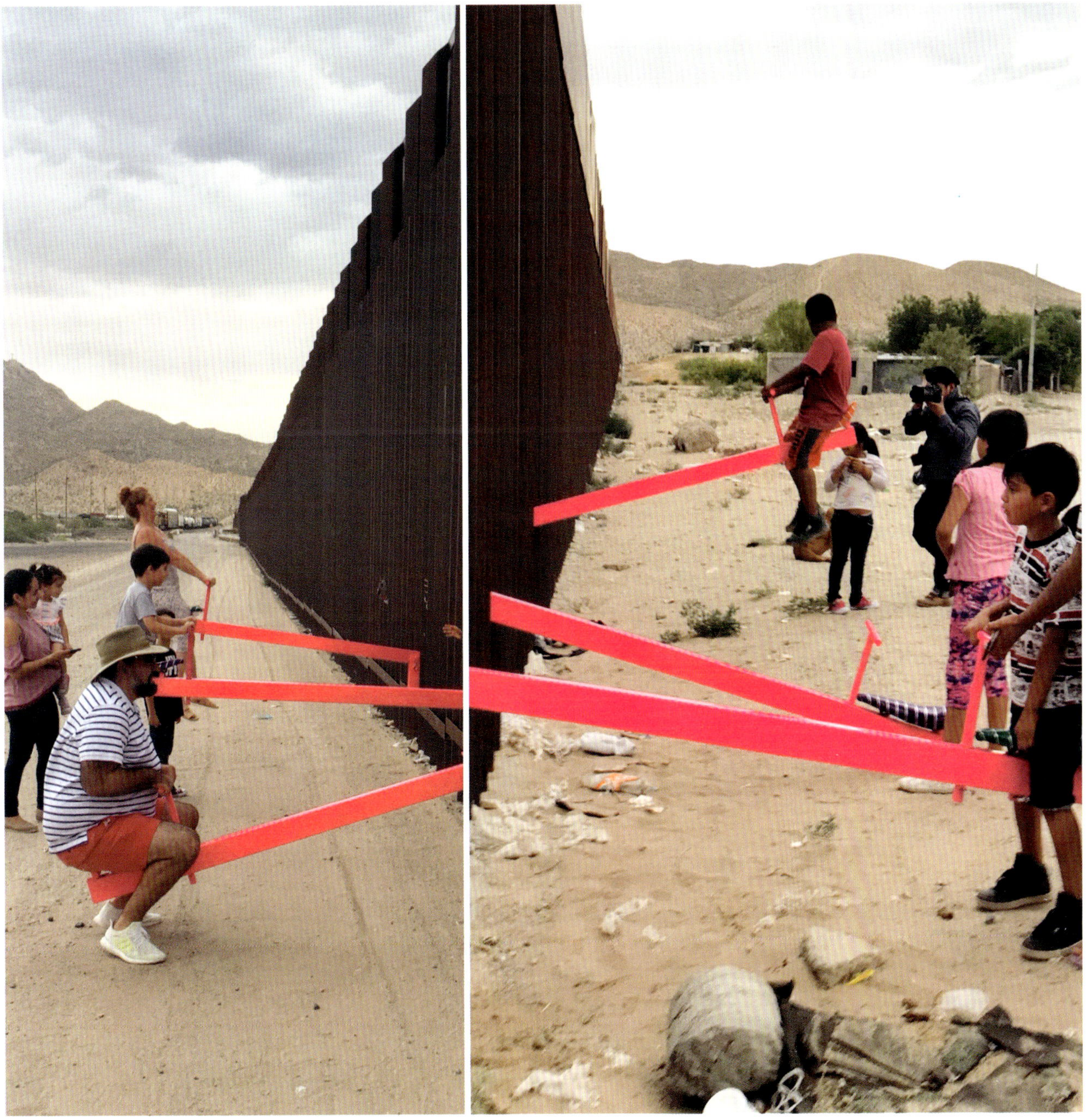

A Note on Terminology

Throughout this volume, I use the terms "Latino" (male), "Latina" (female), and "Latinx" (gender-neutral) to designate individuals of Mexican or Latin American descent who were born in the United States. The term "Chicano/a" denotes Latinx people associated with the Chicano Civil Rights Movement. My use of these terms reflects individuals' self-described designations. I refer to those who have migrated from Mexico during their lifetime as "Mexican migrants" or "immigrants."

1. In particular, the North American Free Trade Agreement (NAFTA), almost a decade in the making at the time it was signed in 1994, marks the reduction of barriers to trade and capital investment between the US, Mexico, and Canada.

2. Jefferson Cowie, *Capital Moves: RCA's Seventy-Year Quest for Cheap Labor* (Ithaca, NY: Cornell University Press, 1999), 103, 170.

3. The Treaty of Guadalupe Hidalgo ended the Mexican-American War, a territorial dispute over Texas. The treaty resulted in the United States' acquisition of present-day Texas and most of present-day California, Colorado, Nevada, Utah, and Wyoming, a region that totals 525,000 square miles. The subsequent Gadsden Purchase of 1854 resulted in the acquisition of present-day Arizona and New Mexico. Since then, the border has been a focus of transnational political attention, especially during the Mexican Revolution of 1910–19 and following the establishment of the US Border Patrol in 1924.

4. Historian Ana Raquel Minian has investigated the exclusion of Mexican migrants from Mexico from 1965 to 1986, an underexplored aspect of the US-Mexico migration narrative and a factor that "helped create a permanent class of displaced, undesirable people that migrant activists rose up to insist that they deserved rights despite [this]." Ana Raquel Minian, *Undocumented Lives: The Untold Story of Mexican Migration* (Cambridge, MA: Harvard University Press, 2018), 3.

5. The US-Mexico border divides the homelands of other Indigenous nations as well. In 2020, the Kumeyaay Nation in Southern California filed a federal lawsuit against the Trump administration to halt the construction of the border wall on their ancestral lands.

6. Miguel Fernández de Castro and Daisy Nam, "Ballroom Marfa: Interview with Miguel Fernández de Castro," trans. Gabriela Carballo, 2020, ballroommarfa.org/wp-content /uploads/MFC_INTERVIEW-1.pdf. Further edited by the author.

7. Fernández de Castro and Nam.

8. For more on the built environment of the border, see C. J. Alvarez, *Border Land, Border Water: A History of Construction on the US-Mexico Divide* (Austin: University of Texas Press, 2019).

9. Ronald Rael, an architecture professor at the University of California, Berkeley, and Virginia San Fratello, an assistant professor at San José State University in California, came up with the idea for a "Teeter-Totter Wall" in 2009.

10. The video is also titled *Teeter-Totter Wall* (2019).

11. Among the accolades, London's Design Museum named the pair the winner of the Beazley Designs of the Year in 2020.

12. These themes are explored fully in the related book, Ronald Rael, *Borderwall as Architecture: A Manifesto for the US-Mexico Boundary* (Oakland: University of California Press, 2017).

1 BORDER STORIES

Throughout the twentieth and twenty-first centuries, conservative agendas have deployed negative characterizations of migrants to advance specific economic and political agendas. Economic downturns have often been exploited to promote the narrative that "illegal aliens" pose serious threats to the US economy—"stealing" jobs from American workers—as well as national security.[1] Especially during the Trump administration, such agendas employed xenophobic stereotypes of migrants and the Latinx population to craft and pass anti-immigrant legislation. Likewise, mass-media portrayals of immigration at our southern border have characterized it as an emergency-level "illegal alien problem" of undocumented migrants "flooding" US borders.[2] While some news media outlets have improved their coverage in recent years, offering more balanced and sensitive reporting that includes migrant voices and perspectives, coverage marked by such anti-immigrant biases persists, especially in conservative news outlets.

Responding to the renewed politicization of the border in the 1960s and the increased media attention that ensued in the decades that followed, artists have created photographic series countering such characterizations. In this chapter I explore migration narratives documented in photo books and photo essays, part of a sizable number of photographic works about the US-Mexico border.[3] Although their imagery spans broad geographical and thematic terrain, these projects are united in their efforts to bring specificity to border life and culture, offering important correctives to mass-media representations of conflicts on the border and throughout Latin America.

US immigration policies underwent a decidedly rightward shift during Ronald Reagan's presidency (1981–89). These years saw escalating anti-immigrant rhetoric promoting the notion of a so-called invasion of illegal aliens that was threatening to become an all-out crisis. This culminated with the 1986 passage of the much-debated Immigration Reform and Control Act (IRCA). Originally introduced by Alan Simpson, Republican senator of Wyoming, and signed into law by President Reagan, the IRCA set stringent parameters for immigration, including an unrealistic annual limit of 270,000 immigrants, with a maximum of 20,000 allowed from any one country.[4] Political leaders and government agencies defended the IRCA's harsh parameters, describing them as preventing a national crisis.[5] The concern with enforcing the IRCA accounted for a dramatic surge in attention to the border in the 1980s.

Around the time the IRCA was signed into law, equipment upgrades and other technological enhancements contributed to the militarization of the US-Mexico border.[6] These enhancements supported the alleged legitimacy of the government's response to the rise in undocumented immigration across the border. An article that appeared in the *Los Angeles Times* in 1986, titled "All-Out Border War to Stem Alien Flow Is High-Tech Affair," reported on the use of new technology and military-style devices at the border.[7] Under a headline that displays the article's explicit bias—referring to undocumented immigrants as "aliens"—the central image shows two patrolmen in the bed of an all-terrain vehicle, set against a wide-angle view of a darkening sky, with the lights of Tijuana in the background (fig. 2).[8] The two patrolmen in the rear of the truck each use the high-tech night-vision gear the piece describes: one stands with goggles raised to his face, while the other bends to look through a periscope-like device mounted on the truck. Below this panoramic scene are two images that further illustrate the infrared technology. On the left, a patrolman is shown behind the periscope, looking through its lens. On the right, we are given access to the view this gadget displays: figures of migrants detected in the desert via their body heat, each being led in handcuffs to a patrol truck. Readers are offered a glimpse of the migrants only through the intermediary night-vision view to which Border Patrol has access. The depiction further aligns the public's "view" with that of Border Patrol, a concept reinforced through the text of the news story and the accompanying captions.

Amid the pristine cleanliness of the vehicles, the almost clinical approach to their target, and the coordinated appearance of their attire, the posed images in this article read as little more than a promotional ad for Border Patrol and their new, modernized equipment. The message the photographs convey is one that artist Esther Parada perceptively pinpoints in her analysis of mainstream news imagery: "*Our* military might or exercise of power is somehow clean, rational, and even constructive."[9] In addition, the imagery shows none of the violence the vehicles and devices were known for bringing to bear on undocumented crossers, nor the intimidation and scare tactics the spotlights, loudspeakers, and weapons mounted on helicopters and vehicles were designed to carry out.[10] The story concludes with a description of one patrolman "on horseback, rounding up a group of people. He was a Border Patrol officer doing his job the way it used to be done."[11] The image of the horseback-riding patrolman—a modern-day American cowboy defending the country against threat and invasion—played well in the media environment of the 1980s, bolstered in part by Reagan's nickname as the "Cowboy President."

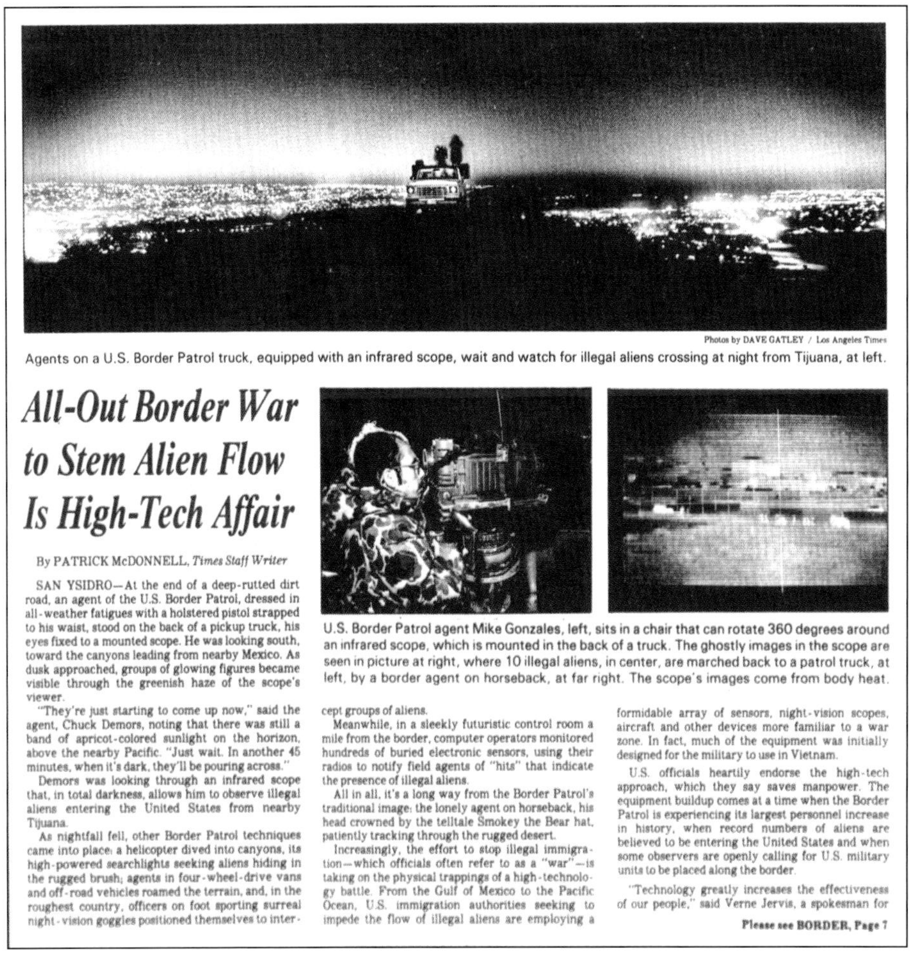

Photos by DAVE GATLEY / Los Angeles Times

Agents on a U.S. Border Patrol truck, equipped with an infrared scope, wait and watch for illegal aliens crossing at night from Tijuana, at left.

All-Out Border War to Stem Alien Flow Is High-Tech Affair

By PATRICK McDONNELL, *Times Staff Writer*

SAN YSIDRO—At the end of a deep-rutted dirt road, an agent of the U.S. Border Patrol, dressed in all-weather fatigues with a holstered pistol strapped to his waist, stood on the back of a pickup truck, his eyes fixed to a mounted scope. He was looking south, toward the canyons leading from nearby Mexico. As dusk approached, groups of glowing figures became visible through the greenish haze of the scope's viewer.

"They're just starting to come up now," said the agent, Chuck Demors, noting that there was still a band of apricot-colored sunlight on the horizon, above the nearby Pacific. "Just wait. In another 45 minutes, when it's dark, they'll be pouring across."

Demors was looking through an infrared scope that, in total darkness, allows him to observe illegal aliens entering the United States from nearby Tijuana.

As nightfall fell, other Border Patrol techniques came into place: a helicopter dived into canyons, its high-powered searchlights seeking aliens hiding in the rugged brush; agents in four-wheel-drive vans and off-road vehicles roamed the terrain, and, in the roughest country, officers on foot sporting surreal night-vision goggles positioned themselves to intercept groups of aliens.

U.S. Border Patrol agent Mike Gonzales, left, sits in a chair that can rotate 360 degrees around an infrared scope, which is mounted in the back of a truck. The ghostly images in the scope are seen in picture at right, where 10 illegal aliens, in center, are marched back to a patrol truck, at left, by a border agent on horseback, at far right. The scope's images come from body heat.

Meanwhile, in a sleekly futuristic control room a mile from the border, computer operators monitored hundreds of buried electronic sensors, using their radios to notify field agents of "hits" that indicate the presence of illegal aliens.

All in all, it's a long way from the Border Patrol's traditional image: the lonely agent on horseback, his head crowned by the telltale Smokey the Bear hat, patiently tracking through the rugged desert.

Increasingly, the effort to stop illegal immigration—which officials often refer to as a "war"—is taking on the physical trappings of a high-technology battle. From the Gulf of Mexico to the Pacific Ocean, U.S. immigration authorities seeking to impede the flow of illegal aliens are employing a formidable array of sensors, night-vision scopes, aircraft and other devices more familiar to a war zone. In fact, much of the equipment was initially designed for the military to use in Vietnam.

U.S. officials heartily endorse the high-tech approach, which they say saves manpower. The equipment buildup comes at a time when the Border Patrol is experiencing its largest personnel increase in history, when record numbers of aliens are believed to be entering the United States and when some observers are openly calling for U.S. military units to be placed along the border.

"Technology greatly increases the effectiveness of our people," said Verne Jervis, a spokesman for

Please see BORDER, Page 7

Figure 2. *Los Angeles Times*, Sunday, April 13, 1986. Photo via newspapers.com

News stories from the Reagan era reveal the consistency with which nativist views of the immigration debate were perpetuated: establishing an "us versus them" binary while keeping the public misinformed as to the reality of the situation. Notably, images and testimonies of migrants were usually absent. When their images were shown, it was in mug shots or other kinds of depictions that reinforced their criminalized, second-class status.

The photo books and series discussed in this chapter provide counternarratives to the newspaper and other media accounts of immigration that sought to dehumanize migrants and glorify the border's increased technological militarization. They document a range of situations, from quotidian

[**7**] *Mixtecos: Norte Sur*. Eniac Martínez (Mexican, 1959–2019), with text by Eduardo Vázquez Martín, 1994. Book, cover; 26 x 26 cm. © Eniac Martínez. Collection of the Cleveland Museum of Art, Ingalls Library. Image courtesy of the Centro de la Imagen Archives

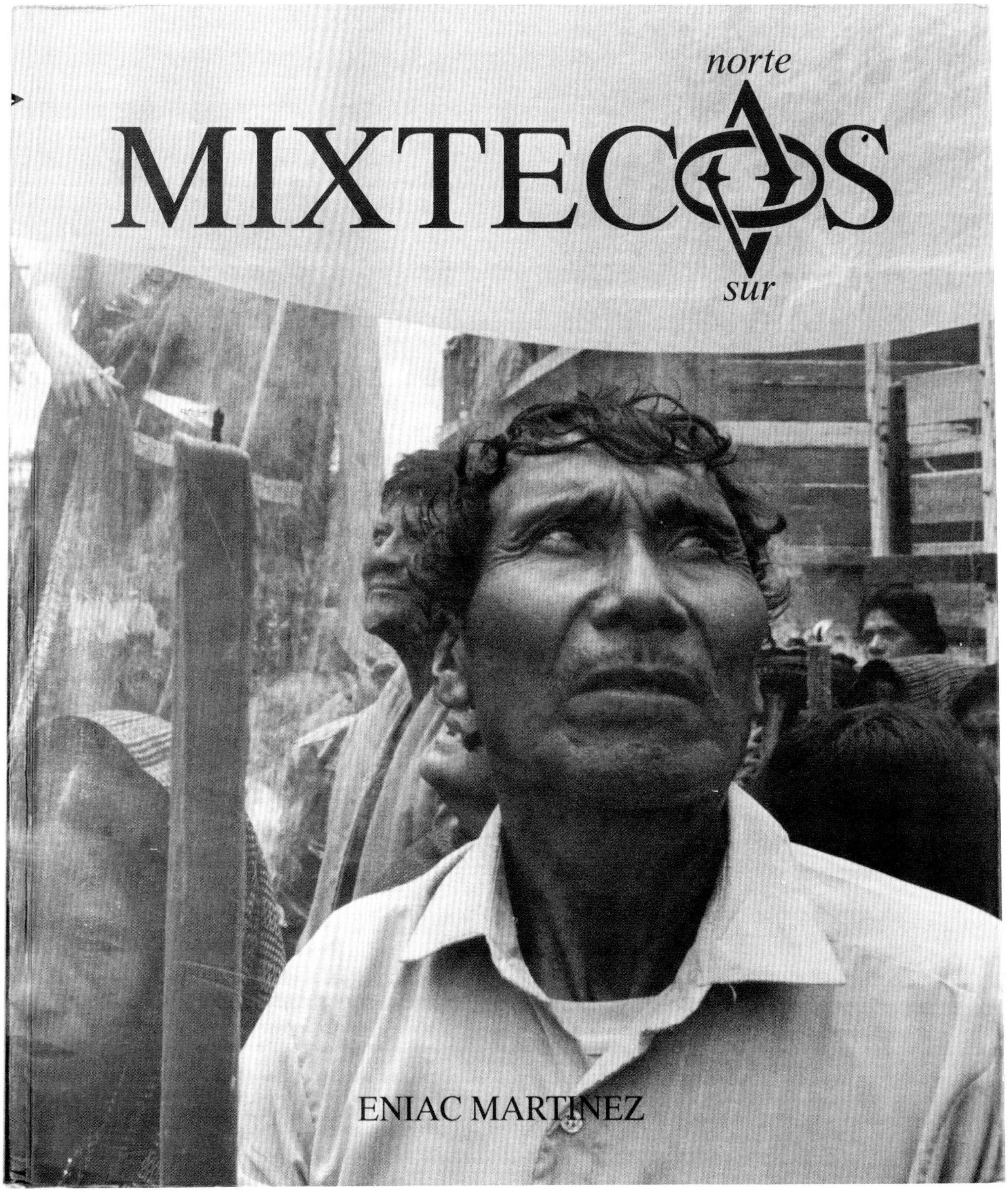

moments of family life to the perils and conflict of border crossings, and, in the process, offer insight into the migrants' reasons for undertaking the dangerous journey across the border. In their individual ways, the artists cast themselves as new makers of meaning amid the ongoing and contentious debates surrounding the border and its milieu, contributing to a radical reconsideration of how its history, spaces, and communities can be understood.

Mexican photographer Eniac Martínez (1959–2019) documented migration and the border from the southern side. Martínez's first long-term project was his *Mixtecos* series (1988–92), for which he spent four years following a group of Indigenous migrants from their native state of Oaxaca in the south of Mexico to various locations throughout California, where families worked as seasonal farmworkers or day laborers. Each winter, the families returned to Oaxaca, and Martínez followed their journey back home, bringing money, goods, and cultural influences from El Norte.

With its emphasis on migration as a cyclical phenomenon, Martínez's photo book *Mixtecos: Norte Sur* (1994) offers a corrective to the unidirectional, cross-border migration propagated in the news media. Inspired by photo books such as Robert Frank's *The Americans* (1959) and Eugene Smith's *Minamata* (1975), Martínez was drawn to the photo-book format as a means to control the narrative stakes of his projects, a control that would have been forfeited had he published the photographs in daily newspapers.[12] His *Mixtecos* book comprises sixty-four black-and-white photographs arranged in three discrete sections: "Sur," "Norte," and "Sur." Thus, the sequence of the images tells the story of a seasonal migratory route, a common one among Indigenous migrants, and allegorizes return, a kind of "coming full circle." Against the forces of colonial legacies, Martínez's volume shows how the Mixteco community's survival, both economically and culturally, is based on migration and offers an informative visual account of how and why migrants cross the border—accounts absent from the mainstream press. And, countering the cultural assimilation that often followed earlier waves of migration, Martínez's photographs, such as his images of the popular Festival of San Juan and Día de los Muertos, suggest that the Mixteco's traditions are kept alive through annual festivals and celebrations [7]. The series is thus a documentary narrative of Indigenous survival and resistance, and the persistence of Mixtecos' long-distance ties to their home communities. This narrative is in line with arguments that social scientists were only beginning to advance in the 1980s.[13]

Photographs throughout the book picture both pro- and anti-immigration demonstrations along the border. An image from a demonstration by members of the Comite Civico Popular Mixtecos (CCPM), an advocacy group for Mixteco migrants established in San Jose, California, in 1987, shows a young man holding a sign that reads, "Alto al Mal Trato a los Inmigrantes Mixtecos" (Stop the Mistreatment of Mixteco Immigrants) [7a]. In the background, a police officer on horseback looks away from the demonstrators with a clear lack of interest, an aversion of gaze that reflects the widespread refusal to acknowledge the immigrant laborers' struggle for recognition and basic human rights.

Another striking image features a young boy in Gilroy, California, on Halloween [7b]. The boy is dressed in a vampire costume, with his face painted, and looks directly at the viewer. Behind the boy, family members play with two dogs. The horizon line of an impending dusk slices through

[**7a**] *Mixtecos: Norte Sur*. Eniac Martínez, Eduardo Vázquez Martín, 1994. "Manifestación de trabajadores mexicanos, San José, California, 1989," page 64. Book; 26 x 26 cm.

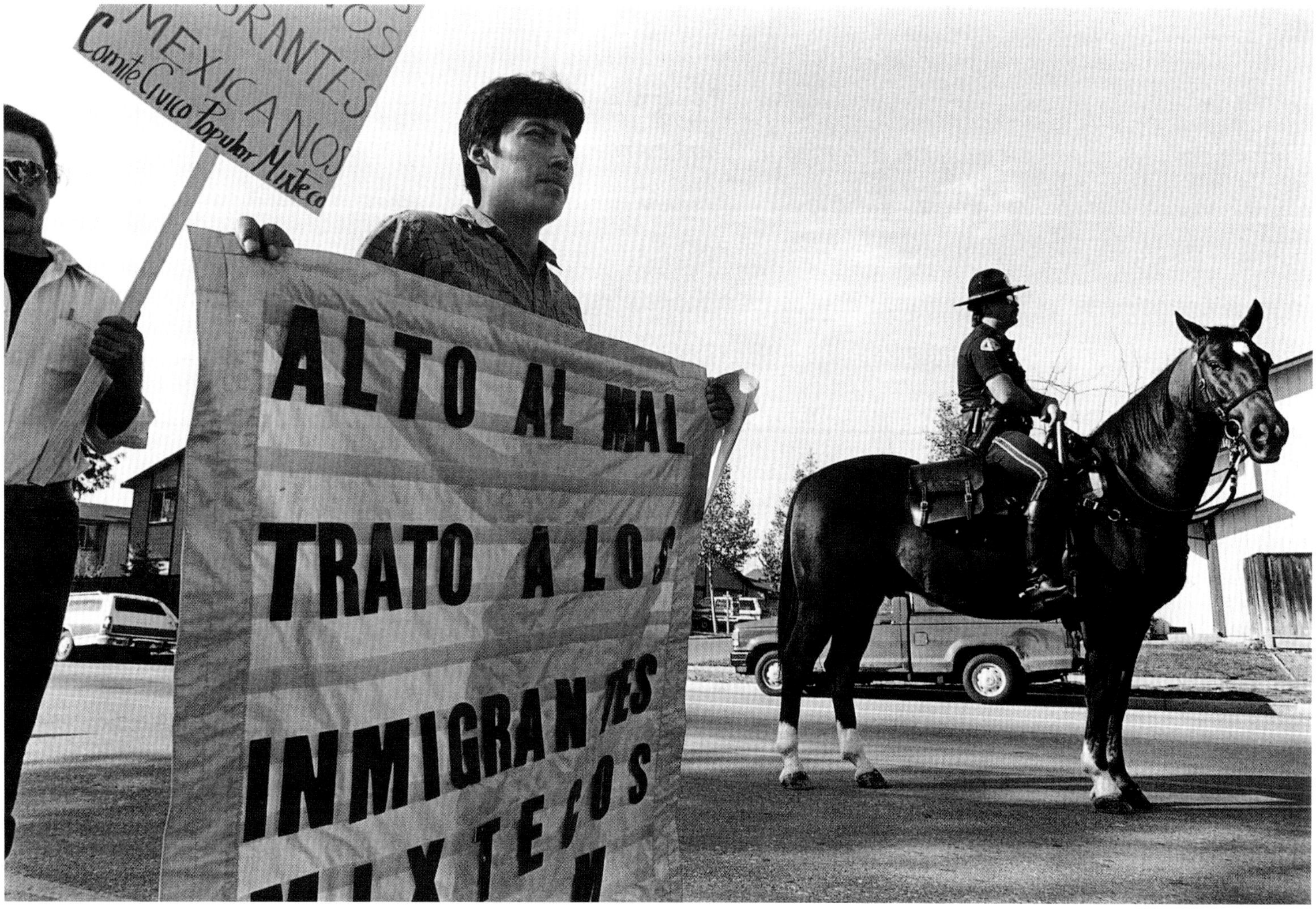

[7b] *Mixtecos: Norte Sur*. Eniac Martínez, Eduardo Vázquez Martín, 1994. "Día de Halloween, Gilroy, California, Estados Unidos," 1989, pages 78–79. Eniac Martínez. Book; 26 x 26 cm. © Eniac Martínez. Image courtesy of the Centro de la Imagen Archives

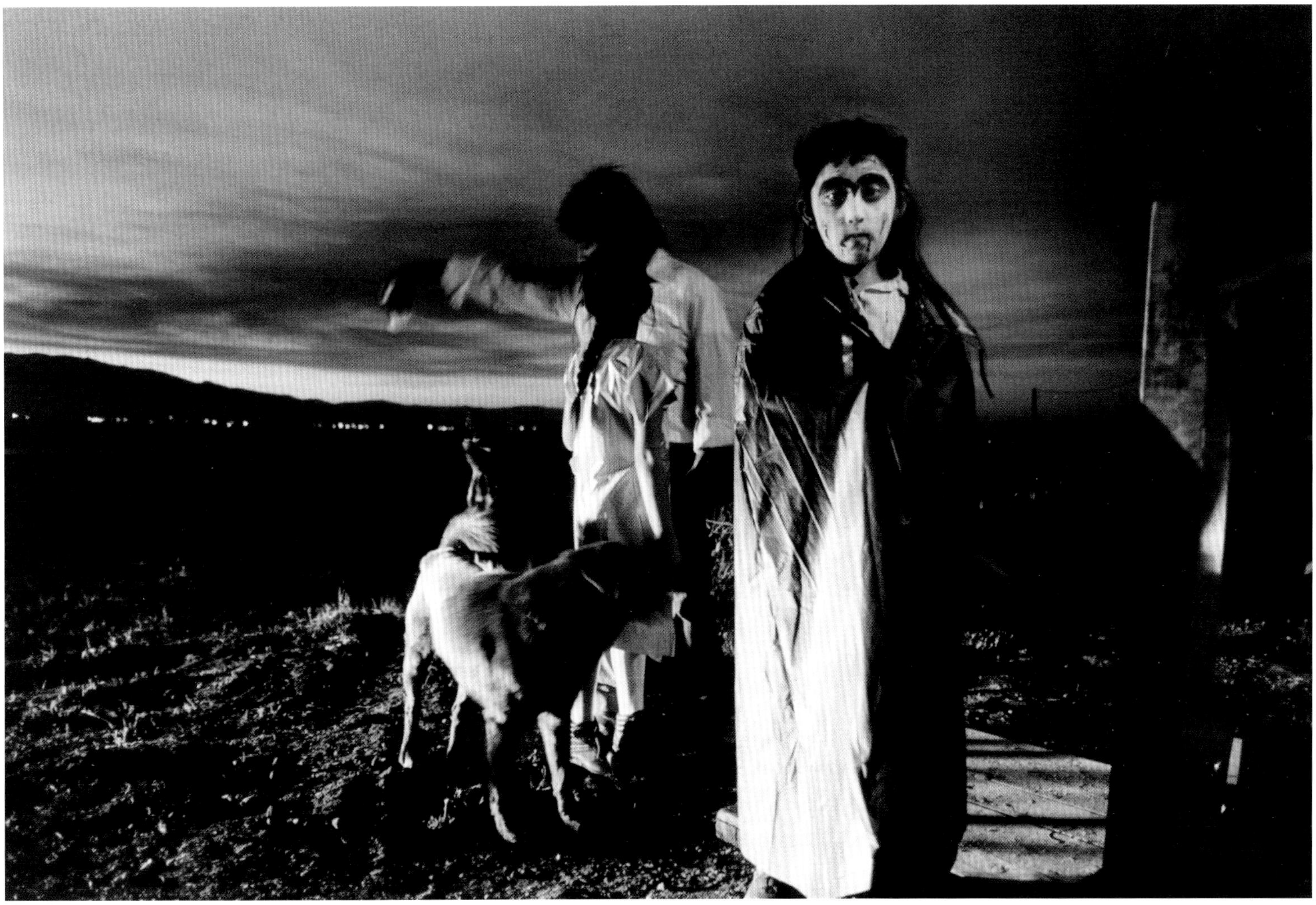

the center of the photograph, and we can see glimmers of light in the darkening background. The boy's frontal pose and sharply outlined figure are offset by the cloudy sky, and his gaze confronts viewers in a frank manner. We may read the photograph as documenting an Americanized stand-in for Día de los Muertos, but, coupled with the boy's direct, steady gaze, the image also signals the resistance to assimilation among Mixteco communities thematized throughout the series.

In 1989, Mexican photographer Lourdes Grobet (1940–2022) collaborated with anthropologist Néstor García Canclini (born 1939) on the book *Tijuana: La casa de toda la gente*; Grobet provided photographs to accompany Canclini's text [8]. Canclini, a longtime resident of Mexico, popularized the term "cultural hybridity" and took a particular interest in the spaces of the US-Mexico border. Throughout, *Tijuana* evokes the duality of the border town as both a place that migrants pass through en route to the United States and a site of American escapism. Following a short essay by Canclini, in which he states that previous literature on the subject by social scientists is inherently limited because it is written rather than seen (in photos), the majority of the book is given over to Grobet's photographs, under the heading "Una Sola Ciudad en Imagénes" (A Single City in Images). Images have as their only caption anonymous quotes from city residents, who offer their impressions of various Tijuana public landmarks and spaces. It is clear from their quotes that all the participants, at all levels of society, are uniquely aware of their position in a global, migratory, hybrid landscape.

A series of seven images and accompanying quotes depict Avenida Revolución, Tijuana's tourist district [8a, b]. The quotes appearing below the photographs of tourists highlight the incongruity of worlds colliding on the Avenida and the place of fantasy tourists anticipate when they enter Mexico. One resident comments, "It refers to the myth that Americans bring, which has to do with crossing the border into the past, into the wilderness, into the idea of being able to ride horseback."[14] Another references the experience the Avenida has become for American tourists, for whom it embodies all exotic experiences they hope to encounter in the country.

Grobet's photographs capture the uncomfortable strangeness of the interactions between tourists and residents. The tourists become caricatures, illustrating the economic and cultural divides within the city's spaces. Because her mother was from El Paso, Texas, Grobet visited the border often when she was growing up and was familiar with its cities. An artist originally trained as a painter, Grobet abandoned painting for photography after witnessing the events of 1968 in Mexico.[15] She was not alone in experiencing the renewed urgency of the moment, as that year's student movements, along with what is now known as the Tlatelolco Massacre, became a catalyzing force for Mexico's artistic and cultural landscape in the years that followed.[16] Grobet's interest in photography was partly prompted by the increased access to cameras and film in 1960s Mexico, although she developed her photographic practice with a distinctly conceptual, feminist slant.

In another striking image from *Tijuana*, taken in a bus station, a group of women are seated on the floor amid piles of their belongings, packed haphazardly in cardboard boxes tied with rope, trash bags, and overloaded shopping bags [8c]. One young woman sits with her chin resting in her palm and looks directly at the camera. Above her head, an

[**8**] *Tijuana: La casa de toda la gente*, 1989. Néstor García Canclini, photographs by Lourdes Grobet (Mexican, 1940–2022), with contributions by Patricia Safa. Book, cover; 25 x 25 cm. © Lourdes Grobet S.C.

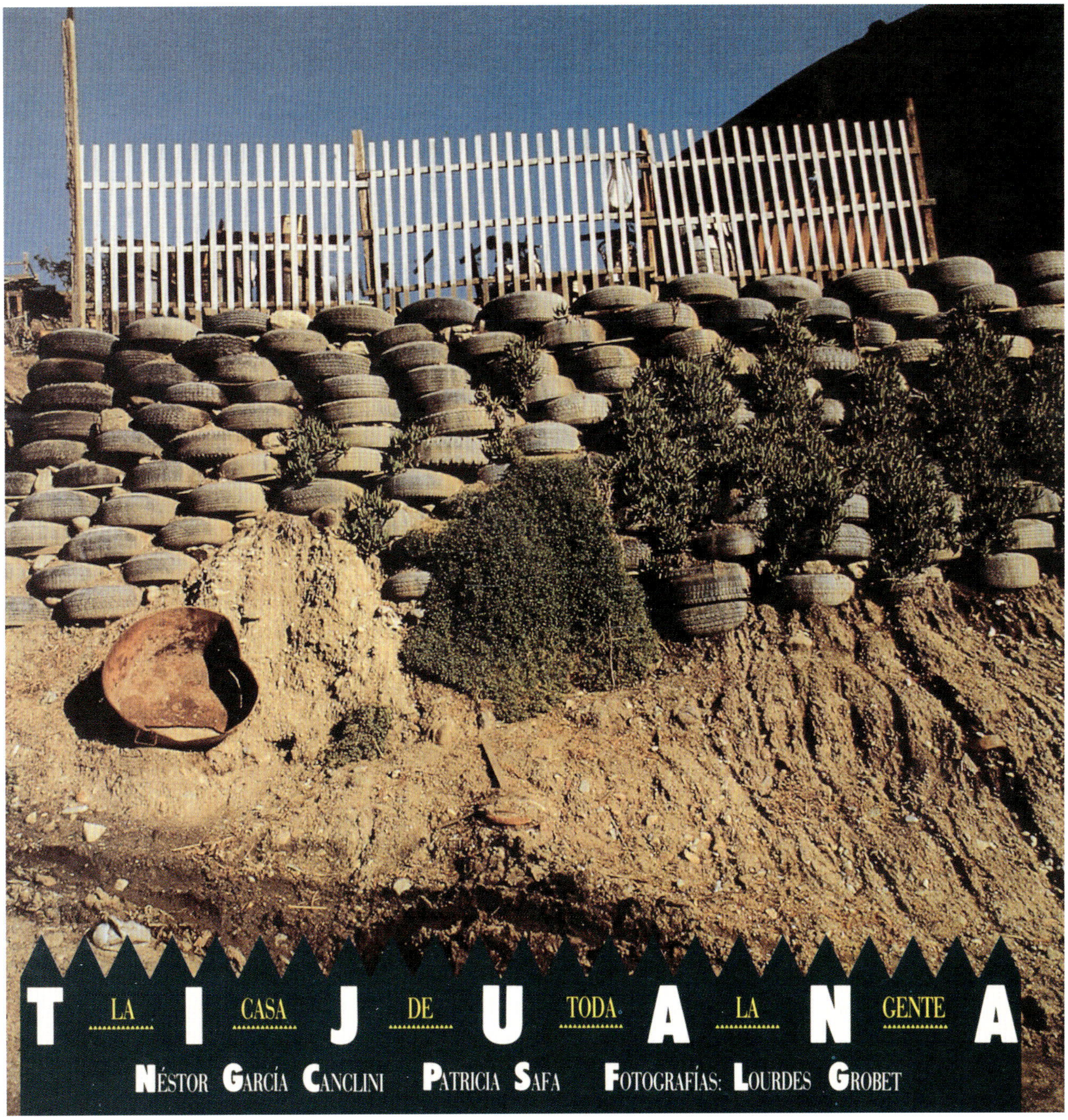

[**8a**] *Tijuana: La casa de toda la gente*, 1989.
Néstor García Canclini, photographs
by Lourdes Grobet, with contributions by
Patricia Safa. Book, page 28; 25 x 25 cm.
© Lourdes Grobet S.C.

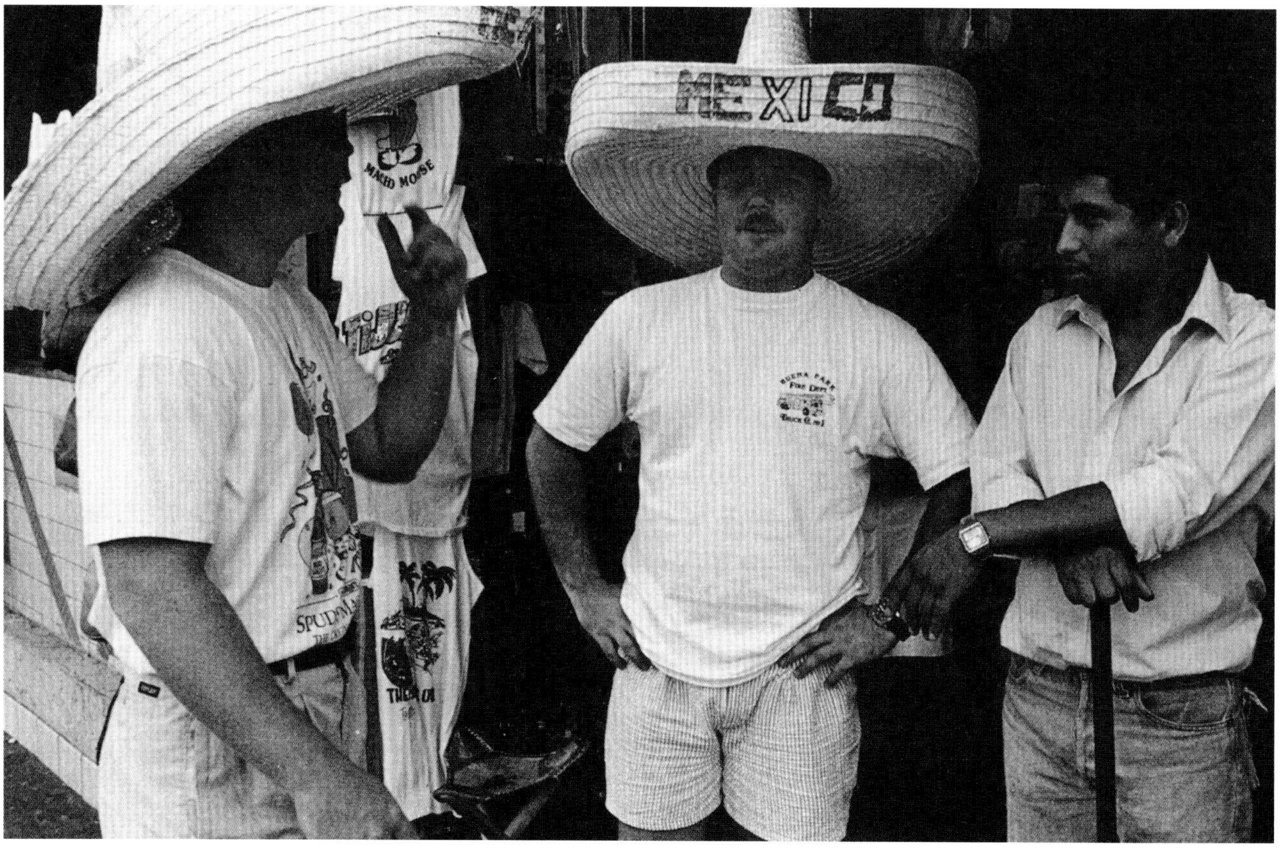

[**8b**] *Tijuana: La casa de toda la gente*, 1989.
Néstor García Canclini, photographs
by Lourdes Grobet, with contributions by
Patricia Safa. Book, page 29; 25 x 25 cm.
© Lourdes Grobet S.C.

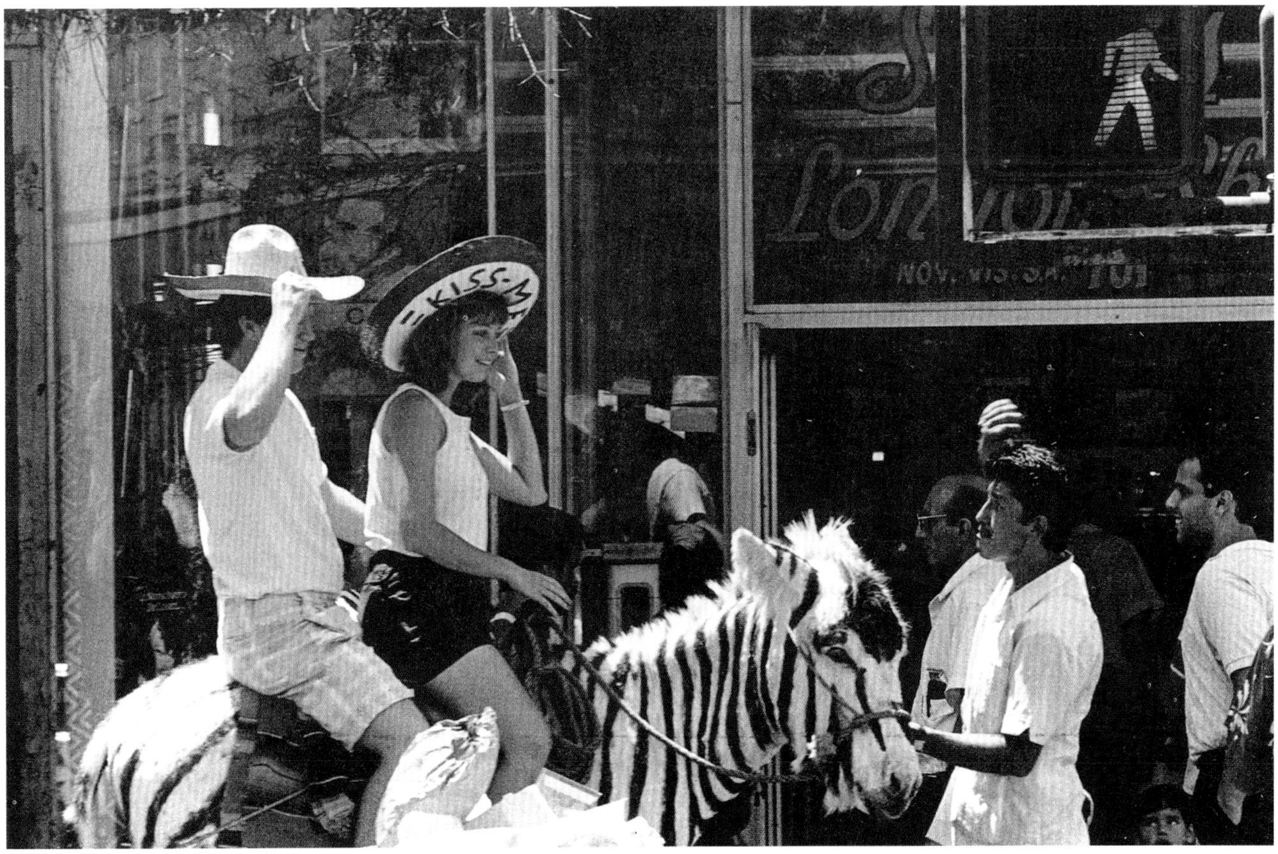

[**8c**] *Tijuana: La casa de toda la gente*, 1989.
Néstor García Canclini, photographs
by Lourdes Grobet, with contributions by
Patricia Safa. Book, page 20; 25 x 25 cm.
© Lourdes Grobet S.C.

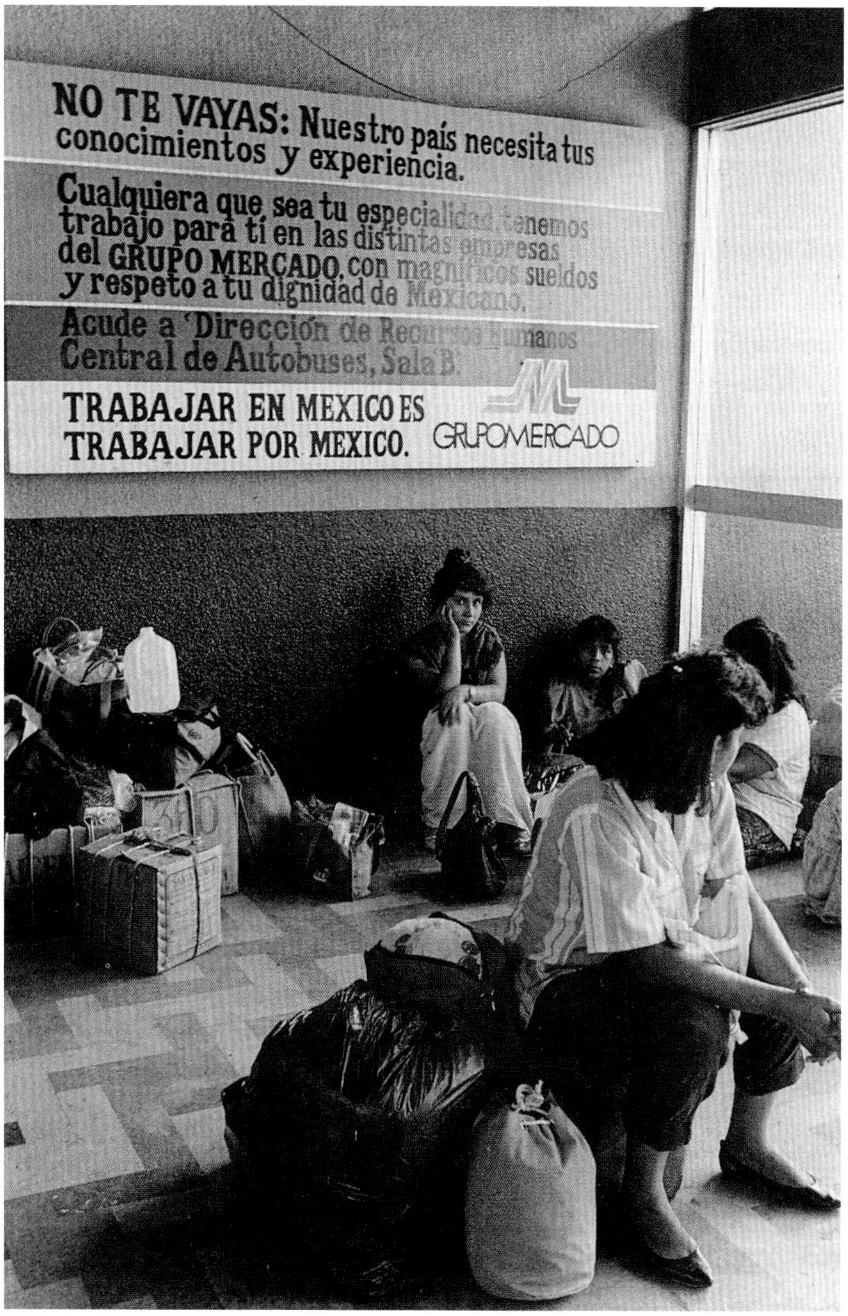

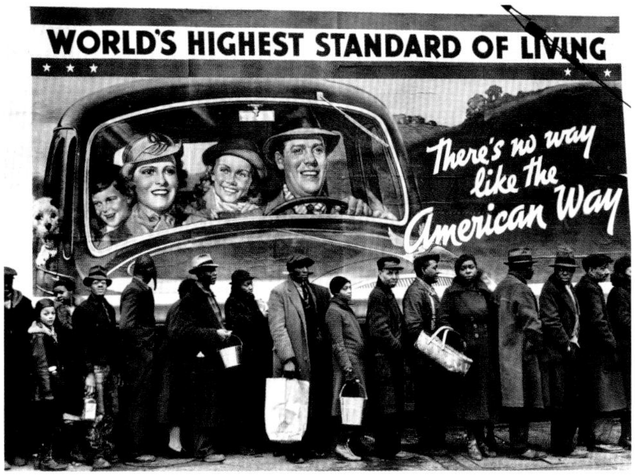

Figure 3. *The American Way, aka Louisville Flood*, 1937. Margaret Bourke-White (American, 1904–1971). Gelatin silver print; 24.9 x 34.1 cm. The Nelson-Atkins Museum of Art, Gift of Hallmark Cards, Inc., 2005.27.2568. © 2024 Estate of Margaret Bourke-White / The LIFE Picture Collection / Shutterstock

advertisement reads, "NO TE VAYAS" [DON'T LEAVE], and appeals to migrants to seek employment in Mexico, for "magnificent wages and respect for [their] dignity as Mexicans." The ironic juxtaposition of the sign and the migrant women is not unlike Depression-era documentary photographs from the United States. An especially close parallel is Margaret Bourke-White's *Louisville Flood* (1937), which depicts a line of African Americans outside a flood-relief agency under a billboard that reads, "World's Highest Standard of Living: There's No Way Like the American Way" (fig. 3).

The irony in Grobet's photograph is reinforced by the fact that the sign makes it seem as if migrants have a choice as to whether or not to leave. By the time they have reached Tijuana, most migrants have traveled great distances, sometimes from as far as Central or South America. In addition, the neoliberal economic policies that took effect in Mexico throughout the 1980s, culminating with the passage of the North American Free Trade Agreement (NAFTA) in 1994, made migration for the sake of livelihood less of a choice than a necessity for many migrants. This condition of forced migration versus the privileged travel of tourism depicted just a few pages later is another duality of Tijuana's social spaces. By featuring a group of women waiting to cross the border, the photograph subverts the typical portrayal of male migrants that often permeate the visual landscapes of Mexico and the United States. As a corrective to mass-media depictions, Grobet's project brings specificity to the cultural landscape of the border through focusing on a single city and highlighting the voices of migrants and border residents, voices typically absent from the mass media at that time.

Magnum photographer Alex Webb's book *Crossings: Photographs from the U.S.-Mexico Border* (2003) features his photographs of the border from the 1970s to 2001 [9]. In 1975, during his first trip to the region from his native New York, Webb (born 1952) writes, "I was fascinated and overwhelmed by experiencing a country, Mexico, so geographically close to and so culturally different than the United States. It was the beginning of a long relationship with the border and with the entirety of Mexico."[17] Webb is a devoted researcher whose notes from his first trip to the border, culled from government data and news stories, display a deep knowledge of his subjects and the perils of border crossing.[18] Webb discovered that the border region, while a distinct cultural landscape, was not unlike other parts of the country in terms of everyday and family life [10]. By emphasizing the prosaic aspects of life on the border in *Crossings*, Webb attempts to bridge the divide between himself, his subjects, and his audience.

The book's ninety-five photographs are roughly arranged by theme or formal affinity. Among the themes that unfold throughout *Crossings* is that of waiting. Border commuters line up, waiting for border-crossing cards at a Mexican federal building in Tijuana. Figures sit on the ground, waiting for nightfall to travel north. In one image, a group of men in the dimming sunlight stand in line on the cement ridge of Tijuana's riverbed overlooking "El Bordo" and the United States [11]. This photograph, titled *Waiting to Cross*, is taken from a low vantage point, which serves to monumentalize the men's figures. As their forms recede into the distance, their figures appear against the sunset backdrop. All facing forward with a resolute expression, focused only on what lies ahead as they wait, they resemble a makeshift army. The sight of

[**9**] *Crossings: Photographs from the U.S.-Mexico Border*, 2003. Alex Webb (American, born 1952). Book; overall: 29.8 x 24.8 cm. Collection of the Cleveland Museum of Art, Ingalls Library. © Alex Webb

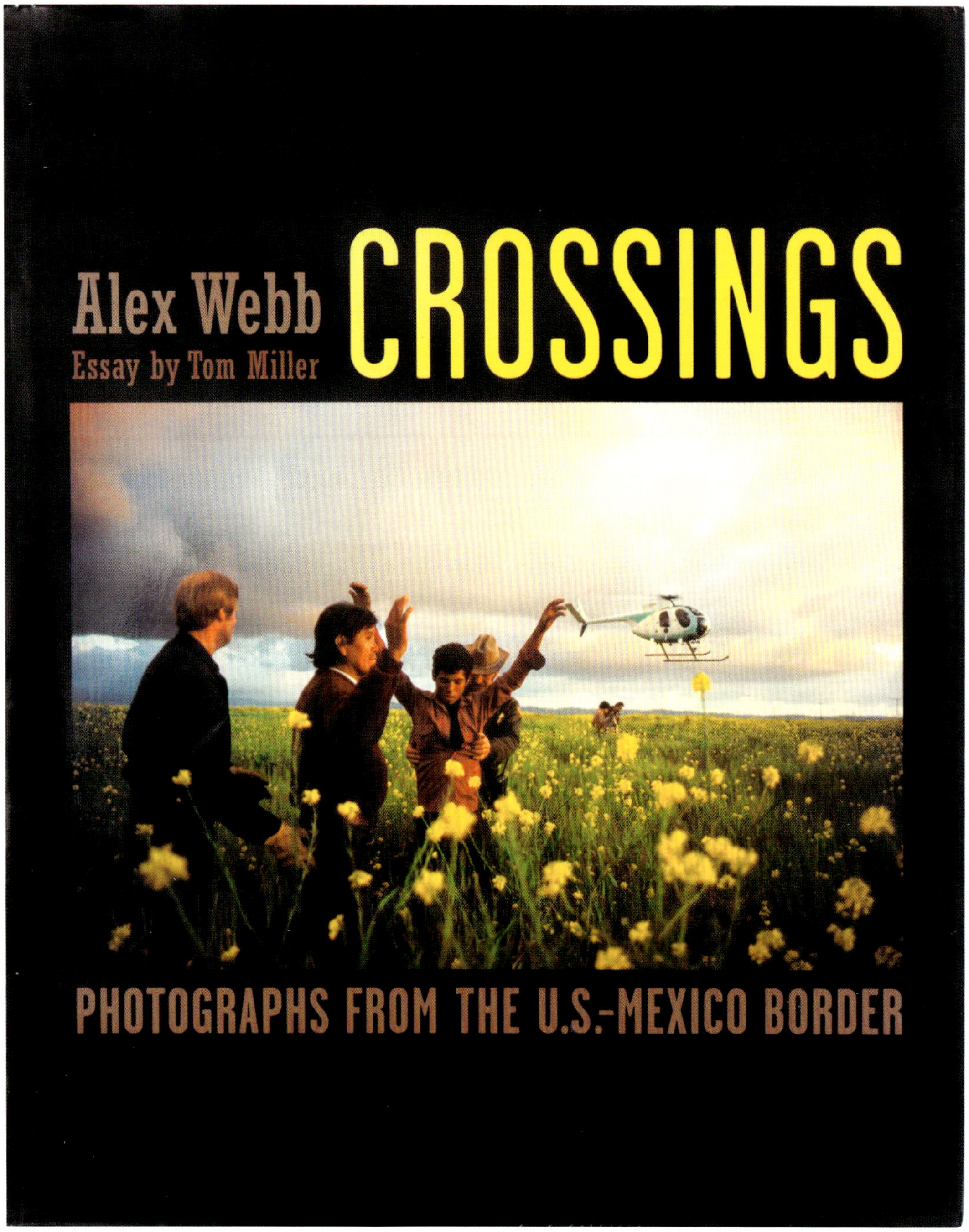

[**10**] *Nuevo Laredo, Tamaulipas*, 1996.
Alex Webb. Digital C-print mounted on
3mm Sintra; 63.5 x 96.5 cm.
Courtesy of the artist. © Alex Webb

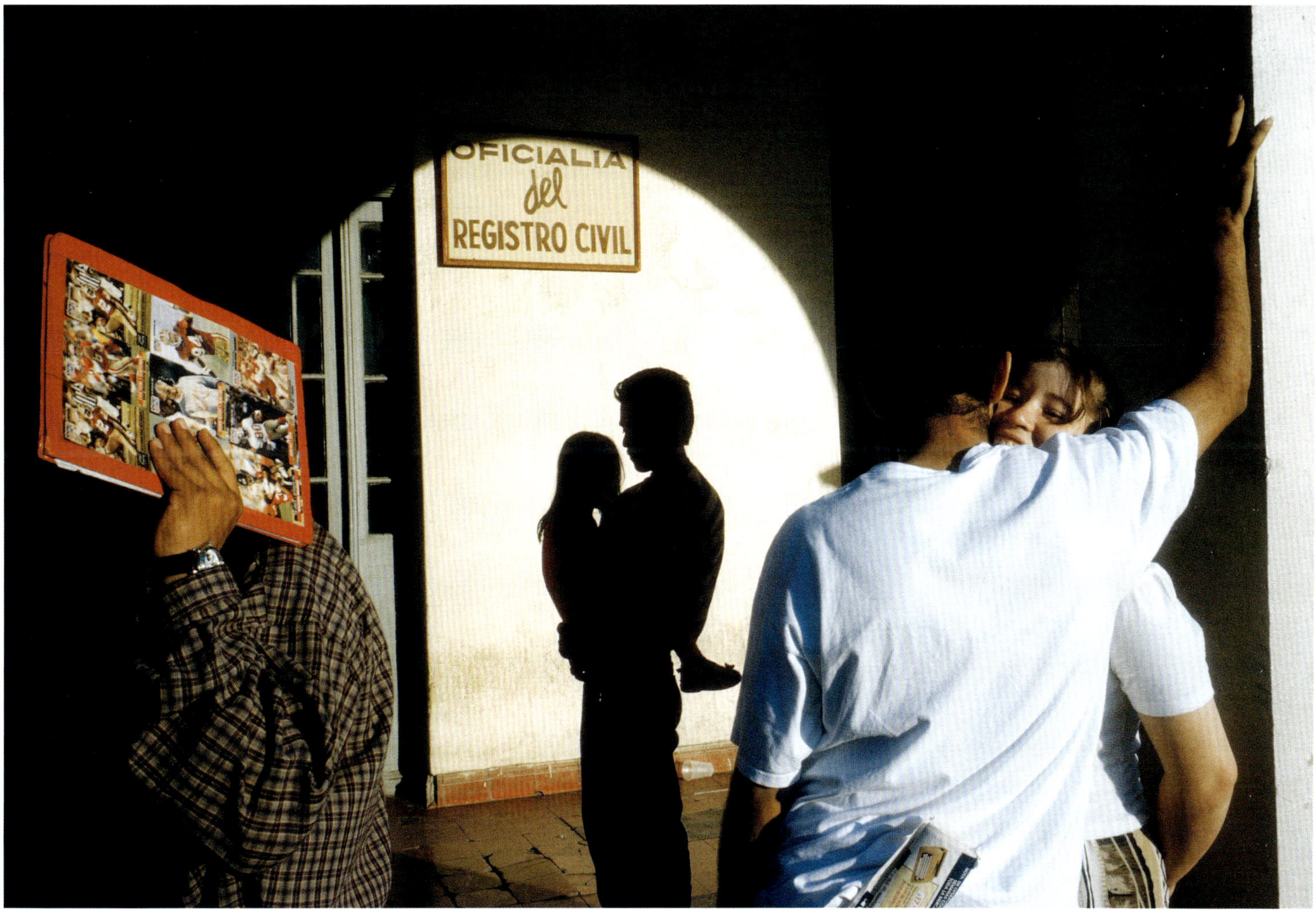

[**11**] *Waiting to Cross, Tijuana*, 1992.
Alex Webb. Digital C-print mounted on 3mm Sintra; 47 x 71.1 cm.
Courtesy of the artist. © Alex Webb

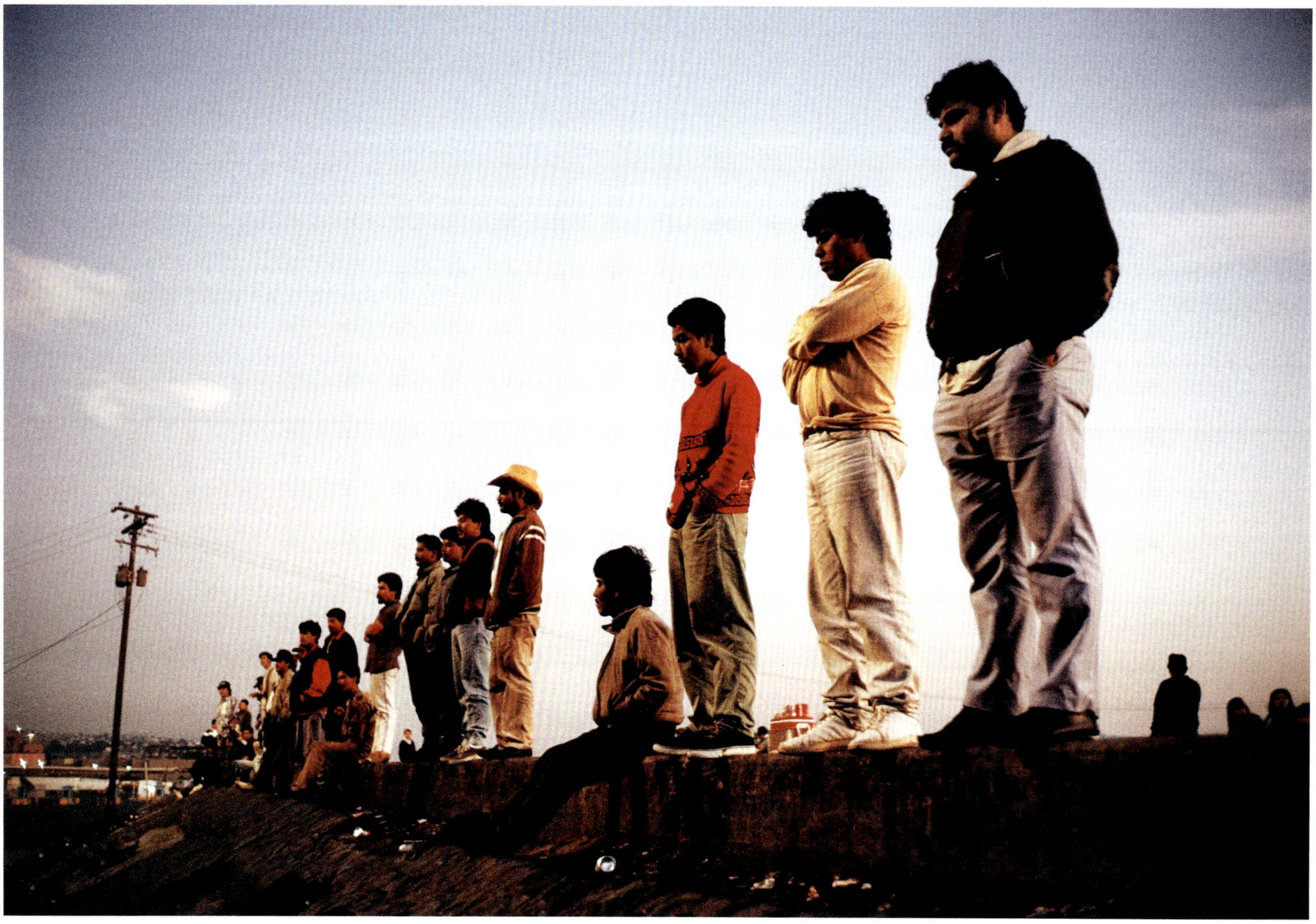

migrants waiting along the border at sunset was a common one. A popular migrant strategy entailed waiting for nightfall, then rushing the border, en masse, with the knowledge that patrolmen could capture only a fraction of crossers amid the darkness and confusion.

Shot in Tijuana, *Waiting to Cross* is reminiscent of a scene Gloria Anzaldúa describes in *Borderlands / La Frontera* (1987): "Trembling with fear, yet filled with courage. . . . Mexicans with hands like boot soles gather at night by the river where two worlds merge creating what Reagan calls a frontline, a war zone. The convergence has created a shock, a border culture, a third country, a closed country."[19] Read in conjunction with Webb's photograph, Anzaldúa's characterization, at once calm and geopolitically resonant, emphasizes the charged moment of this nocturnal ritual, with both likening the gathering figures of migrants to a line of soldiers in a war zone awaiting battle.

The manner in which Webb positioned the figures in the frame, erect and statuesque against the skyline, underscores their resistance to the army of patrolmen one can imagine positioned right across the border and humanizes the magnitude of their sacrifice. Down the line, the men appear with nothing more than the clothes they wear: a variegated array of khakis and denim, sneakers and oxfords, sweaters and sports jackets. As the photo was taken in 1992, we know they are facing the militarized outfit of Border Patrol, now equipped with movement-sensory surveillance devices, night-vision goggles, trucks, helicopters, and high-powered rifles. It is telling that Webb chose to photograph this side of the "battle" as opposed to the US side, creating a record of migrant resistance. It was also in 1992 that the ten-foot-tall steel wall along the border between San Diego and Tijuana was newly constructed, a significant escalation over the chain-link fence and national monuments that had previously delineated the border. Webb's image contrasts the vertical thrust of the wall with the verticality of the individuals preparing to confront it with their own upright postures. They present a human wall, a flesh-and-blood resistance to the inanimate steel structures that block, repel, and demean them.

Made shortly after the IRCA had gone into effect, Susan Meiselas's *Crossings* (1989) series documents the effects of this reactionary law.[20] Meiselas (born 1948) is a New York–based photographer who has belonged to the Magnum photo agency since 1976. From her beginnings as a photographer, she has drawn on her background as an anthropology major at Sarah Lawrence for her socially engaged documentary practice, which incorporates narrative strategies such as interviews and extensive research to supplement the images. Her experience photographing the Nicaraguan Revolution of 1970 made her deeply aware of the complexities and paradoxes of US-sponsored interventions in Central America, and how they produced refugees who entered the United States through the border with Mexico.

In 1989, Meiselas spent several weeks following border patrolmen around the clock as they conducted their duties [12]. She shot the series with panoramic film, explaining, "There was something theatrical in the whole active choreography of moving, [and I] wanted to get that energy into every frame."[21] One frame from Meiselas's *Crossings* series captures the moment when, at 2:00 a.m. one morning, Border Patrol apprehended a twelve-year-old boy and then took him to a detention center in San Diego [13]. The photograph depicts two figures in a stark, brightly lit room. The young boy in the image both affirms and contradicts the typical "Mexican

[**12**] *7:30 a.m. Arrest of undocumented worker by U.S. Border Patrol in downtown San Diego, CA*, from the series *Crossings*, 1989. Susan Meiselas (American, born 1948). Gelatin silver print; 44.5 x 73.7 cm. Courtesy of and © Susan Meiselas / Magnum Photos

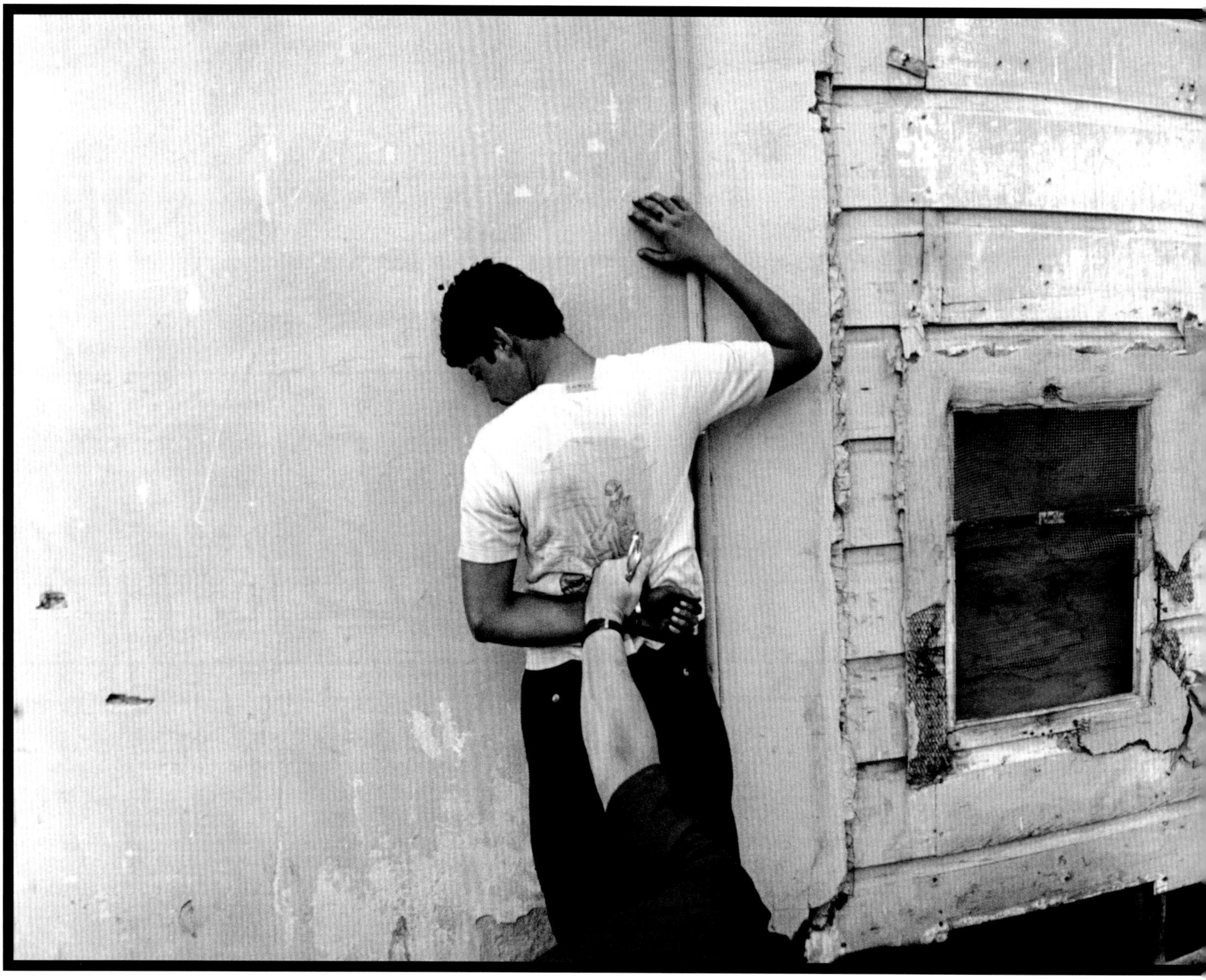

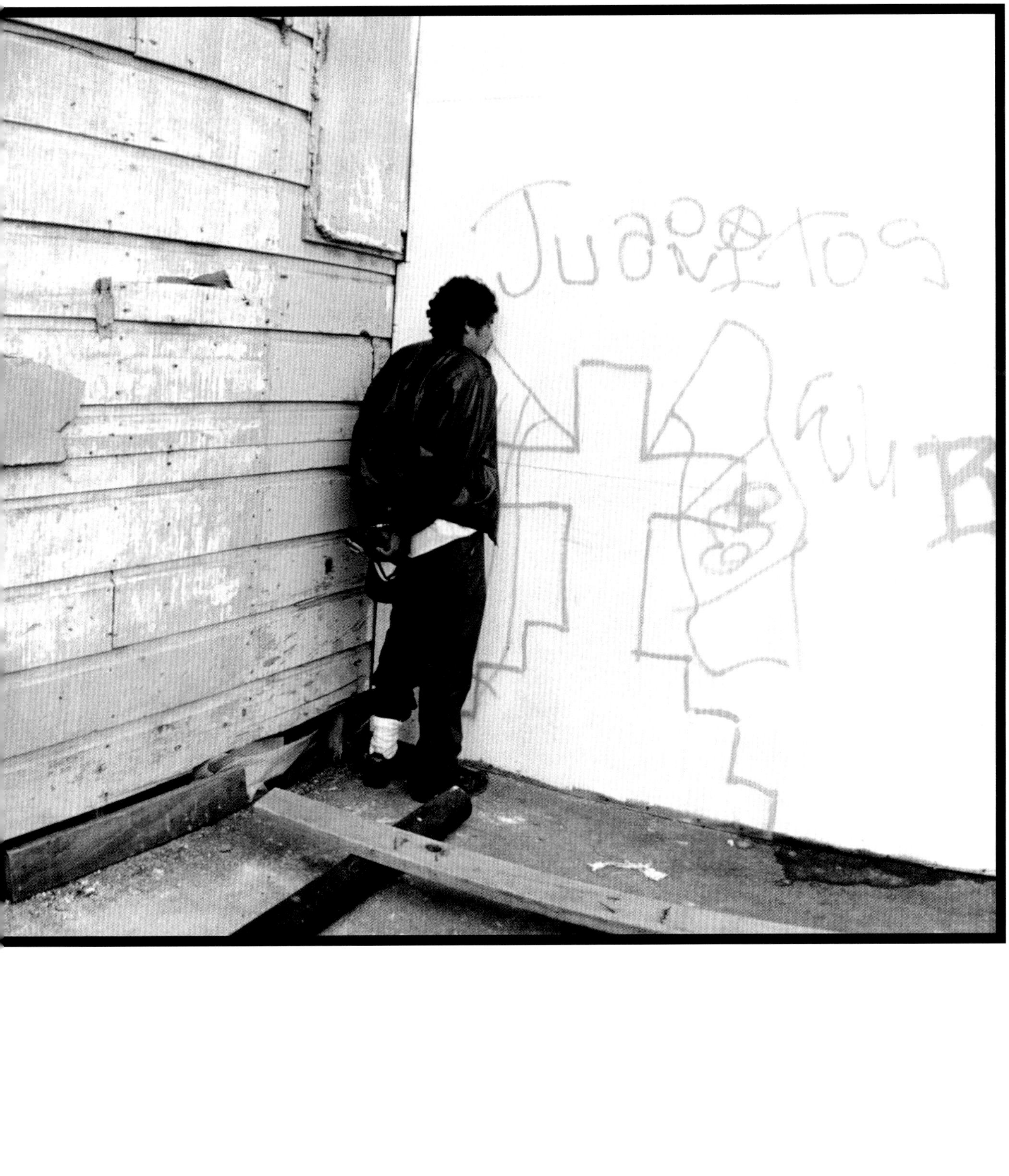

[**13**] *2:00 a.m. Arrest and documentation of twelve-year-old boy, Imperial Beach, California*, from the series *Crossings*, 1989. Susan Meiselas. Gelatin silver print; 44.5 x 73.7 cm. Courtesy of and © Susan Meiselas / Magnum Photos

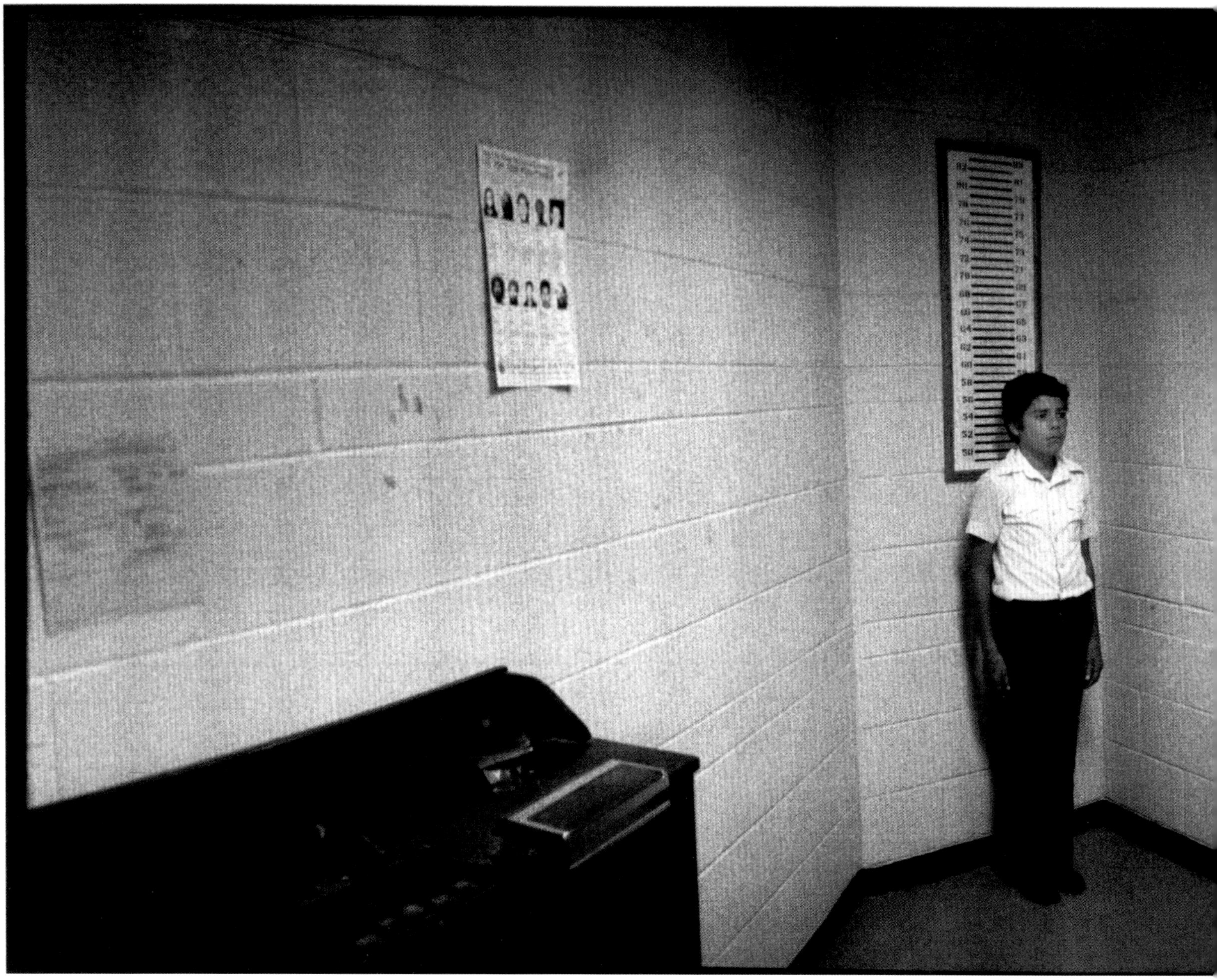

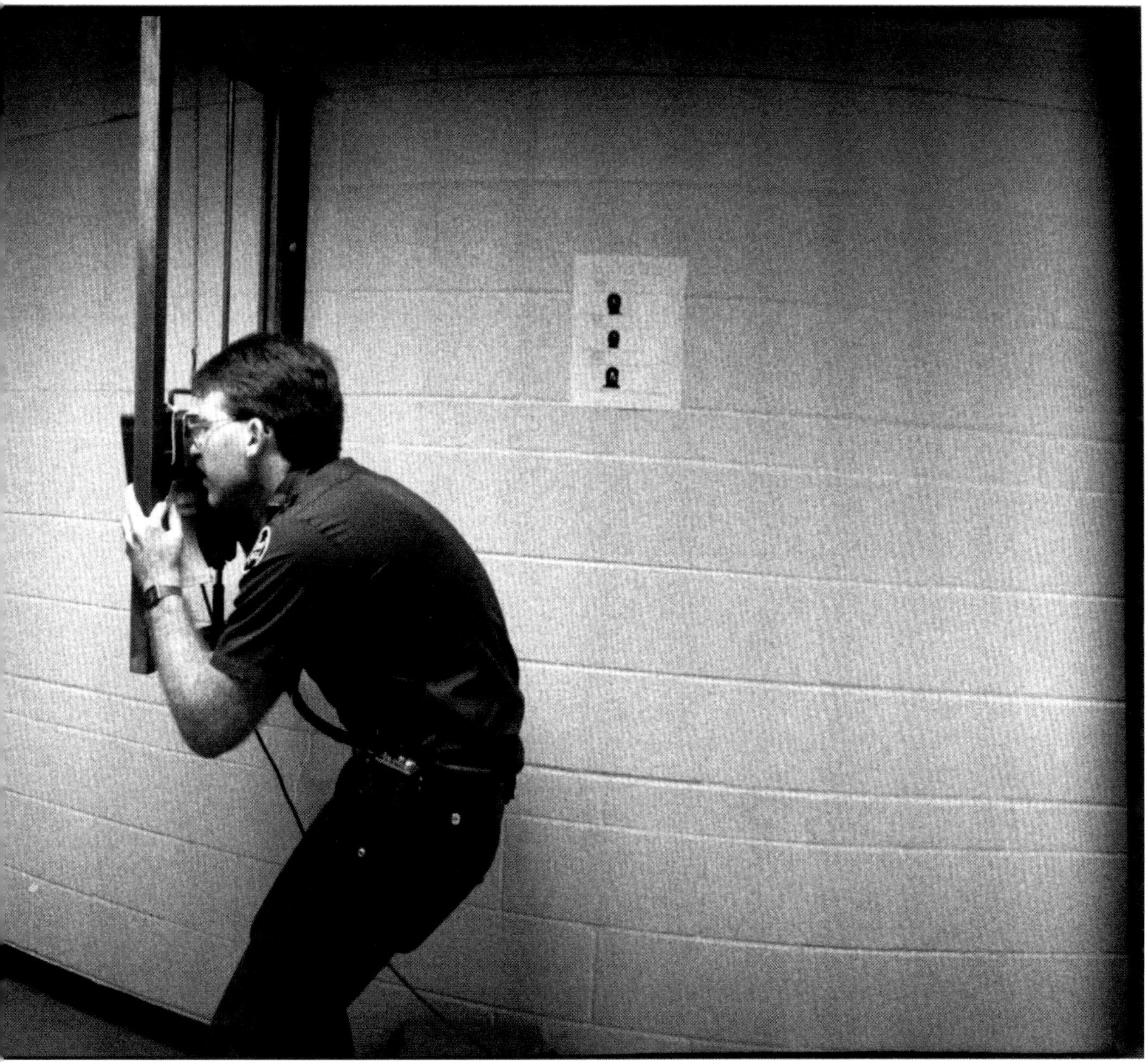

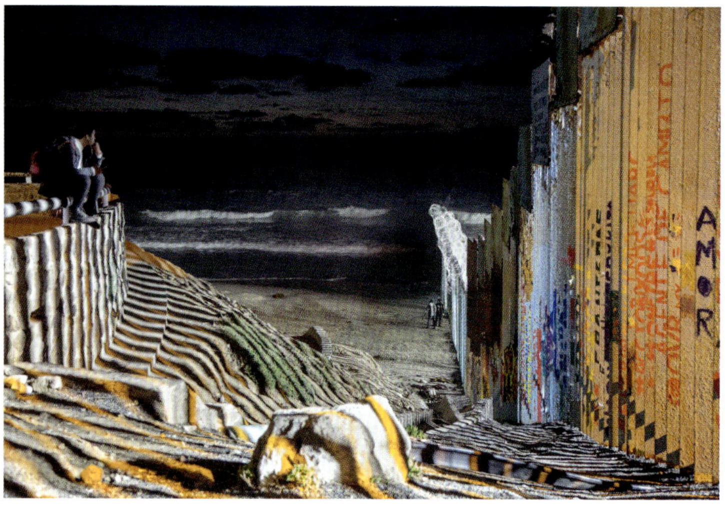

Figure 4. *The wall dividing the US and Mexico at Freedom Park, Tijuana Beach, Tijuana, Mexico*, 2018. Susan Meiselas. C-print; dimensions variable. Photo: Susan Meiselas / Magnum Photos

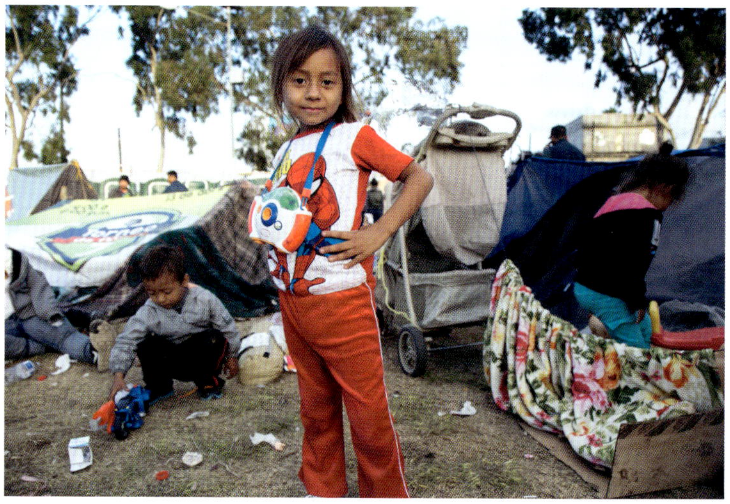

Figure 5. *Genesy, 5, getting ready to leave the Benito Juárez shelter, Tijuana, Mexico*, 2018. Susan Meiselas. C-print; dimensions variable. Photo: Susan Meiselas / Magnum Photos

Brown" person the patrol officers often targeted.[22] Although he is a male of dark complexion he is also a child, his short stature underscored by the height chart behind him and the stooping figure of the patrol officer who photographs him. He wears a neatly pressed white shirt tucked into black slacks, with black dress shoes. Before him an officer operates a camera employed for the consistency of standardized image making, and to the left, a surface for obtaining his fingerprints represents a further method of categorizing his criminal existence. The frame functions as a meta-image of sorts of the relationship between photographer and photographed subject, making explicit and symbolic the power relations between them. In particular Meiselas draws attention to the operations of the gaze, making the very act of photographing the subject of the photograph.

An artist whose practice values the importance of returning to places and communities where she has previously worked, Meiselas has returned to the borderlands many times since 1989. Most recently, in 2018, she returned to document the arrival at the US-Mexico border of the first Migrant Caravan, which originated in Honduras and arrived, on foot, in Tijuana, six-thousand migrants strong (fig. 4). One image stands as a powerful bookend to the *2 a.m. arrest* photograph of the young boy: that of Genesy, a five-year-old girl and member of the Caravan, posing proudly with a toy camera around her neck in front of her family's encampment at the Benito Juárez complex (fig. 5). In contrast to the photograph of the young boy, Genesy gazes directly at the camera, confidently posed, in prominent possession of her own image-making device. An accompanying quote from her mother, Maria, which appeared in an extended *Vogue* feature on Meiselas's photographs, praises Genesy's bravery in the face of travel and uncertainty. "I'm really proud to be her mom. Genesy is really creative. There have been a lot of obstacles traveling with the kids. . . . Back in [San Pedro Sula,] Honduras, we didn't have enough money to eat. I worked cleaning and ironing clothes—on a good day I made $12."[23] The mother's words lend credence to the reality of their sacrifices in their journey to the US-Mexico border, as well as her daughter's strength and tenacity against all odds.

In 2016, the artist Zoe Leonard (born 1961) embarked on an extensive project documenting the Rio Grande / Río Bravo, specifically that portion of the river that functions as the border between Texas and Mexico. A New York–based artist, Leonard spent four years (2016–20) traveling through the borderlands, taking pictures with her hand-held 35mm camera. Leonard's desire to examine the politics of representation vis-à-vis themes such as gender, sexuality, migration, and displacement made the spaces of the borderlands of particular interest to the artist. She explains, "I wanted to challenge popular misconceptions about the borderlands, constructed and reified through popular culture, and through news media accounts."[24]

The result is the two-volume publication *Al río / To the River* (2022), featuring a broad selection of essays by various writers and more than three hundred pages of photographs.[25] The images are shown uncropped, printed to the edges, and without any accompanying text. They appear in sequences that suggest movement—the photographer's movement, the movement of actors in the borderlands, the flow of the river (fig. 6). At times, the montages are cinematic in their arrangement, like storyboard layouts. Among the themes depicted are the construction of border walls, Border Patrol, and national landmarks, but also, perhaps unexpectedly, moments of everyday life, like ranchers herding animals in

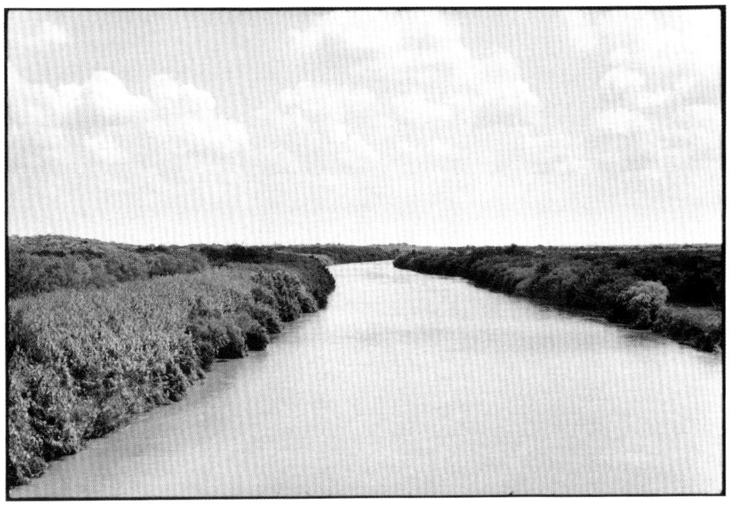

Figure 6. Detail from Tim Johnson, ed., *Zoe Leonard: Al río / To the River* (Luxembourg: Mudam Luxembourg- Musée d'Art Moderne Grand-Duc Jean; Berlin: Hatje Cantz, 2022). Zoe Leonard (American, born 1961). Gelatin silver print. © Zoe Leonard. Courtesy of the artist, Galerie Gisela Capitain, Cologne, and Hauser & Wirth

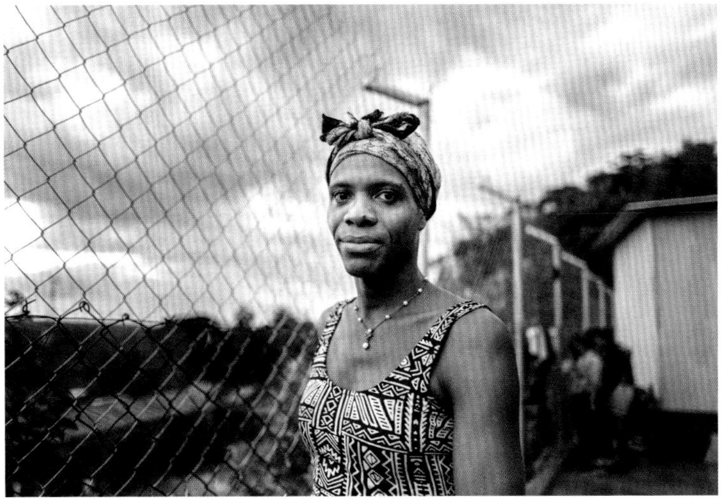

Figure 7. *Ashley, Trans, whose life was threatened in Honduras, seeks safety in the US*, plate 72 in *La Caravana del Diablo*, 2020. Ada Trillo (Mexican American, born 1976). Archival pigment print; 66 x 102 cm. © Ada Trillo. Image courtesy of the artist

the landscape and children playing in the river on a hot day. The image sequences enable us to gain access to the artist's conceptual exploration of observation itself and how she is attuned to the choreographies of the border. *Al río* reveals the ways in which the river and its tributaries move one way, while the actors who live and labor there move in other ways. In following these activities, Leonard metaphorizes the heterogeneous qualities of the border and how "despite the history of barricading . . . the border region has always been a space of movement."[26]

As an outsider in the borderlands, Leonard was cognizant of the stories that typically define the border and instead chose to highlight other micro-narratives or landscapes. In a sequence of six photographs early on in the book, families swim in the river in Ciudad Juárez, their cars pulled up to the water's edge, trunks open, as children and adults wade and splash in the water on a sunny day [14]. For the artist, it was important to include images of the joy and leisure that were a part of daily life on the border. In documenting such private moments, Leonard remained respectful of her subjects, keeping a distance and putting her camera down or pointing it away from residents in scenarios she knew they may not wish to be photographed. In this way, she was careful not to replicate with her camera the intense surveillance with which these individuals were no doubt well familiar.

In recent years, and in the wake of climate change, COVID-19, and a global recession, the distance that migrants have traveled to reach the US-Mexico border has increased. Ada Trillo's photo book *La Caravana del Diablo* (2022) traces the path of migration from northern Central America to the United States. Trillo, who was born in El Paso in 1976 and grew up in Ciudad Juárez, was inspired to embark on her project after hearing a campaign speech by Donald Trump referring to Mexicans and Central Americans as "drug dealers, criminals, and rapists," and sought to counter such dehumanizing rhetoric. *La Caravana del Diablo* begins by documenting riders on *La Bestia* (The Beast), the ominously nicknamed freight trains on which many migrants from Mexico and Central America hitch a ride to travel to the US border. The photographs, made when she was riding alongside migrants on *La Bestia*, are a primer for the long and terrifying journeys migrants undertake. The black-and-white photographs in the 116-page volume are arranged chronologically, charting the four years Trillo spent taking them (2017–20). All the images are simply captioned with descriptive text. Often, the captions include the names of the subjects, reflecting the photographer's engagement with them. While traveling with the Migrant Caravan from Honduras to California, Trillo also photographed and recorded the stories of many LGBTQ+ migrants whom she met along the way, whose sexuality compounded their struggles as asylum seekers (fig. 7). Trillo explains, "I am Queer, so this was very personal to me. . . . I realized the hostility and mistreatment towards trans-women [during the Caravan]. Things got so bad that upon the Caravan's arrival in Mexico City, LGBTQ communities of the US and Mexico provided them with separate transportation and accommodations in Tijuana to protect them."[27]

In one image from 2020, a naked toddler sleeps on a pile of clothing on the banks of the Usumacinta River, the waterway that forms the border between Guatemala and Mexico [15]. In the shade of a tree, the child is surrounded by evidence of hundreds of asylum seekers' journey, with clothing hung up to dry on makeshift clotheslines, while people bathe in the river in the background. Besides recording the

[**14**] Detail from Tim Johnson, ed., *Zoe Leonard: Al río / To the River* (Luxembourg: Mudam Luxembourg- Musée d'Art Moderne Grand-Duc Jean; Berlin: Hatje Cantz, 2022). Zoe Leonard. Gelatin silver prints, C-prints, and inkjet prints. © Zoe Leonard. Courtesy of the artist, Galerie Gisela Capitain, Cologne, and Hauser & Wirth

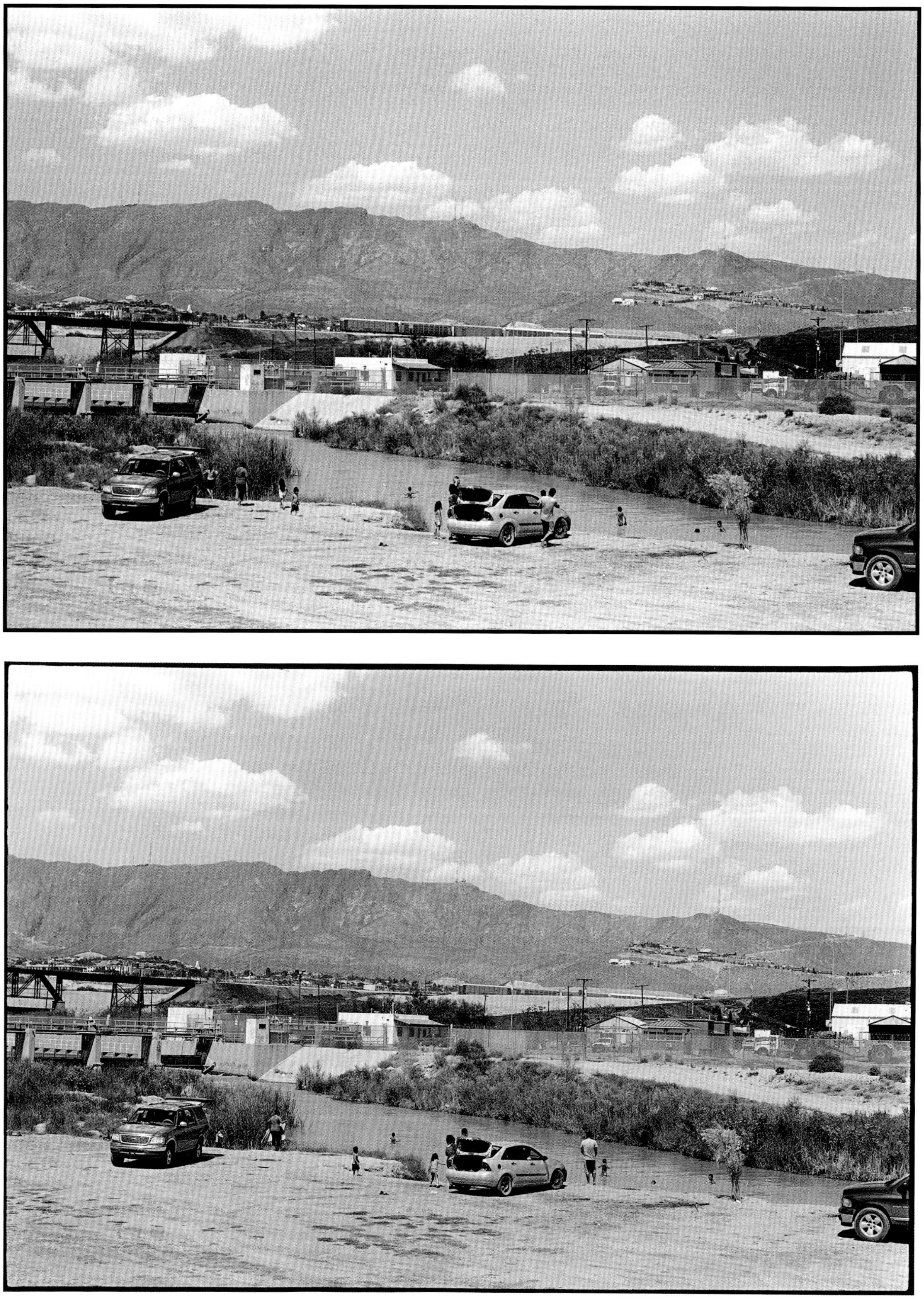

[15] *Sleeping by the River, Tecun-Uman Guatemala*, 2020. Ada Trillo. Digital print; 50.8 x 76.2 cm. The Cleveland Museum of Art, Gift of the artist. © Ada Trillo. Image courtesy of the artist

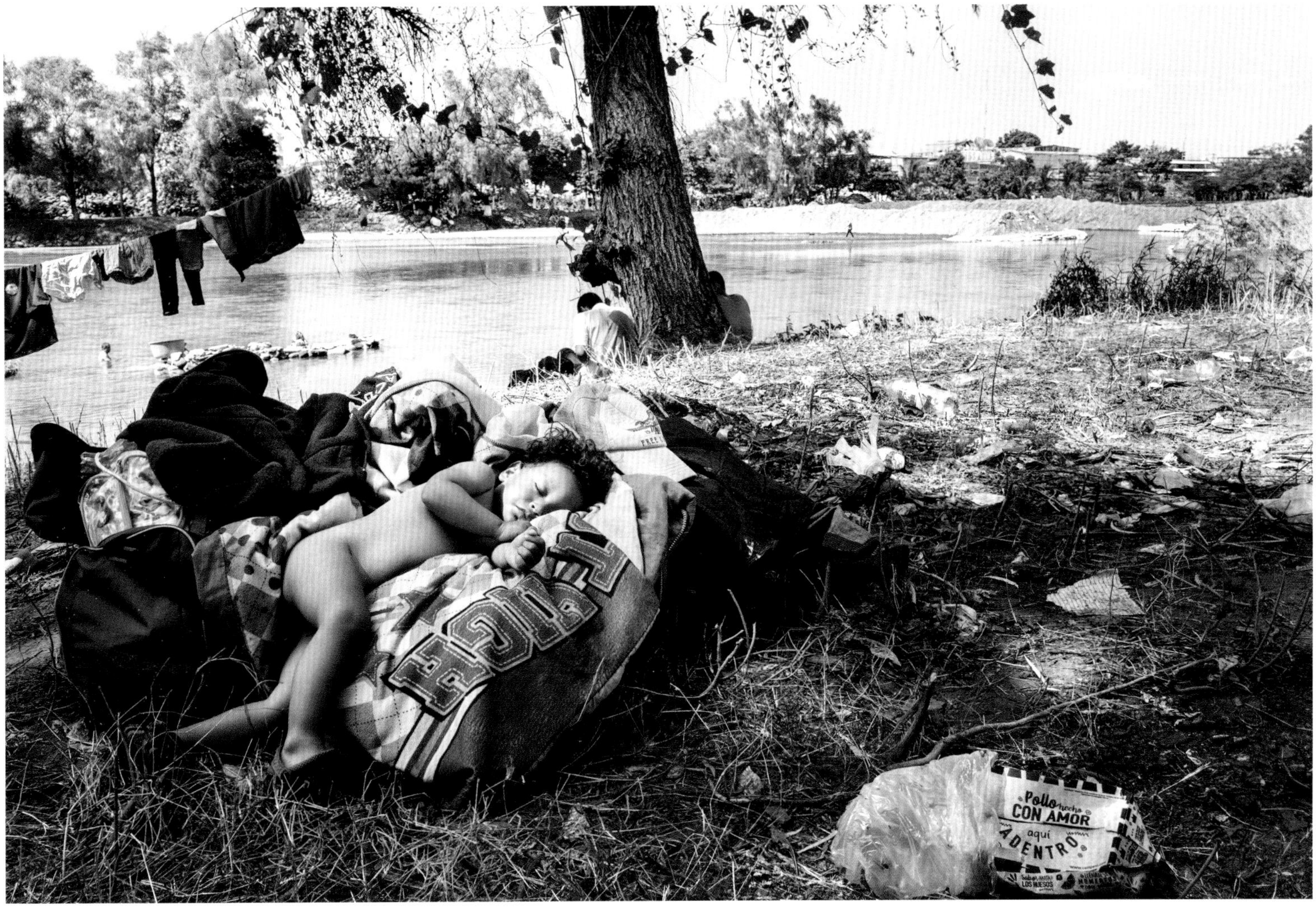

labor and sacrifice of transporting a young child a distance of nearly three thousand miles, the image offers a rare moment of peaceful repose. It also speaks to the vast distances that families with young children traverse and to the many miles that still lie ahead of the caravan in their journey to the US border. In humanizing the reality of the migrants' journey, the photographs provide "a glimpse into the plight of asylum seekers and migrants, hard-working people banded together for a chance at a better life."[28]

The artists discussed in this chapter offer narratives that are instrumental in the context of contemporary politics, as they resist and subvert what the photographers understand as spurious collaboration between governmental institutions and the news media on the handling and depiction of the border. In effect, their images cannot be easily manipulated to serve the political agendas of the Border Patrol, or a given presidential administration. Countering the ephemeral nature of news stories produced for mass audiences, these photographers appropriate the format of the photo book or essay to intervene in and make lasting contributions to the polarized media landscape. In so doing, they challenge the press's narrative closure and its focus on fear and hysteria, prompting readers to reconsider what they think they know about the border and immigration.

1. Daniel J. Tichenor, *Dividing Lines: The Politics of Immigration Control in America* (Princeton, NJ: Princeton University Press, 2009), 224. See also Timothy J. Dunn, *The Militarization of the U.S.-Mexico Border, 1978–1992: Low-Intensity Conflict Doctrine Comes Home* (Austin: University of Texas Press, 1996), 3.

2. Many articles deploy the imagery of a deluge to describe the crisis or "invasion" of US borders, with phrases like "pouring into the US," "floods of illegal aliens," "waves . . . beyond calculation," "surge," "flow," and "tide."

3. Some notable photo books from this period devoted to the US-Mexico border not included in this chapter are: Max Aguilera-Hellweg, *Max Aguilera-Hellweg: La Frontera Sin Sonrisa* (El Paso, TX: El Paso Museum of Art, 1995); Don Bartletti, *Between Two Worlds: The People of the Border* (Oakland, CA: Oakland Museum, 1992); Alan Weisman and Jay Dusard, *La Frontera: The United States Border with Mexico* (Tucson: University of Arizona Press, 1991); Douglas Kent Hall, *The Border: Life on the Line* (New York: Abbeville, 1988); Peter Goin, *Tracing the Line: A Photographic Survey of the Mexican-American Border* (Reno: Library, University of Nevada–Reno, 1987); Patricia Preciado Martin and Louis Carlos Bernal, *Images and Conversations: Mexican Americans Recall a Southwestern Past* (Tucson: University of Arizona Press, 1983); Pablo Ortiz Monasterio and Marisa Giménez Cacho, *Testigos y complices* (Mexico City: Martín Casillas, 1982).

4. The law also imposed strict penalties on employers who knowingly hired undocumented immigrants. Around the passage of the IRCA, Reagan's declaration of a War on Drugs—which was taken up with equal enthusiasm by his successor, George H. W. Bush—became a prominent element of national security, and border security was highlighted as a safeguard against narcotics trafficking from Mexico and Central America.

5. George Russell et al., "The Policy Dilemma: Trying to Stem the Illegal Tide; Congress, Once Again, Prepares to Tackle Reform Proposals," *Time* (July 8, 1985): 50–54.

6. These upgrades included introducing helicopters with high-powered spotlights and fixed-wing aircraft to monitor the border; electronic intrusion-detection ground sensors and transmitters; closed-circuit television systems with accompanying cameras stationed along the border; radar- and infrared-detection systems; high-powered semiautomatic rifles; an expanded fleet of trucks and vehicles; and newly built and expanded-capacity detention facilities. Dunn, *Militarization of the U.S.-Mexico Border*, 30–31.

7. Patrick McDonnell, "All-Out Border War to Stem Alien Flow Is High-Tech Affair," *Los Angeles Times*, April 13, 1986.

8. This article includes many recurring elements of media stories on undocumented migrants from this period: Border Patrol, politicians, and INS officials issued all the quotes; an Anglo-surnamed individual wrote the stories; and the term "illegal alien," rather than the more politically correct "undocumented migrant," is used. These trends are extensively discussed in Celestino Fernández and Lawrence Pedroza, "The Border Patrol and News Media Coverage of Undocumented Mexican Immigrants during the 1970s: A Quantitative Content Analysis in the Sociology of Knowledge," *Mexican American Studies and Research Center* 2 (1981): 1–29.

9. Esther Parada, "C/Overt Ideology: Two Images of Revolution," in *The Contest of Meaning: Critical Histories of Photography*, ed. Richard Bolton (Cambridge, MA: MIT Press, 1989), 225. This essay was originally published in *Afterimage* 11, no. 8 (March 1984). See also David Avalos, "The Donkey Cart Caper: Some Thoughts on Socially Conscious Art in Anti-social Public Space," *Community Murals: An International Visual Arts Magazine* 11 (Fall 1986): 14–15.

10. In *The Tarnished Door: The New Immigrants and the Transformation of America* (New York: Times Books, 1983), *New York Times* correspondent John Crewdson details the multiple instances of Border Patrol misconduct he and colleagues had witnessed in covering the border.

11. McDonnell, "All-Out Border War."

12. Martínez worked as a staff photographer at the newly established progressive newspaper *La Jornada* in Mexico City for several months in 1987 and 1988, but left to pursue his own projects. Author's interview with Eniac Martínez, August 26, 2016.

13. See Jonathan Fox, "Indigenous Mexican Migrants," in *Beyond La Frontera: The History of Mexico-U.S. Migration*, ed. Mark Overmyer-Velázquez (New York: Oxford University Press, 2011), 161–78.

14. Lourdes Grobet and Néstor García Canclini, *Tijuana: La casa de toda la gente* (Tijuana: Instituto Nacional de Antropología e Historia, 1989), 28 (author's translation).

15. Author's interview with Lourdes Grobet, August 25, 2016.

16. It is estimated that the Mexican police killed between thirty and three hundred students and civilians on October 2, 1968, and arrested over thirteen hundred. However, given the lack of transparent and accurate documentation, the number of deaths was likely far greater.

17. Alex Webb, email to the author, August 13, 2016.

18. Magnum Photo Archive, New York.

19. Gloria Anzaldúa, *Borderlands / La Frontera: The New Mestiza* (San Francisco: Aunt Lute, 1987), 11.

20. The series was partially exhibited in *Los Vecinos*, held at the Museum of Photographic Arts, San Diego, in 1989, but Meiselas also exhibited the work as a solo show titled *Crossings*, which was presented at the Art Institute of Chicago in 1990 and toured multiple venues throughout the US and internationally.

21. Author's interview with Susan Meiselas, August 10, 2016.

22. In her book *Migra! A History of the U.S. Border Patrol*, Kelly Lytle Hernández introduces the term "Mexican Brown" to refer to the Border Patrol's tendency since the 1940s to police based on class, complexion, and national origin. Kelly Lytle Hernández, *Migra! A History of the U.S. Border Patrol* (Berkeley: University of California Press, 2010), 10.

23. Bridget Read, "Where the Border Ends," *Vogue* (December 7, 2018), https://www.vogue.com/projects/13547630/asylum-seekers-waiting-to-enter-the-united-states-in-tijuana.

24. Author's interview with Zoe Leonard, August 16, 2022.

25. Tim Johnson, ed., *Zoe Leonard: Al río / To the River*, texts by C. J. Alvarez, Ariella Azoulay, Cecilia Ballí et al. (Luxembourg: Mudam Luxembourg-Musée d'Art Moderne Grand-Duc Jean; Berlin: Hatje Cantz, 2022).

26. C. J. Alvarez, *Border Land, Border Water: A History of Construction on the US-Mexico Divide* (Austin: University of Texas Press, 2019), 5.

27. Ada Trillo, email to the author, October 17, 2023.

28. Helen Cunningham Newbold, "Preface," in Ada Trillo, *La Caravan del Diablo: On the Run from the Northern Triangle to America* (The Hague: Komma No Ordinary, 2021), 11.

2 THE URBAN BORDER

In *Whittier Boulevard* (1979), photographer Ricardo Valverde displays his fascination with the lowrider car culture of East Los Angeles and the idiosyncratic fashion of the cholo/as, the Chicanos associated with lowrider subculture, known for their custom of cruising neighborhood thoroughfares [16].[1] In this image, taken at night, a young woman—an extra on the set of a movie being filmed on Whittier Boulevard—turns to confront the camera at the moment Valverde snaps his shutter. Valverde (1946–1998) captures her defiant expression, reinforcing the markers of an oppositional counterculture that surround her. The young woman's gaze toward the camera, equal parts assertive and vulnerable, draws viewers into the scene. Dressed in an open-back black outfit that reveals a tattoo, Marlboro cigarettes in hand, and with dark, heavy eye makeup, the woman stands at the door of a lowrider that is equally remarkable in its outfitting. The car's exterior is expertly painted with stripes and flames, and has been polished to a high sheen, reflecting the lights and storefronts of the East LA thoroughfare in its windows and body. The skewed angle of the street in the background and the distorted reflections in the lowrider's surface create an abstract and otherworldly aura.

Here, the car itself becomes a fetishized art object, a quality seen in other photographs by Valverde that revel in the sumptuousness of the cars' embellished surfaces, venerating the people who ride them [17]. In this way, and in line with his political views, Valverde highlights the Latinx community's appropriation and transformation of an iconic American product, the automobile, into something all their own—an artistic object of street life in LA. The car is no longer merely a mode of transportation; it has become a magnificent foil to the isolating obstacles that the city's highway system and overpasses were creating in these neighborhoods since the 1950s.[2]

In this chapter I focus on photographs of the distinctive urban environments of Los Angeles as a border city. Located 130 miles from the border with Mexico, Los Angeles is considered a "border city" or "border community" based on the large contingent of Mexican immigrants who live there, a population whose labor transformed LA into a city at the turn of the twentieth century.[3] The excessive policing of the border as a tool to reinforce discriminatory treatment of migrants in cities far from the border itself brings the lived realities of the border into communities such as East LA, whose residents have long generational lineages of Mexican heritage even if they are not migrants themselves. In this way, the effects of our national boundaries are both literally and metaphorically far-reaching.

Latinx photographers working in the 1970s and 1980s, including Ricardo Valverde, Laura Aguilar (1959–2018), Harry Gamboa Jr. (born 1951), and George Rodriguez (born 1937), approached the border's urban environments fully attuned to the way in which their city is mapped out and where

[16] *Whittier Boulevard*, 1979. Ricardo Valverde (American, 1946–1998). Gelatin silver print; 18.8 x 27.9 cm. The J. Paul Getty Museum, Los Angeles, 2016.31.2. © Esperanza Valverde and Christopher Jude Valverde

[17] *La Reina—16 de Septiembre*, 1976. Ricardo Valverde. Gelatin silver print; 27.9 x 35.6 cm. Collection of Esperanza Valverde and Christopher J. Valverde, Ricardo Valverde Estate. © Esperanza Valverde and Christopher Jude Valverde

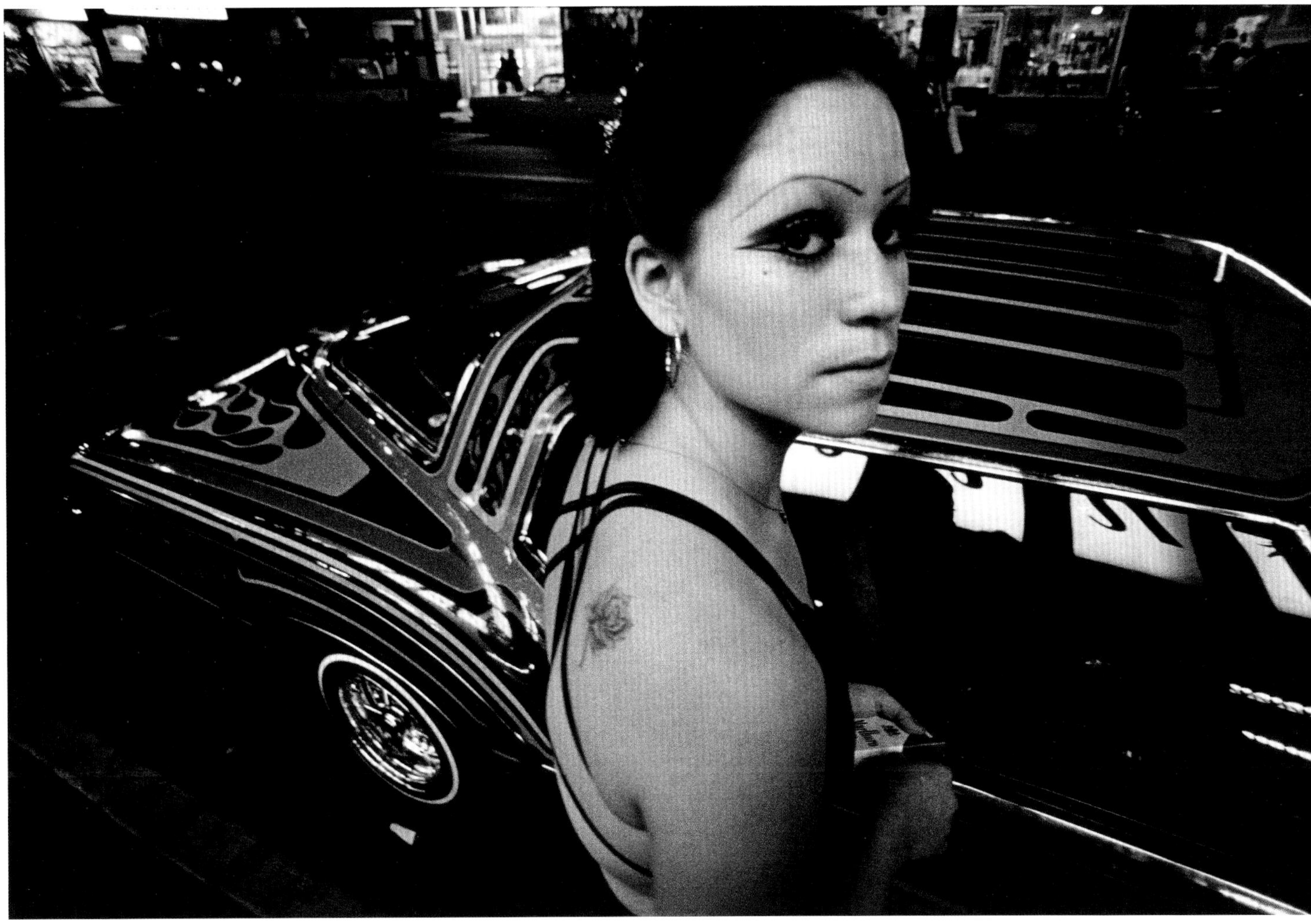

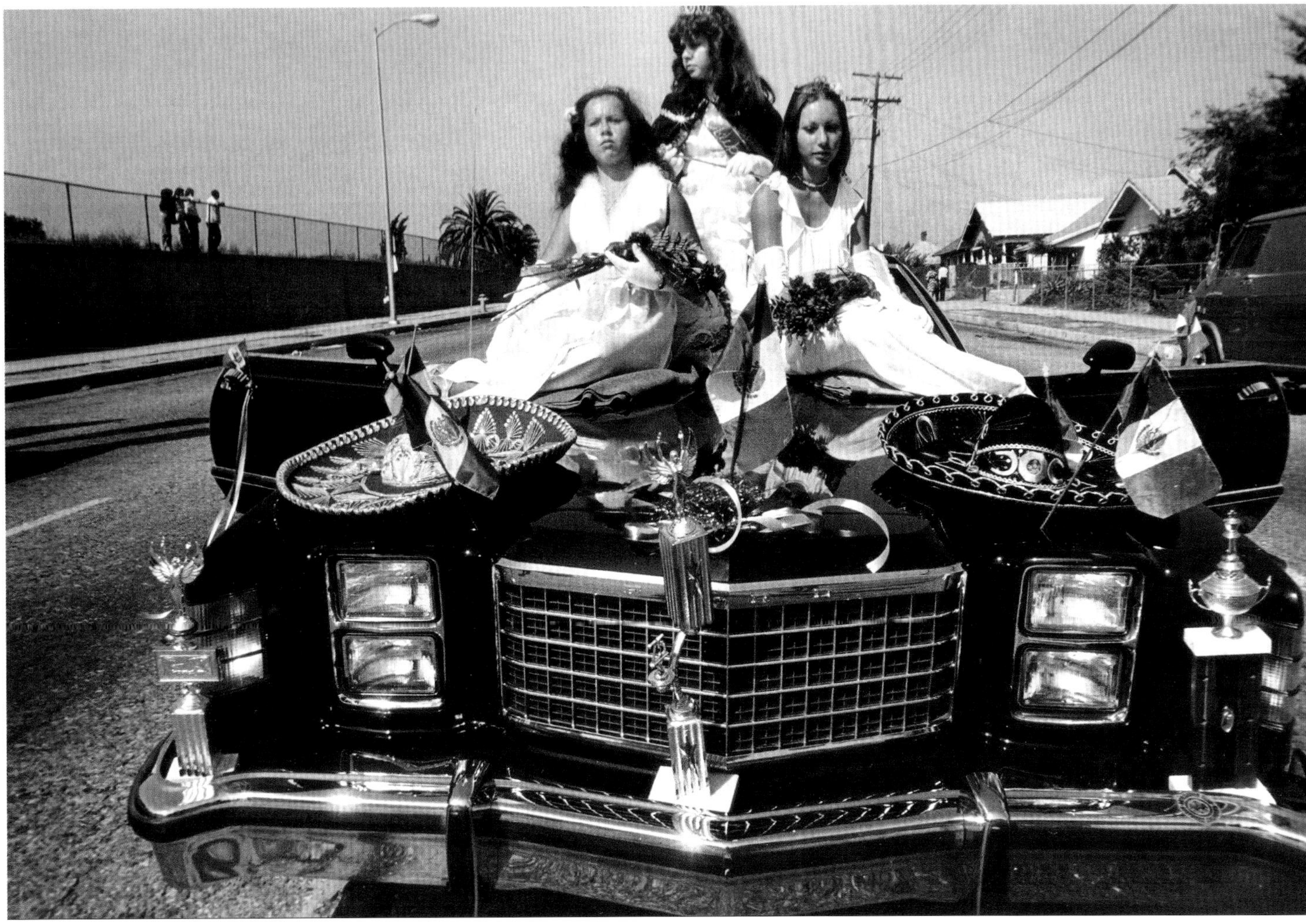

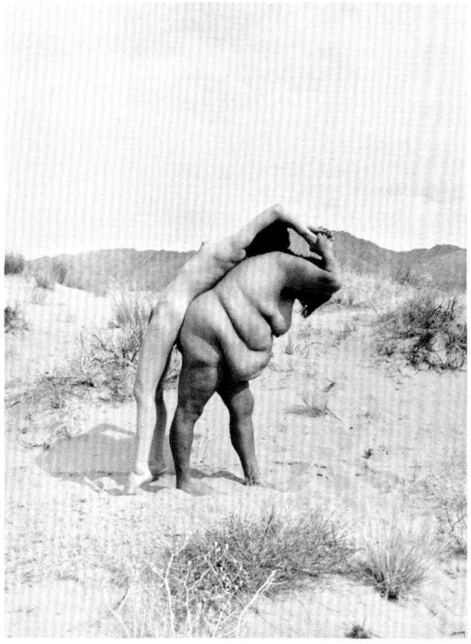

Figure 8. *Stillness #27,* 1996. Laura Aguilar (American, 1959–2018). Gelatin silver print; 30.5 x 22.9. The Cleveland Museum of Art, Karl P. Goldfield Trust, 2023.11. © The Laura Aguilar Trust

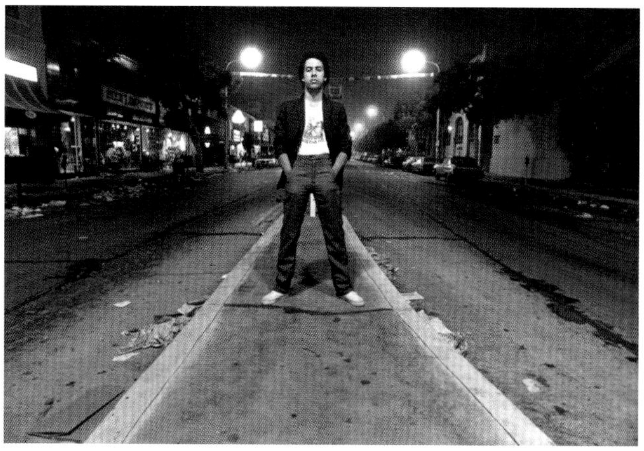

Figure 9. *Nocturnal Niche, Westwood, CA* [featuring the performer Humberto Sandoval], from the series *Urban Exiles,* 1980. Harry Gamboa Jr. (American, born 1951). Gelatin silver print; 40.6 x 50.8 cm. © 1980, Harry Gamboa Jr. Image courtesy of the Centro de la Imagen

Latinx populations reside within it. This is due in part to their unique perspectives as Angelenos but it also stems from the rising urbanization of the borderlands underway at this time.[4] The theme of mobility in border cities—exemplified in photographs of freeways and car culture in Los Angeles—coincided with contemporaneous writing on social mobility (or lack thereof) for Latinxs and migrants, and a socio-spatial understanding of urbanism that was just beginning to be theorized.[5] Artists are keenly aware of the areas from which the Latinx community has been historically, socioeconomically, and culturally excluded throughout the greater LA cityscape. Through spatial explorations of their urban milieu that paralleled real-life displacements and deterritorializations, the earliest of the photographs discussed in this chapter anticipate the recent topicality of space and exclusion as it relates to Latinx identity at the present moment.

The enduring history of Mexican populations in Los Angeles can be seen in the heritage of the Latinx photographers featured in *Picturing the Border.* Although Valverde moved to LA while still a young child, his family had deep roots in the state of Arizona that predate its incorporation into the United States. Likewise, Louis Carlos Bernal (whose work is discussed in chapter 3) was from the border town of Douglas, Arizona, an area where his family had lived for generations. Laura Aguilar has often discussed the natural landscapes that are the backdrop to her self-portraits as influenced by her deep maternal ties to California (fig. 8).[6]

In these instances, it was a case of the border crossing the artist's families rather than the other way around, a product of the shifting border line that occurred in 1848 and 1854 with the Treaty of Guadalupe Hidalgo and the Gadsden Purchase, respectively. The history of the contested spaces between the United States and Mexico, and the oppression of the populations who suffered through resettlement there, was a predominant theme of the Chicano Civil Rights Movement. Activists began referring to this area of the Southwest as Aztlán, a name referenced in the sixteenth-century Codex Ramírez that historians gave to the area north of Mexico from where their ancestors originated.[7] As one aspect of their resistance to decades of inequality and racism, Chicanos claimed Aztlán as a historical homeland where they would become the majority and reverse the balance of power over their Anglo oppressors. Aztlán thus became a potent symbol of Chicano nationalism throughout the 1960s and 1970s.[8] The movement rejected the emphasis on American patriotism and assimilation practiced by earlier generations of migrants, instead emphasizing a cultural nationalism that united all people of Mexican origin.

In the 1970s, several Latinx photographers began focusing on the contemporary urban landscape of the border city of Los Angeles with a politicized eye, albeit in varying ways. Harry Gamboa Jr. was aware of the divisive nature of the city's layout, meant to segregate Latinx communities into the eastern portions and block their mobility outside of these neighborhoods. The freeways constituted one means by which this separation was enacted. Reflecting on this feature of LA in 1989, Gamboa writes, "The city is a sprawling mass of concrete, asphalt, lawn chairs, palm trees, television antennas, and segregated neighborhoods that are defined by obvious streets of gold or graffiti/blood-stained sidewalks. . . . The foundation of this major metropolis is gift wrapped with ribbons of freeways, on-ramps, and off-ramps that lead to cultural isolation."[9]

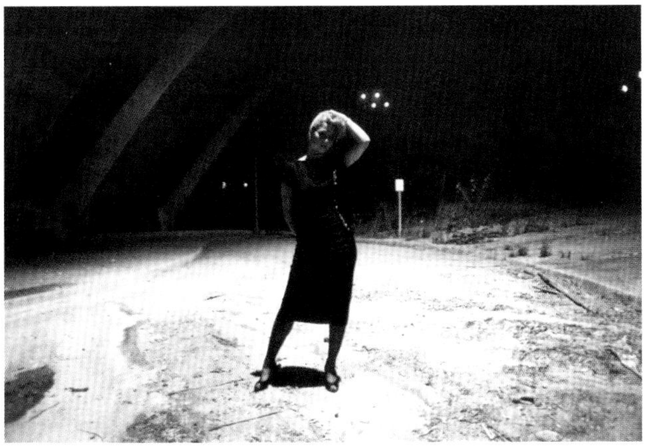

Figure 10. *Missing Venus, Pasadena, CA* [featuring the performer Cindy Herrón], from the series *Urban Exiles*, 1980. Harry Gamboa Jr. Gelatin silver print; 40.6 x 50.8 cm. © 1980 Harry Gamboa Jr. Image courtesy of the Centro de la Imagen

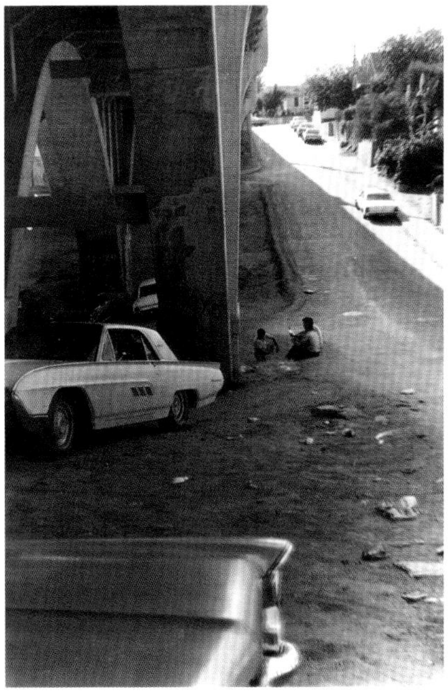

Figure 11. *Underpass in Los Angeles*, c. 1978. Ricardo Valverde. Gelatin silver print; 25.4 x 20.3 cm. © Esperanza Valverde and Christopher Jude Valverde

Intensely aware of the marginalizing effects of the city's topography, he strove to incorporate an understanding of this phenomenon into his art. Gamboa's *Urban Exiles* (1980) series is set throughout the city's spaces (figs. 9, 10). The nocturnal portraits that make up the series depict their subjects in the center of the image and from a low vantage point. Each figure is rendered with an attitude of defiance, occupying the streets of LA at a time of night when the spaces are devoid of people. Visually akin to film stills, these staged nighttime scenes make striking use of, and impart an empty and artificial quality to, these public spaces.

Ricardo Valverde also made work that distinctly captures his awareness of LA's oppressive spaces. For example, in *Underpass in Los Angeles* (c. 1978), Valverde emphasizes the concrete barriers that physically divide East LA from the rest of the city (fig. 11). The photograph was taken from street level with a vertical orientation that accentuates the towering height of a cement structure supporting the freeway overpass under which Valverde stands. Three men sit together at the base of one concrete pillar, dwarfed by its imposing size. Valverde highlights the highway's proximity to residences; along the right-hand side of the image, we see a row of well-kept homes and sunlight-bathed front yards that line the inclining street, a striking contradiction to the harshness of the bare concrete structure and the scale of its looming presence.

Various twentieth-century photographers who documented the American city emphasize urban structures as symbols of modernization, the transformation of cities under capitalism (fig. 12), or the unique beauty of Hollywood (fig. 13). Photographers such as Gamboa and Valverde sought to upend these precedents. Their photographs set forth a visual vocabulary that subverts modernism's heroic treatment of urban structures, focusing on the breadth and height of the overpasses that have entrapped and blocked LA's poor and immigrant inhabitants. Valverde in particular drew inspiration from Roy DeCarava's (1919–2009) work, which often employs shadows as both a formal and a symbolic device to break down binaries and subvert Black tropes and conceptions of otherness, while also employing a tonal range that implicates the "underground" or otherwise hidden, often dimly lit areas of Black Harlem (fig. 14). Valverde's *Underpass* also plays on the symbolic device of the shadow, signaling

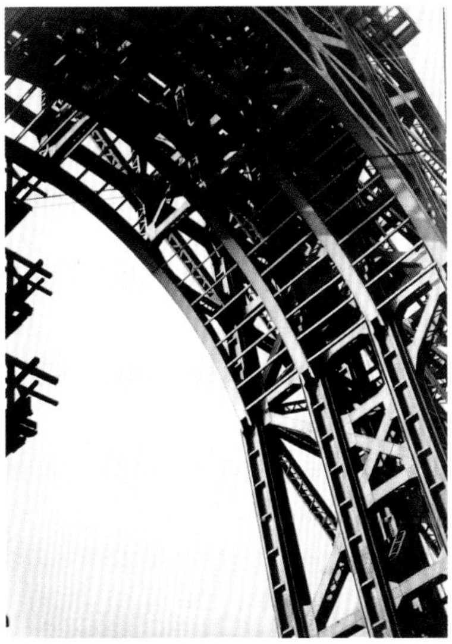

Figure 12. *Hudson River Bridge*, 1930. Berenice Abbott (American, 1898–1991). Gelatin silver print; 23.7 x 17.3 cm. The Cleveland Museum of Art, John L. Severance Fund, 2007.20. Photo © Berenice Abbott / Getty Images

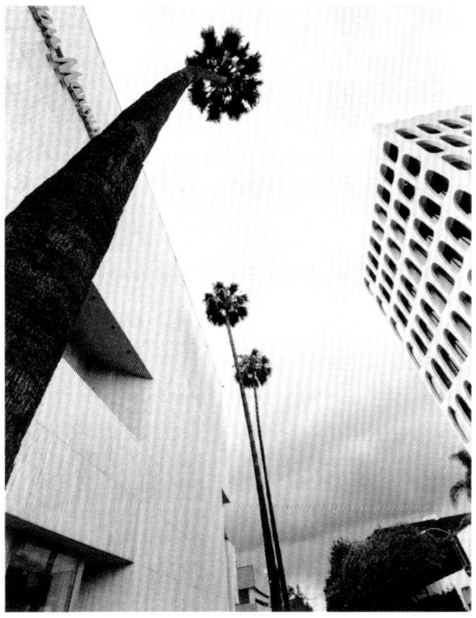

Figure 13. *Nature of Los Angeles: Untitled*, 2008. Bruce Davidson (American, born 1933). Gelatin silver print; 57.9 x 46 cm. The Cleveland Museum of Art, Gift of an anonymous donor, 2018.774. Photo: Bruce Davidson / Magnum Photos

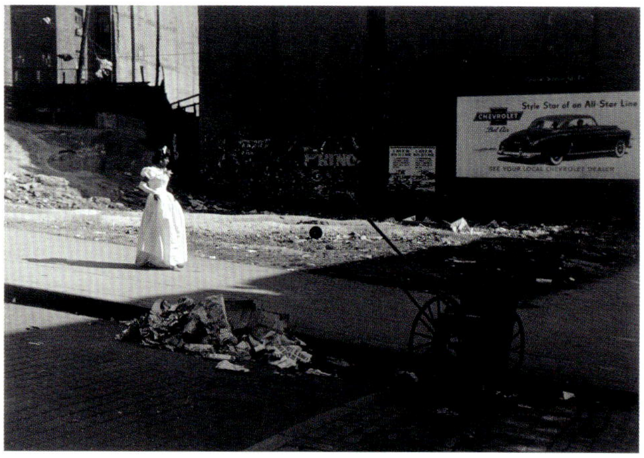

Figure 14. *Graduation, New York*, 1949, printed 1982. Roy DeCarava (American, 1919–2009). Gelatin silver print; 22.4 x 32.9 cm. The Museum of Fine Arts, Houston, Museum purchase funded by Photo Forum 1994, 94.746. © Sherry DeCarava, courtesy of the DeCarava Archives www.decarava.org

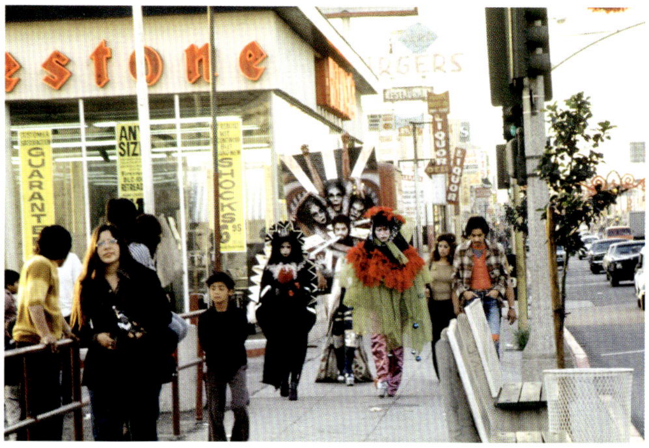

Figure 15. *Walking Mural* [featuring the performers Glugio "Gronk" Nicandro (American, born 1954), Willie F. Herrón III (American, born 1951), and Patssi Valdez (American, born 1951)], Whittier Boulevard, East Los Angeles, December 24, 1972. Harry Gamboa Jr. FujiFlex Lightjet print; 40.6 x 50.8 cm. © 1972 Harry Gamboa Jr. Photo courtesy of the artist

"borders" between dark and light, chaos and order, detritus and affluence to imply that poverty and cultural wealth can coexist in his own borderland barrio.

The invisibility of Latinxs in mainstream media was a motivating factor at a time when visualizations of race, gender, and sexuality were increasingly at stake, in particular for artists of color. In 1979, a group of LA photographers, including Valverde, Gamboa, Louis Carlos Bernal (1941–1993), Isabel Castro (born 1954), and Roberto Gil de Montes (born 1950), founded the Council for Latino Photography/USA, or CLP/USA, which was active through 1985. The CLP/USA members' participation in the Chicano Civil Rights Movement informed their political stance regarding Latinx representation, and their mission statement suggests they viewed photography as a means of counteracting the imagery of Latinxs circulating in the mainstream media and press.[10] In many ways, the CLP/USA's commitment to community, visibility, and empowerment, and their ability to disseminate their photographs through a transnational network of artists, transcended their time. By banding together with fellow photographers through the formation of the CLP/USA, the group worked against the nativist conceptions of so-called "American" identity, activating the transgressive nature of seeing and being seen. Valverde explains, "We are constantly being bombarded by stereotyped images of Latinos . . . as individuals who can be kept in a mold. I think my work is evidence that we Latinos, as all other people of color, are in a struggle to be seen, to be recognized as a vital element of force in our society."[11]

Beginning in the 1970s and 1980s, East LA's celebration of Día de los Muertos, or Day of the Dead, became a major annual event. A syncretic merging of Halloween and the Mexican Día de los Muertos celebration, the festival held particular meaning for LA's large Mexican communities. Following the Chicano Civil Rights Movement, it became a symbol of nationalism and pride of place among members of the community. This notion was reinforced by the annual celebrations organized by Self-Help Graphics, a Chicano art-and-cultural space in East LA established in 1973. Annually from that year on, Self-Help organized a large procession that began at Evergreen Cemetery and concluded at their space, where community members would host a large party and set up altars to commemorate deceased friends and family members. Early photographs of the event drew crucial attention to the reclamation of urban space among residents, contextualized their actions within social movements occurring elsewhere at that moment, and created a place for visualizations of the Latinx experience in East LA.

In 1972, Gamboa and fellow artists Gronk (born 1954), Willie Herrón (born 1951), and Patssi Valdez (born 1951) formed the art collective Asco, known for their performances and interventions in the city's public spaces. Shortly after their formation, Asco's performances and costumes were closely tied to the annual festivities associated with the Día de los Muertos celebration, resisting the cultural-symbolic tropes that had become associated with the event, the Mexican community, and Chicano nationalism. The group's *Day of the Dead* (1974) performance, in which they crashed the Day of the Dead mass held at Self-Help Graphics in costumes that pushed clichés of Mexican nationalism in LA to the extreme, caused a considerable disruption to the scheduled events. It followed in much the same spirit as previous performances, including *Walking Mural* (1972) and *Instant Mural* (1973).

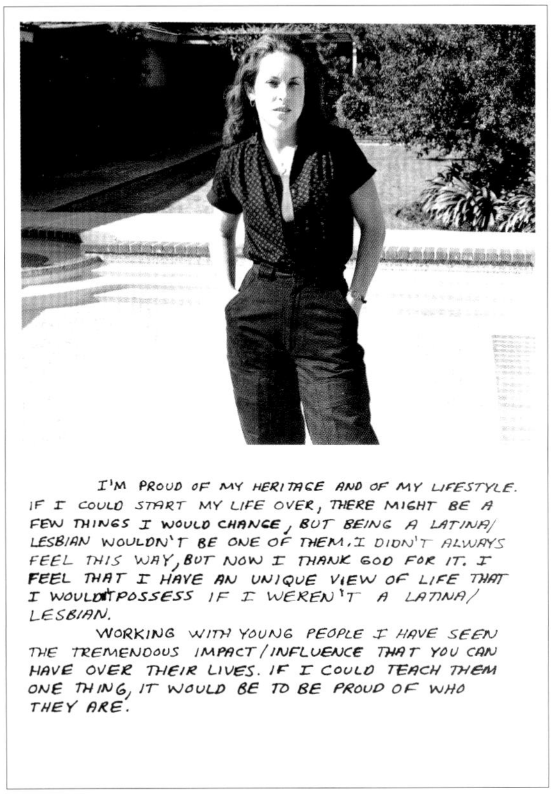

Figure 16. *Laura V*, from the series *Latina Lesbians*, 1988. Laura Aguilar. Gelatin silver print; 35.6 x 27.8 cm. © The Laura Aguilar Trust

In *Walking Mural*, Valdez, dressed all in black as the Virgin of Guadalupe and surrounded by costumed fellow members of Asco, walked down Whittier Boulevard in an impromptu performance meant to challenge the static nature of muralism, an art form that had become closely associated with the Chicano community, instead embracing a vibrant, experimental art form that intervened in the neighborhood's public, social spaces (fig. 15).

A close friend and collaborator of the group's members, Valverde documented Asco's performances over the years, including their over-the-top costumes, which often featured traditional *calavera*, or skull-face, makeup [18]. One photograph from 1981 captures Gronk riding a decorated float during a Day of the Dead procession [19]. Gronk's masked figure, a menacing presence who floats in the center-left portion of the image and whose body is cut off at the waist, leans toward the camera. He appears to ride a flaming structure down the street, although viewers are clued in to the constructed nature of the event given his papier-mâché mask and the vehicle's painted cardboard encasement. Valverde took the photograph from close to ground level, framing Gronk against the California sky and positioning the top of an adjacent church so that it appears to emerge from the flames, imbuing the image with a sense of irreverence and iconoclasm.

Pushing against tropes of gender and sexuality, the East LA–based Latinx photographer Laura Aguilar asserted control over her own identity and that of those in her community in her *Latina Lesbian* (1986–90) series, consisting of seventeen portraits paired with handwritten statements from her sitters. Such pairing was a growing strategy in conceptual photography that allowed for "self-authorship" by photographed subjects.[12] In each portrait, sitters comment on prevailing perceptions from outsiders, the media, and even family members they have had to overcome due to their Latina and lesbian identities. Gazing directly at the camera and portrayed in poses of self-assuredness, they become powerful role models for a subsequent generation. One sitter, Laura V., writes: "Working with young people I have seen the tremendous impact/influence that you can have over their lives. If I could teach them one thing, it would be to be proud of who they are" (fig. 16).

Aguilar's triptych *Three Eagles Flying* (1990) is a formidable self-portrait of being trapped between identities spanning gender, race, culture, and nationhood [20]. Presented against a black background, a bound, partially nude Aguilar stands between the American and Mexican flags. The American flag is wrapped around her waist and the Mexican flag is wrapped around her head; the eagle and the serpent on the Mexican flag appear over the artist's obscured face, becoming a symbolic play on the artist's name, derived from *águila*, Spanish for "eagle." The photograph implores viewers to contemplate the double bind of being Mexican American in the United States and feeling constrained by norms of sexuality, body image, and ability, the latter stemming from the artist's struggles with auditory dyslexia.

[**18**] *Asco Days of the Dead Performance, Termites y Guerrero*, 1975. Ricardo Valverde. Gelatin silver print; 40.6 x 50.8 cm. Collection of Esperanza Valverde and Christopher J. Valverde, Ricardo Valverde Estate. © Esperanza Valverde and Christopher Jude Valverde

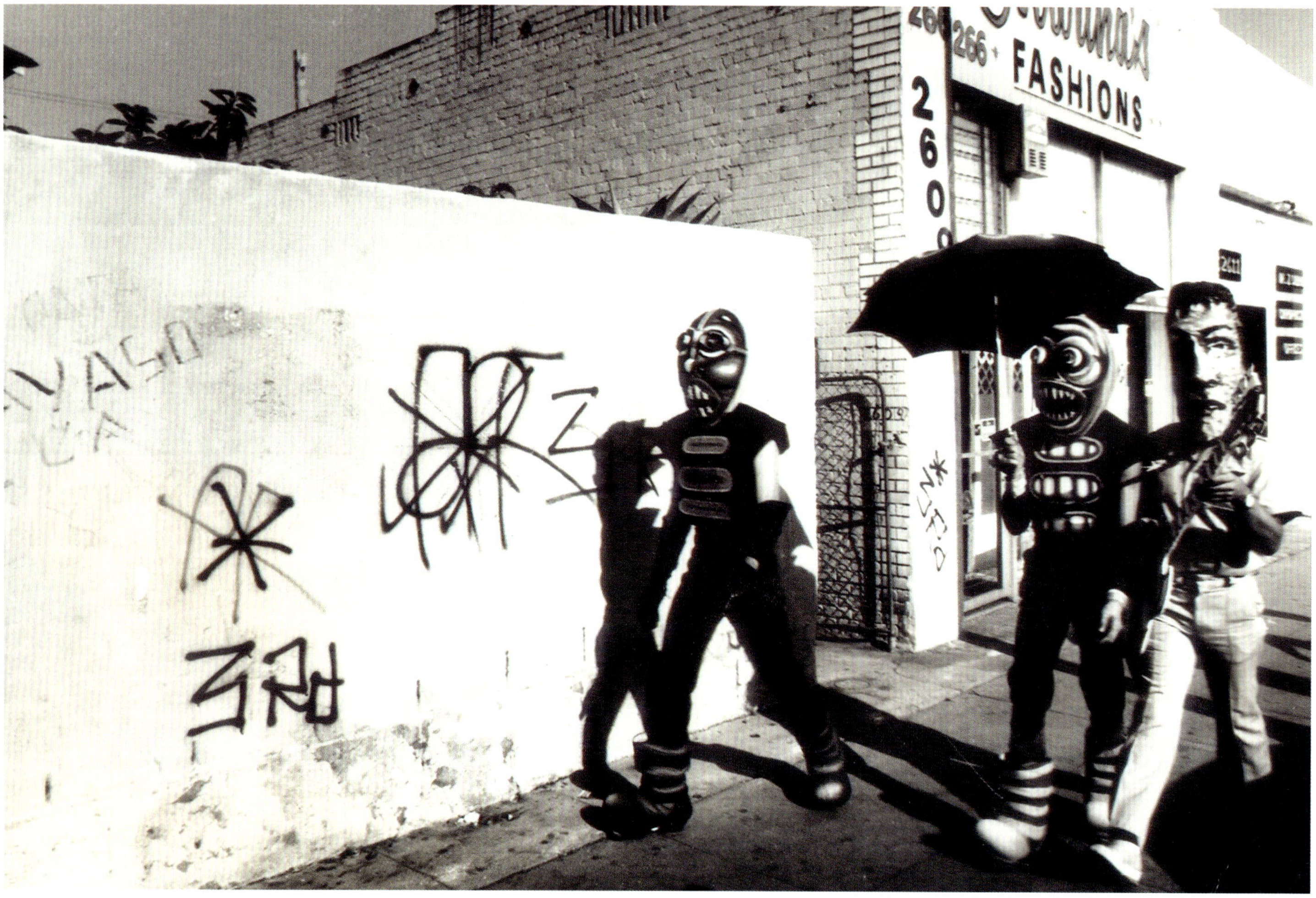

[**19**] *Gronk: Día de los Muertos, East LA*, 1981. Ricardo Valverde. Gelatin silver print; 40.6 x 50.8 cm. Collection of Esperanza Valverde and Christopher J. Valverde, Ricardo Valverde Estate. © Esperanza Valverde and Christopher Jude Valverde

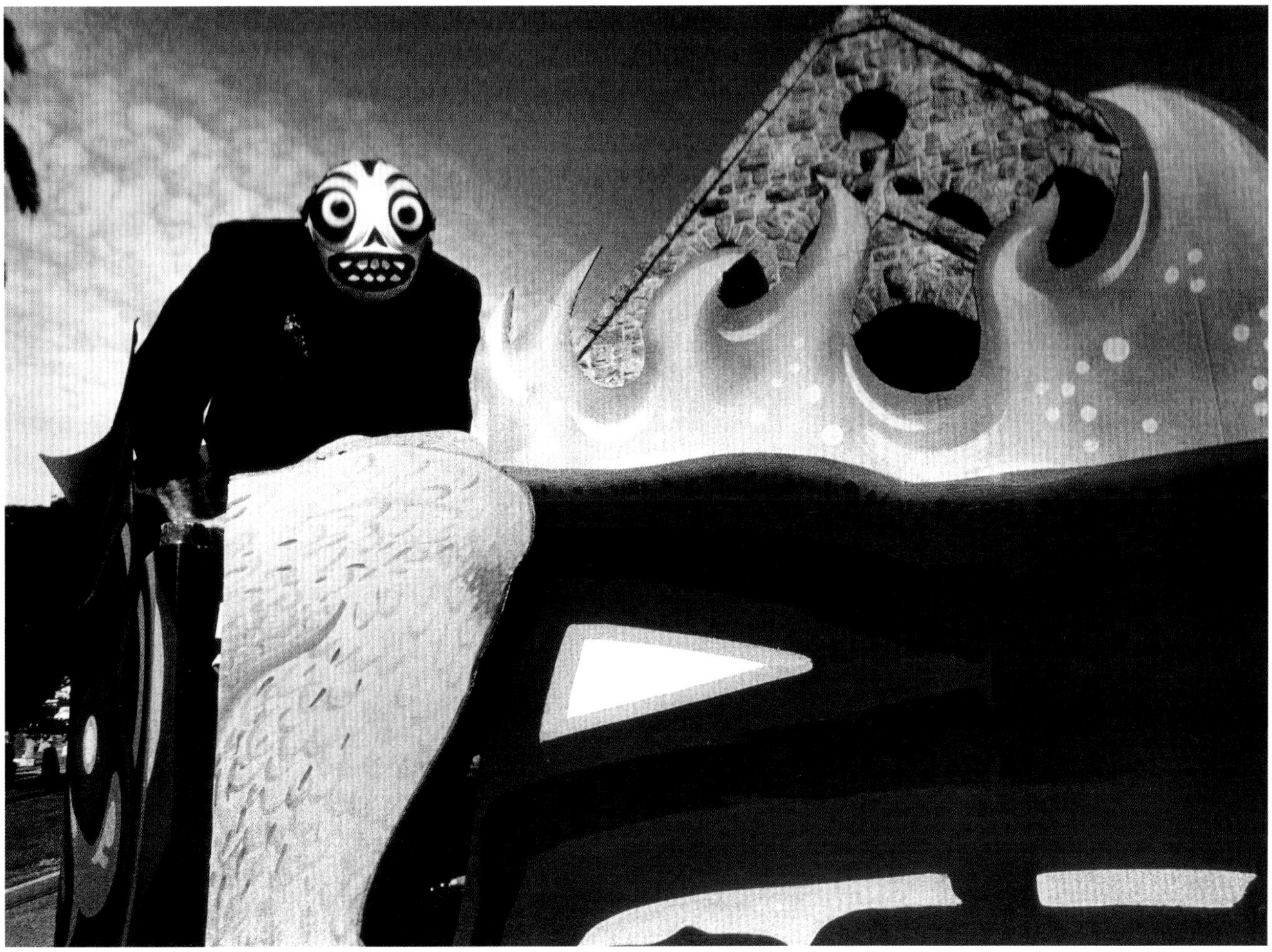

[**20**] *Three Eagles Flying*, 1990. Laura Aguilar. Gelatin silver print; triptych; each 61 x 50.8 cm. © The Laura Aguilar Trust

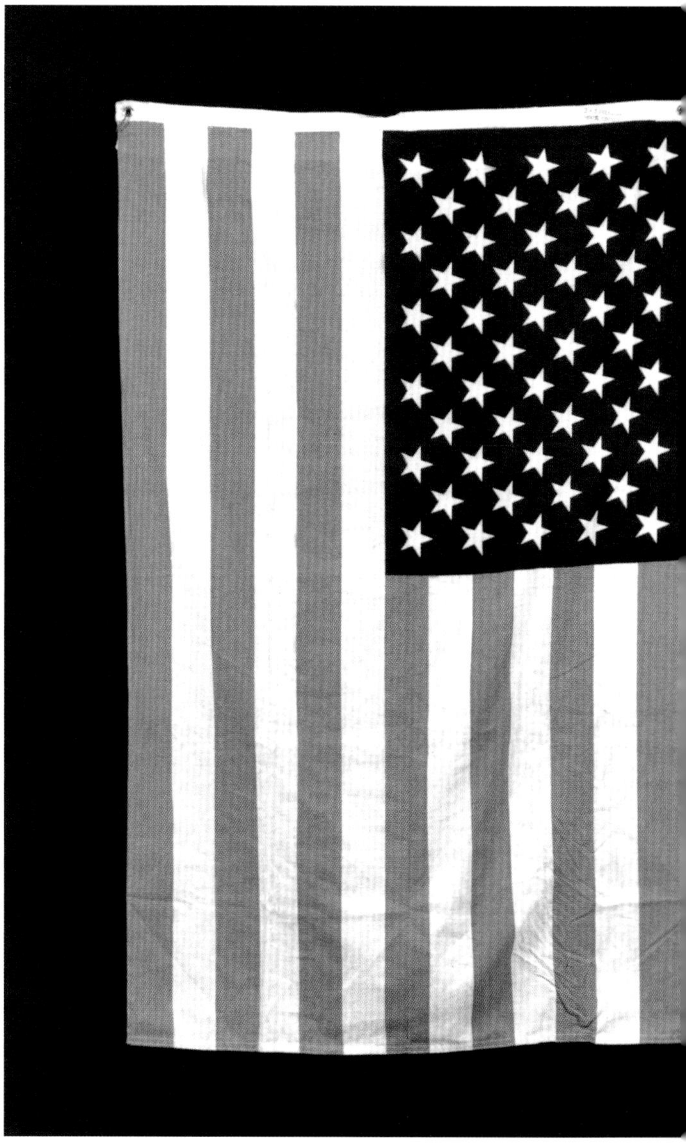

In Los Angeles, events of the Chicano Civil Rights Movement prompted a sea change in young artists' level of political engagement. As a high school student, Harry Gamboa Jr. helped organize the mass walkout of over fifteen thousand students from seven East LA high schools on March 1–8, 1968, an event now known as the Chicano Blowouts. The action quickly spread to other high schools in LA, with thousands of students protesting the lack of equality in the city's public school system, where only one-quarter of the Mexican students were expected to graduate. Signs posted outside schools read, "Education Not Eradication," "Ya Basta Con Reagan," and "Viva La Raza!"[13] The walkout had a direct impact on the rise of the Brown Berets, a nationwide organization that advocates for immigrants' rights, labor rights, minority education, and health care as it concerns Chicano communities.

Two years later, many of the same groups and activists organized the Chicano Moratorium, a movement made up of Mexican American groups who opposed the Vietnam War. George Rodriguez, a resident of South Los Angeles and a first-generation Mexican American who learned photography in high school, documented key moments of the massive protest and related gatherings. Over the course of his decades-long career, often on assignments for LA-based magazines and film studios, he would record events and social movements on the streets of LA in his free time. Rodriguez made powerful images of the Chicano Moratorium March in this fashion, taking panoramic views of the protesters' signs and banners as they occupied the streets of Boyle Heights [21]. In one image from the series, a Chicano protester is led from behind by a police officer, hands restrained behind his back, while two bystanders look on [22]. The image documents the transformation of the peaceful protest into a violent confrontation with the Los Angeles County Sheriff's Department, in which three protesters, including *Los Angeles Times* journalist Rubén Salazar, were killed and many others injured. This weighty moment, frozen in time, is a poignant reminder of the discriminatory policing strategies that have targeted Mexican Americans in borderland cities such as Los Angeles, far beyond the actual border.

The photographic projects addressed in this chapter are especially resonant today, when the border is again a fixture in the daily news cycle. Recipients of the Deferred Action for Childhood Arrivals (DACA) program—which the Trump administration attempted to end in September 2017 and which is still threatened by legal challenges in 2023—have articulated

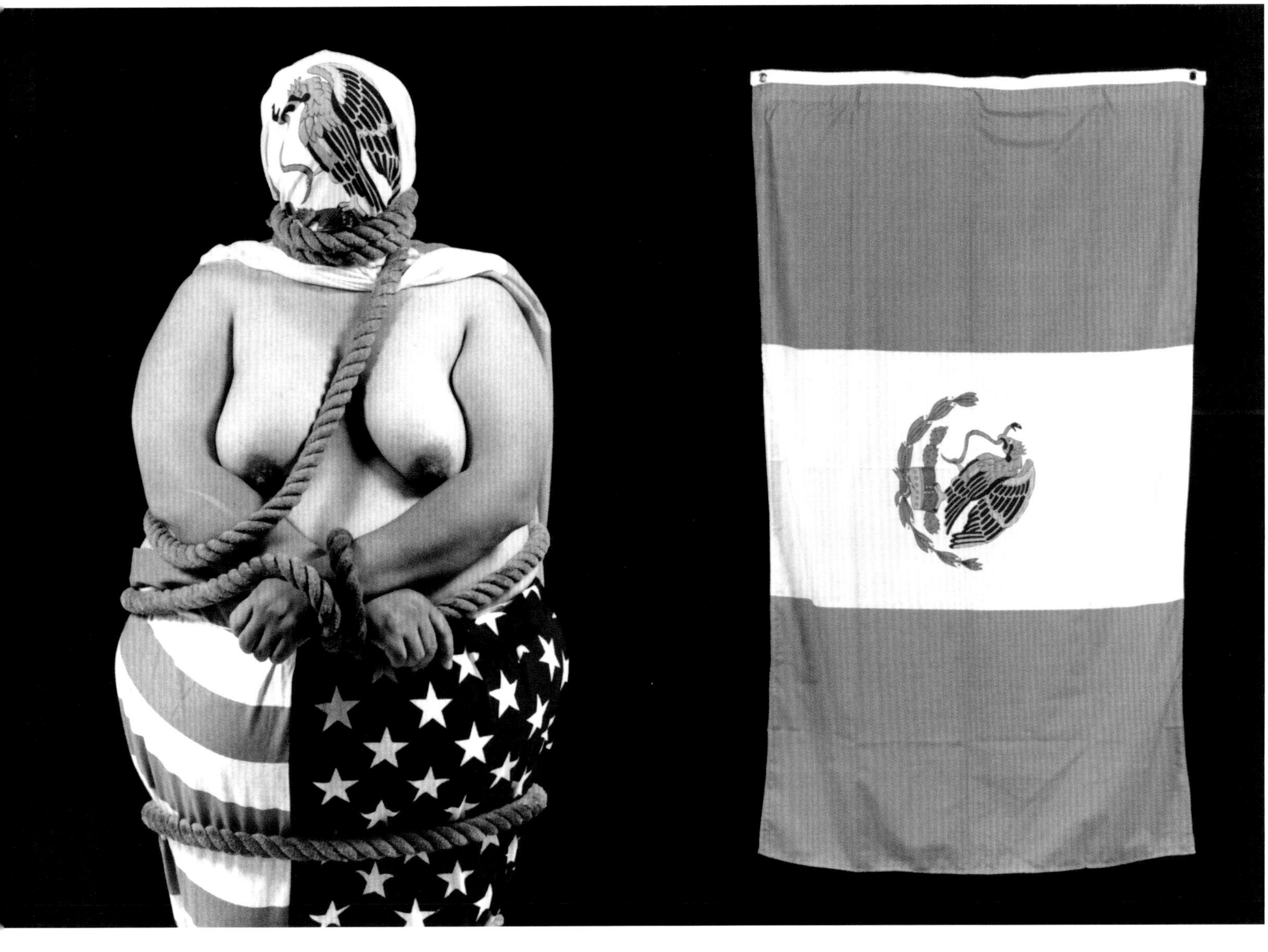

[**21**] *Chicano Moratorium, Boyle Heights*, negative 1970, printed 2021. George Rodriguez (American, born 1937). Gelatin silver print; 22.3 x 33 cm. The J. Paul Getty Museum, Los Angeles, 2021.31.8. © George Rodriguez

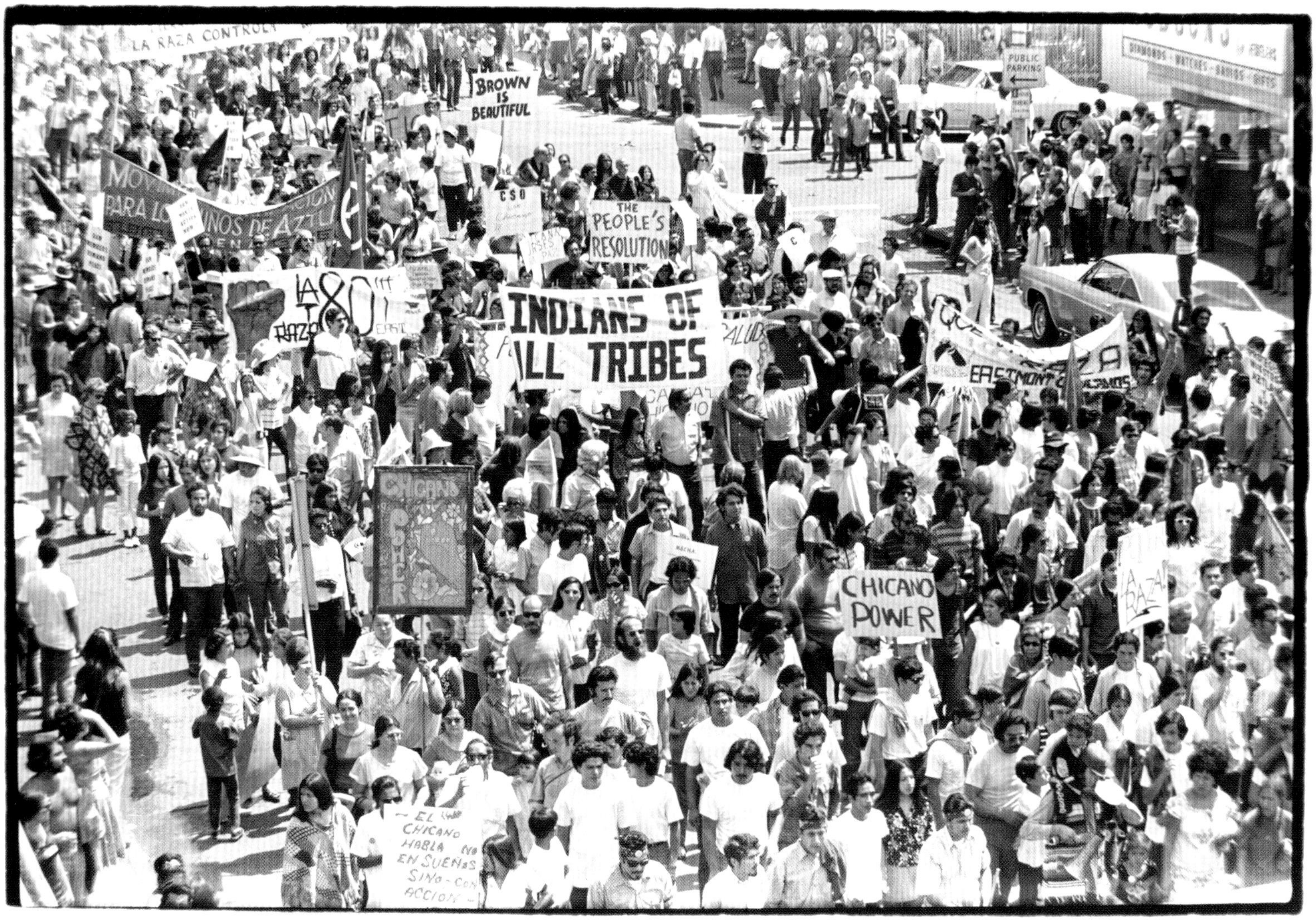

[**22**] *LAPD Arresting a Chicano Student Protester, Boyle Heights*, negative 1970, printed 2021. George Rodriguez. Gelatin silver print; 22.1 x 32.8 cm. The J. Paul Getty Museum, Los Angeles, 2021.31.6. © George Rodriguez

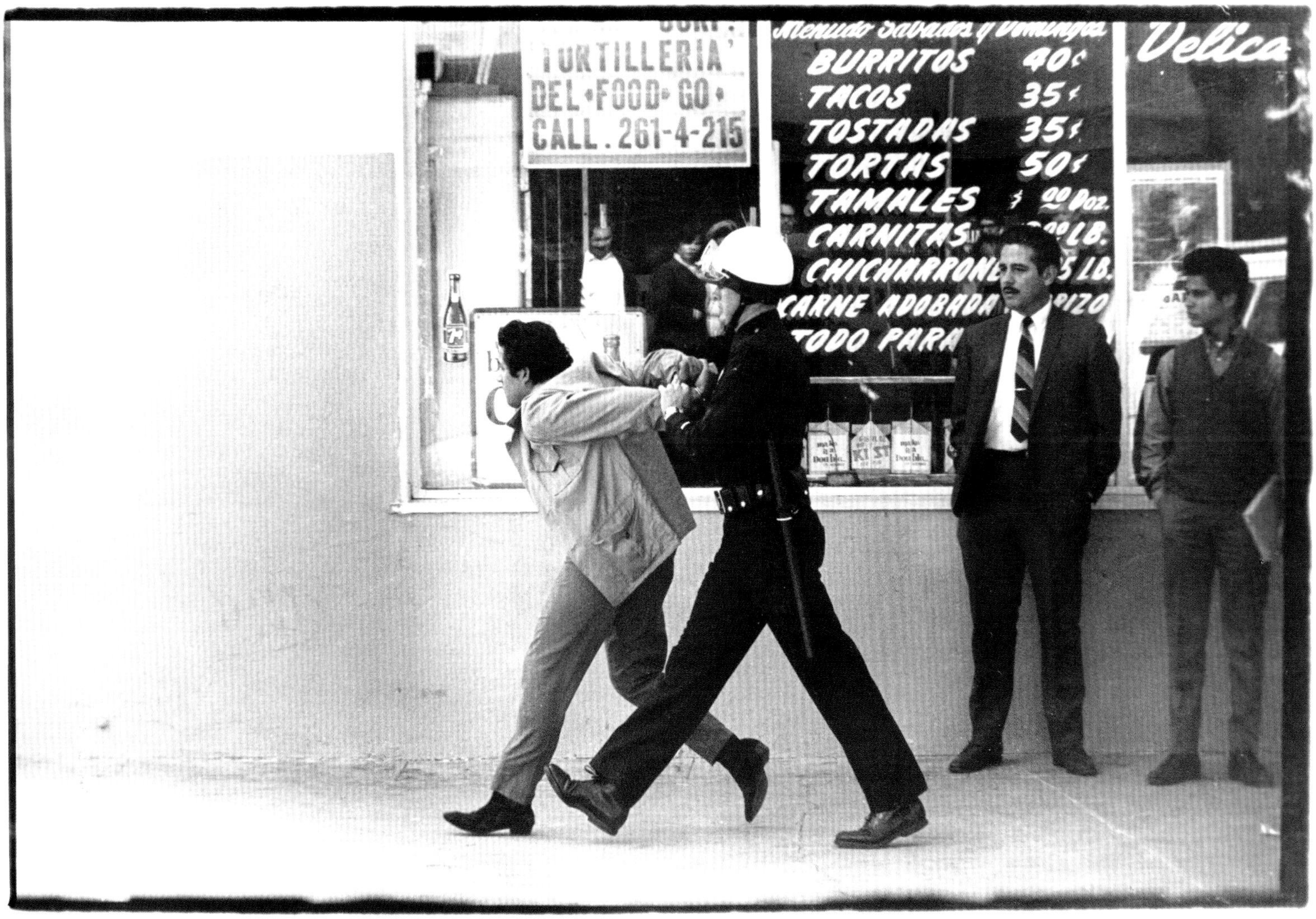

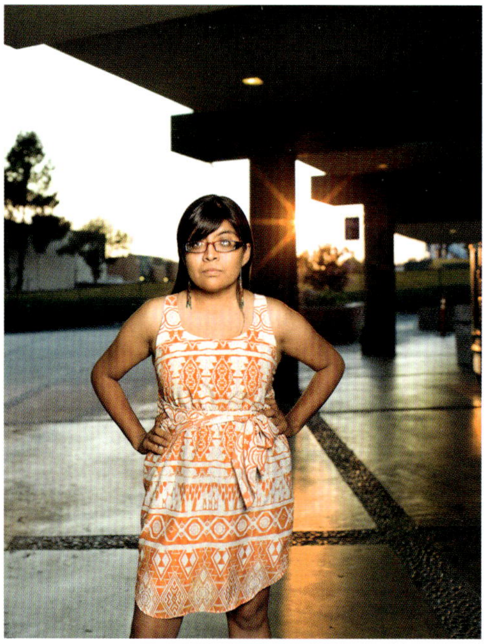

Figure 17. *Adriana Aguilar, 2013*, 2013.
Sam Comen (American, born 1980).
Digital C-print; 91.4 x 71.1 cm. © Sam Comen.
Image courtesy of the artist

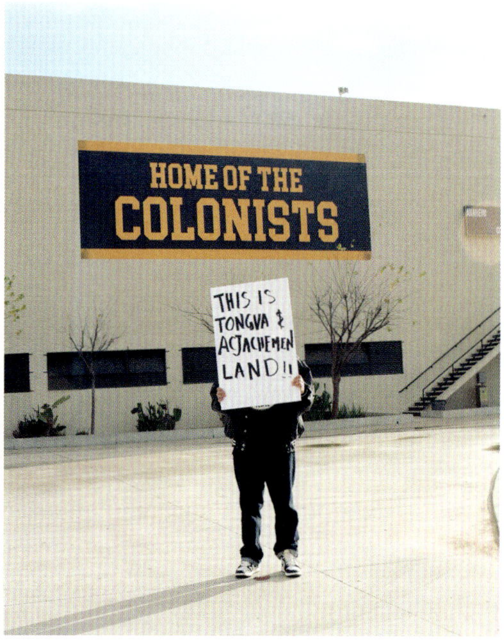

Figure 18. *A Colonist Is a Colonist Is a Colonist*,
2019. William Camargo (American, born 1989).
Archival inkjet print; 101.6 x 81.3 cm.
© William Camargo. Image courtesy of the artist

the profound feelings of displacement and deterritorialization they have experienced in their own homes.[14] Similarly, ongoing waves of ICE raids and the separation of children from their parents at the US-Mexico border have replicated the exclusionary methods meant to filter, block, deport, and dehumanize immigrants based on nativist immigration policies.

In the photographic series *Dreamers: Undocumented & Unafraid* (2013), the LA-based photographer Sam Comen (born 1980) documents DACA recipients from all over the world. Each photograph is paired with a quote by his subject, an approach reminiscent of Laura Aguilar's *Latina Lesbian* series. In one image, a twenty-three-year-old named Adriana is shown on the East Los Angeles College campus with the silhouette of a highway overpass in the background (fig. 17). Her quoted statement recounts the story of her family's migration from Mexico to LA and ends on an optimistic note for the future: "I intend to always work with communities that are systematically disadvantaged and plant seeds of love, awareness and consciousness in new generations to one day have a world free of injustice."

William Camargo's (born 1989) photographic practice is also highly attuned to Latinx identity and urban spaces. In a series of photographs from 2019 made in the artist's home city of Anaheim, California, he stands in different public spaces holding large signs with statements related to each location. "This Area Will Gentrify Soon," reads the sign in one photograph, taken in front of a fenced-off construction site. Another sign references the ancestral homelands of Indigenous nations: "This Is Tongva and Acjachemen Land!!" Camargo holds the sign in front of the local high school, whose banner announces their team's name, the Colonists (fig. 18). In each instance, the placard subsumes the artist's face and torso, transforming his figure into a universalized stand-in for displaced populations and their insistence on recognition. As a native resident of the city, "my body navigated those spaces," explains Camargo, accounting for the personal connections he feels to spaces he photographs.[15] His staged interventions in public places also carry forward many of the practices of Latinx artists included in *Picturing the Border*.

As border city residents themselves, the artists discussed in this chapter have made photographs that are distinct from those by outsiders. Their images' dual emphasis on marginalization and defiant empowerment proposes an alternative conception of Latinx identity in the borderlands and advocates on behalf of those commonly marginalized from mass media and mainstream culture. These artists are uniquely aware that spatial displacement from border cities is just one step in cultural erasure, a process that threatens to excise the stories and experiences of Latinx people from this history in the United States.

1. For an extended discussion of the term "cholo/a," see chapter 4.

2. One way city planners in Southern California reinforced neighborhood segregation was through the intricate and notoriously inefficient freeway system. LA's highways cut through traditionally impoverished immigrant neighborhoods, displacing their residents. See Eric Avila, *The Folklore of the Freeway: Race and Revolt in the Modernist City* (Minneapolis: University of Minnesota Press, 2014); and Eric Avila, *Popular Culture in the Age of White Flight: Fear and Fantasy in Suburban Los Angeles* (Berkeley: University of California Press, 2006).

3. Kelly Lytle Hernández, *Bad Mexicans: Race, Empire, and Revolution in the Borderlands* (New York: W. W. Norton, 2022), 208.

4. Urbanization is characterized by rapid, centralized population growth, often resulting from the influx of laborers drawn by the promise of industrial jobs. Since 1965, the Border Industrialization Program has resulted in the construction of hundreds of foreign-owned factories, or maquiladoras, in and around border cities, attracting huge numbers of rural migrants from the border region and throughout Mexico. See Oscar J. Martínez, *Border People: Life and Society in the U.S.-Mexico Borderlands* (Tucson: University of Arizona Press, 1994); and María Patricia Fernández-Kelly, *For We Are Sold, I and My People: Women and Industry in Mexico's Frontier* (Albany: State University of New York Press, 1983).

5. See Néstor García Canclini, *Hybrid Cultures: Strategies for Entering and Leaving Modernity* (Minneapolis: University of Minnesota Press, 1989); David A. Harvey, *Social Justice and the City* (London: Edward Arnold, 1973); and Henri Lefebvre, *The Urban Revolution* (Paris: Gallimard, 1970).

6. Rebecca Epstein, Sybil Venegas, Pilar Tompkins Rivas, et al., *Laura Aguilar: Show and Tell* (Los Angeles: UCLA Chicano Studies Research Center Press, 2017), 9.

7. Juan González, *Harvest of Empire: A History of Latinos in America* (New York: Penguin, 2011), 105.

8. Armendo B. Rendon, "El Plan Espiritual de Aztlán" [The Spiritual Plan of Aztlán], 1969, in *Takin' It to the Streets: A Sixties Reader*, ed. Alexander Bloom and Wini Breines (New York: Oxford University Press, 1995), 177–80; see also Gloria Anzaldúa, *Borderlands / La Frontera: The New Mestiza* (San Francisco: Aunt Lute, 1987). The term "Chicano" was appropriated and transformed from one of class-based derision to one of ethnic pride among Mexican American and Latinx communities, and emphasized Mexicans' Indigenous roots to differentiate their history of migration from that of European immigrants.

9. Harry Gamboa Jr., "Serpents in the City of Los Angeles," 1989, in *Urban Exiles: The Collected Writings of Harry Gamboa Jr.*, ed. Chon A. Noriega (Minneapolis: University of Minnesota Press, 1998), 64.

10. Ricardo Valverde, "First Communication Meeting Held," *CLP/USA Newsletter* 2 (January 1980), Esperanza Valverde Archive, Los Angeles.

11. Ricardo Valverde quoted in Alejandro Rosas, *Chicano and Latino Artists of Los Angeles* (Los Angeles: Los Angeles Department of Cultural Affairs, 1993), 46.

12. Allan Sekula, "Dismantling Modernism, Reinventing Documentary (Notes on the Politics of Representation)." Massachusetts Review 19, no. 4 (1978): 882.

13. C. Ondine Chavoya, "Orphans of Modernism: The Performance Art of Asco," in *Corpus Delecti: Performance Art of the Americas*, ed. Coco Fusco (London and New York: Routledge, 2003), 241.

14. Maya Rhodan and Emma Talkoff, "We Are Americans, Revisited: The Dreamers, Five Years Later," *Time* (September 4, 2017), time.com/daca-dream-act-jose-antonio-vargas-time-cover-revisited/.

15. Author's interview with William Camargo, October 20, 2023.

3 FAMILIAL SPACES ON

Louis Carlos Bernal's color photograph *Dos Mujeres* (1978) shows two women seated in adjacent rooms of a house in Douglas, Arizona (Bernal's hometown), lit by the ambient light of their home [23]. In the foreground, an adolescent girl sits in a living room with green walls. She looks directly at the camera and is caught in the midst of sewing a garment, a needle poised between the thumb and the index finger of her right hand. Bernal's photograph records the minute details of the interior space, from the surface texture of the plaster wall behind her to the frayed fabric of the upholstered chair she sits on, all bathed in the cool, reflecting light of the green walls.

To the right, an open doorway beckons viewers toward a recessed interior. In the background is a young woman, the older sister, sitting on a bed in a room with red walls, bathed in a warm tone that contrasts with the cool green tones of the adjacent room.[1] The coloristic contrast is striking, and Bernal deftly uses his color film to capture his sitters in two different lights, and thus two different moods and characters. The older sister in the back is brushing her hair, the brush positioned against her head in mid-stroke. Her tilted head and light-brown hair catch the light so as to create a halo effect on the wall behind her. The figures' actions parallel one another, as each subject is caught in the middle of a domestic activity. Each body is independently lit by the midday light in the home, resulting in two separate yet complementary portraits. While Bernal experimented with the spatial, compositional, and lighting aspects of the photograph, he also created a scene that shows the two sisters in roles that reach beyond their young ages. The title of the image—*Two Women*—acknowledges this, and bestows upon the younger sitter a status equal to that of her older sister. The two sitters are shown as poised and assertive, in control of the modest but tidy household that surrounds them.

Hanging on the wall in the living room is a calendar advertising the Harinera Estrella flour company based in Agua Prieta, a town in Mexico just south of the border, the southern "sister city" to Douglas. The text of the calendar is in Spanish, and its pages are set to the first two months of 1978. Its presence in the photograph is an implicit marker of time and place. The calendar features a photograph of a young boy dressed in baseball gear seated with a sandwich, a glass of milk, and a puppy. This staged, stock image is at odds with the candid domesticity of Bernal's photograph. The surrounding scene acts as a foil to the embedded image, a rejection of the cliché, idealized "American" childhood fantasy. In the years after it was made, *Dos Mujeres* circulated widely on both sides of the border as a striking representation of Latinx communities in the borderlands.[2]

During the inception of the Chicano Civil Rights Movement, activists, scholars, and early leaders such as Reies López Tijerina (1926–2015) and José Armas (1944–2002) often equated the community with the family, implying they were one and the same.[3] Author Richard Rodríguez posits kinship and family as crucial sites for political struggle among Latinxs. He explains, "If there is a single issue almost always at stake in Chicano/a cultural politics since the Chicano movement of the 1960s and 1970s, it is the family in some shape, form, or fashion. Indeed, the family is a crucial symbol and organizing principle that by and large frames the history of Mexican Americans in the United States."[4]

[23] *Dos Mujeres, Douglas, Arizona*, 1978. Louis Carlos Bernal. Chromogenic print; 22.9 x 22.9 cm. Collection of the Center for Creative Photography, University of Arizona, Gift of the artist, 80.45.2. © Lisa Bernal Brethour and Katrina Ann Bernal

THE BORDER

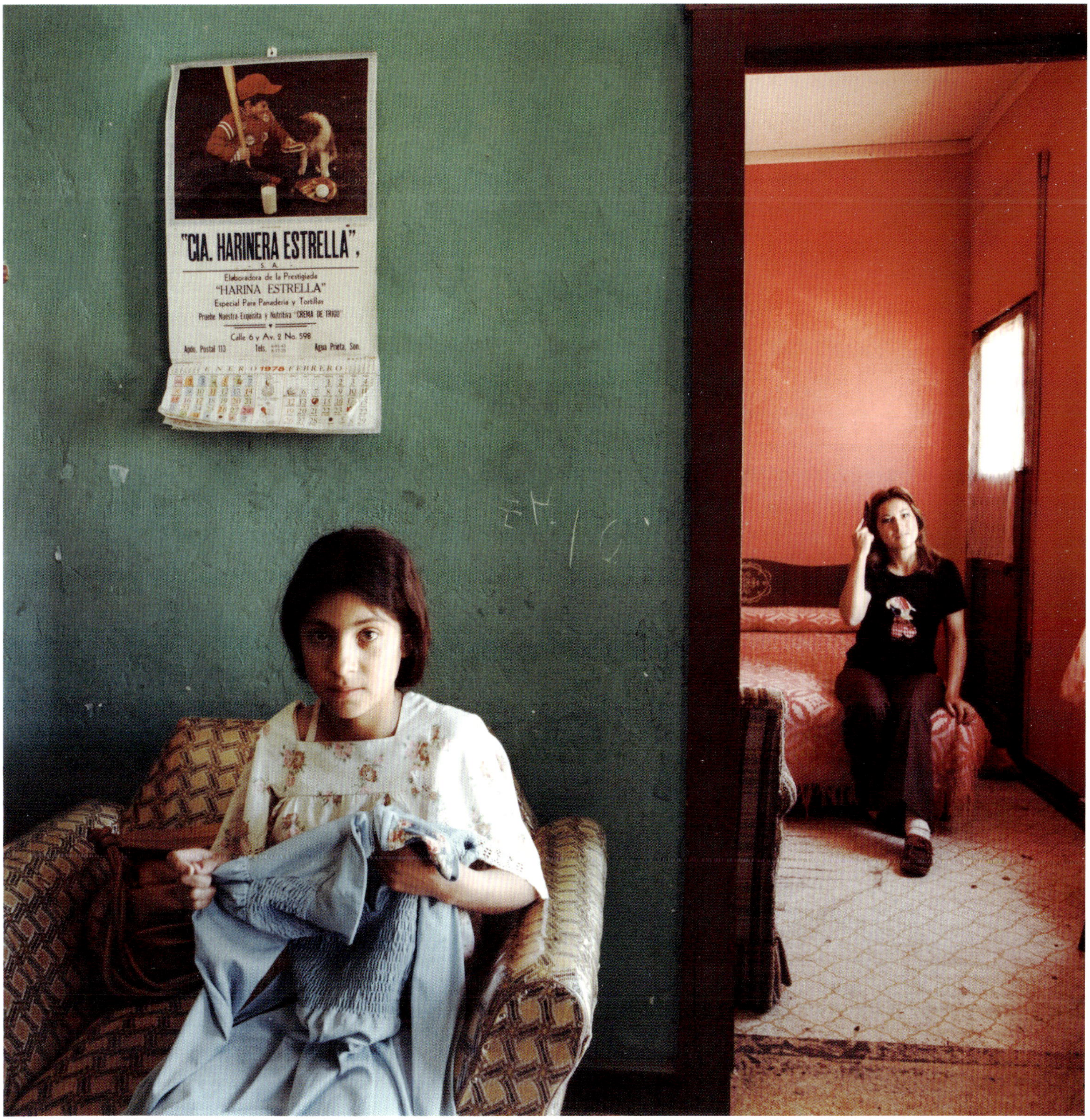
"CIA. HARINERA ESTRELLA",
S.A.
Elaboradora de la Prestigiada
"HARINA ESTRELLA"
Especial Para Panaderia y Tortillas
Pruebe Nuestra Exquisita y Nutritiva "CREMA DE TRIGO"
Calle 6 y Av. 2 No. 598
Apdo. Postal 113
Tels.
Agua Prieta, Son.
ENERO 1978 FEBRERO

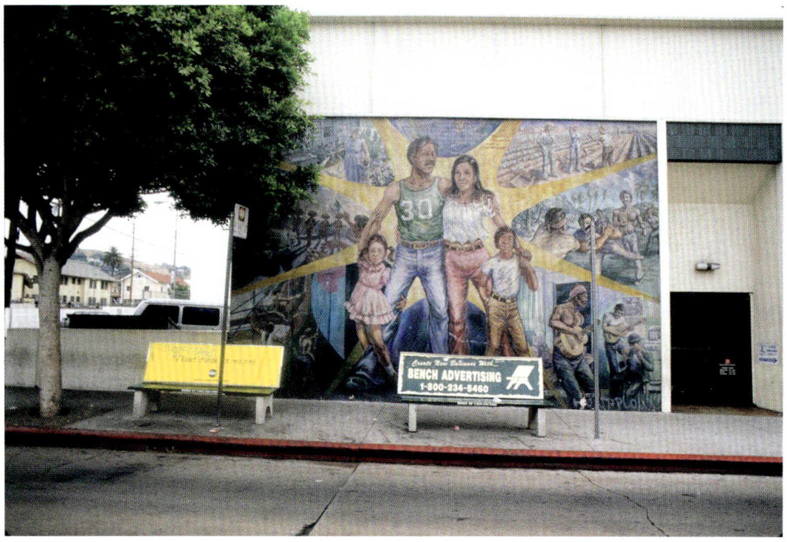

Figure 19. *Chicano time trip* (detail), 1977. Wayne Healy (American, born 1946), David Rivas Botello (American, born 1946). Mural (showing one panel), 2601 North Broadway (at Daly Boulevard), Los Angeles, 1977. Photo: Robin J. Dunitz, courtesy of the USC Digital Library, Robin Dunitz Slides of Los Angeles Murals Collection

Rodríguez's statement draws on a concept popularized during the early days of the Chicano movement: *la familia de la raza* (the family of the race). A metaphor meant to fuse familial cultural values with the Chicano Civil Rights Movement, *la familia de la raza* was an important element of Chicano cultural nationalism in the 1960s and 1970s.[5] *La familia de la raza* embraced all people of Mexican heritage regardless of their citizenship or status and centered on the nuclear family as a bedrock of Mexican American identity. Chicano artists who tackled this theme include Joaquín Chiñas, whose iconic drawing *La Familia* (1962) circulated widely as an early Chicano movement poster, and Wayne Healy (born 1946) and David Rivas Botello (born 1946), whose mural *Chicano time trip* (1977) is located in the Lincoln Heights neighborhood of Los Angeles (fig. 19). In the mural, the father is portrayed as strong and virile; he occupies a central, towering position, and embraces his wife and daughter. His son, though smaller, mirrors his father's confident stance, while his sister clings shyly to her father's enormous leg. Scenes of genealogy—other Chicano families, the history of the movement—surround and radiate from the family. A quote at the top reads, "Our Heritage is the foundation of our destiny. The power of our desires and imagination will determine the future." "The future," the mural suggests, can only be propagated by the heteronormative, nuclear family unit, guided by the machismo of a strong, male-headed household.[6]

In the years since *la familia de la raza*'s popularization, Chicana feminist scholarship and activism that emerged in the 1980s—including Gloria Anzaldúa's book *Borderlands / La Frontera: The New Mestiza* (1987)—has critiqued the concept as perpetuating the notion of a nuclear family and male-headed household at the expense of alternative, feminist, and queer models. In fact, family structures in borderland communities—whether in the small border town of Douglas, Arizona, or the urban neighborhoods of East Los Angeles—are often unconventionally structured, with female-led households and extended networks of multigenerational families or non-biological chosen families living together. Dispersed networks of family members living on both sides of the border are kept in close proximity to their loved ones via photographs and memorabilia that adorn their homes, placed prominently among their belongings.

The artists addressed in this chapter envision cultural empowerment in a way that better reflects the social realities of working-class families in the US-Mexico borderlands: through portraits of maternal domestic governance. Through their photographic practices, the artists discussed here reimagine *la familia* to accommodate expanded notions and alternative understandings of "family" that are important social structures of survival and that simultaneously challenge both Chicano cultural nationalism and American expectations regarding the nuclear family. These family structures range from the alternative to the experimental, the latter reflected in the gender-defying and queer identities of many portraits included in *Picturing the Border*.

In 1979, Roberto Gil de Montes analyzed the appeal of Louis Carlos Bernal's home interiors in the context of current events and media depictions of Latinxs: "There has been much media coverage of late about Latin culture and particularly about its problems. The coverage has predominately occurred in media controlled by non-Latins, making one wonder what other images of the Latin community might look like. [Latinx photographers] bring forth visions [of their own communities] far more rich, far more complicated and hence less easy to dismiss as those images presented to the public by the mass media."[7] Gil de Montes suggests that Bernal's photographs should be understood in relation to increased and largely negative media coverage of Latinx culture from that decade.

Bernal's images of border-home interiors contain multiple layers of meaning and convey his subjects' self-reliance, cultural power, and pride, employing techniques of color photography to reflect the vibrancy of the decorated interiors he visited. When shooting in someone's house, he almost always used a medium- or large-format camera without a flash, manipulating the interior, ambient light to brilliant effect. He was opposed to cropping his frames in the darkroom, where he often printed his images at 9 by 9 inches or larger. In Bernal's case, the avoidance of cropping was also economical, as there was less work involved in processing the film in the darkroom [24].

Around this time, Bernal's photographic practice began to harmonize with his political outlook, which was shaped by his identity as a Mexican American. A Chicano artist and Arizona native with deep ties to the Mexican American communities he photographed, Bernal often said that his photographs are "made *for* the people I have photographed," and that he hoped his images "provide some small contribution to my people—*La Raza*."[8] Significantly, he both articulates and (through his photographs) visualizes the site of Chicano identity as negotiated in the *spaces* of the family, a concept he would develop over time. Bernal always spent time getting to know his subjects before photographing them, an aspect apparent in the access they granted him to their personal and private spaces. He credited this ease of access to his ability to speak Spanish and to understand the culture as a result of having grown up there.[9]

Over the course of his lifetime, which was tragically cut short in 1993 following a bicycling accident, Bernal established and maintained networks with photographers throughout Mexico and the Southwestern United States, and gained notoriety as an established photographer. Despite his international acclaim, his subject matter retained a consistent focus on portraits of the communities throughout the Southwest with which he had grown up. Bernal's affinity for documenting families in the private spaces of their homes and at informal, public gatherings are hallmarks of his oeuvre. So, too, is his use of the saturated hues of color photography, which add tangible veracity to the racialized identities and intimate, self-made spaces of his sitters.

One woman Bernal photographed in Barrio Anita in Tucson, Arizona, posed seated beside a small home altar in a room filled with religious imagery [25]. Between likenesses of Christ and the Virgin Mary are family photographs from multiple generations. The modest furnishings of her home intermingle with the carefully placed pictures, an indication of how every inch of space is given over to decoration. On the wall to the right is a framed image of the Last Supper. This image—a popular decoration found in stores and markets throughout the Southwest and Latin America—marks the photograph as recording vernacular forms of home décor that were inexpensive and thus extraordinarily common. The red walls impart a sense of artificiality, while the Mickey Mouse balloon, hanging from a bare bulb in the center of the room, becomes a makeshift light fixture, adding to the chromatic saturation of the image. The objects' concentration in a corner of the home emphasizes the cramped nature

[**24**] Lubbock, Texas, 1987. Louis Carlos Bernal. Color contact sheet; 27.9 x 21.6 cm. Collection of the Center for Creative Photography, University of Arizona, Louis Carlos Bernal Archive. © Lisa Bernal Brethour and Katrina Ann Bernal

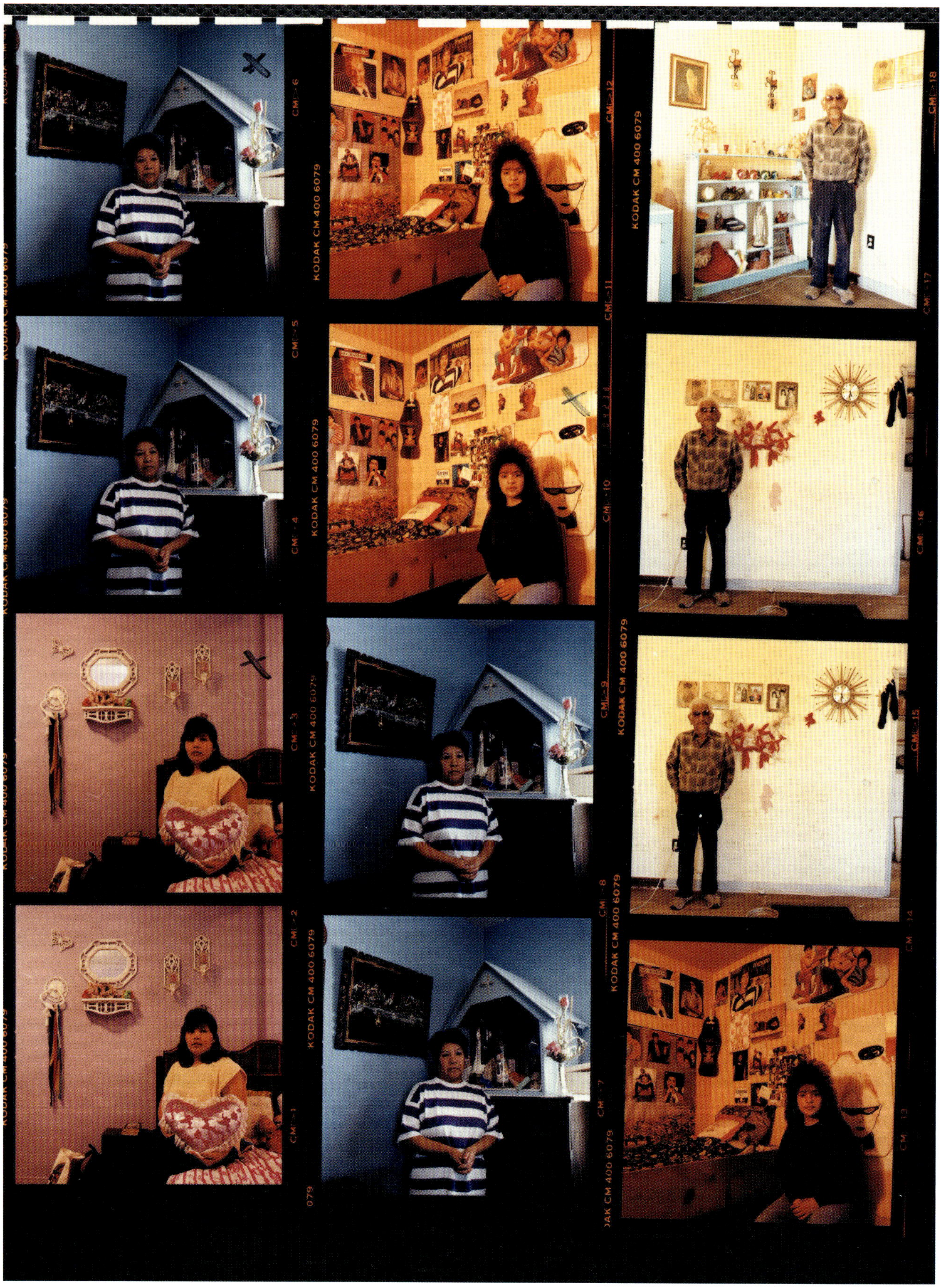

[**25**] *Nanita Mendibles, Barrio Anita*, 1978.
Louis Carlos Bernal. Chromogenic print;
23 x 23 cm. Collection of the Center for
Creative Photography, University of Arizona,
Gift of the Mexican American Legal
Defense and Educational Fund, 82.77.67.
© Lisa Bernal Brethour and Katrina Ann Bernal

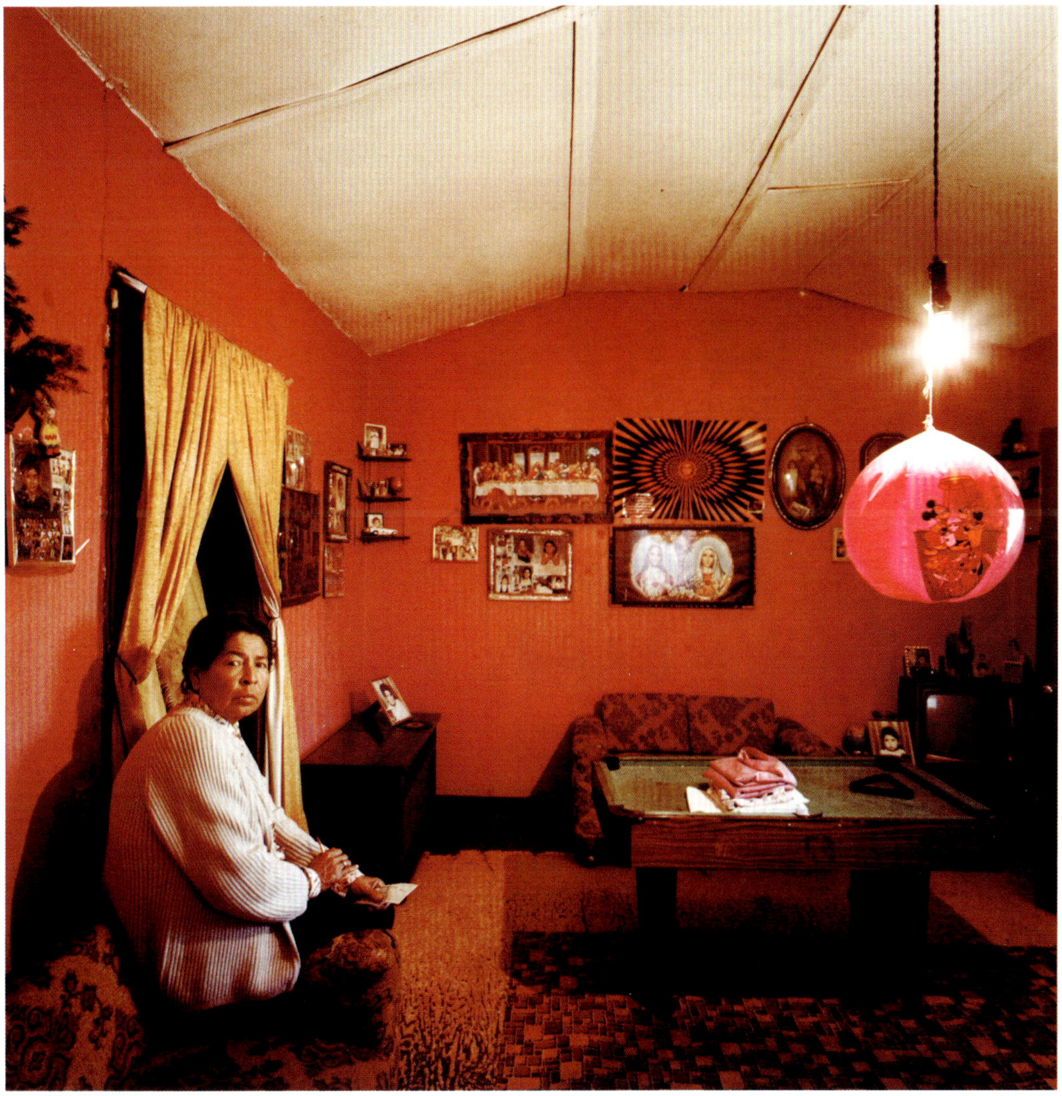

[**26**] *Untitled*, 1979. Louis Carlos Bernal.
Chromogenic print; 22.9 x 22.9 cm.
Collection of the Center for Creative Photography, University of Arizona, Gift of Morrie Camhi, 97.46.36.

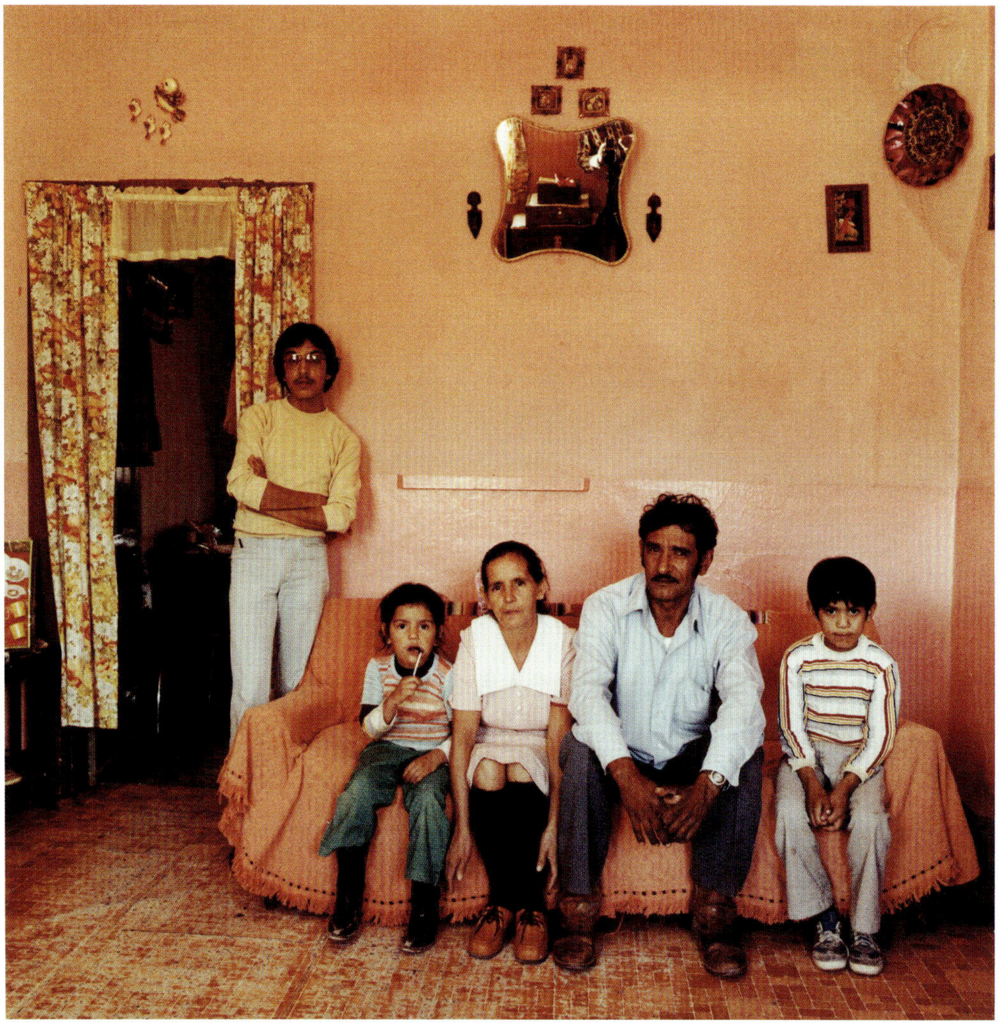

[**27**] *Recamara de Catalina Olomos, Phoenix, Arizona*, 1978. Louis Carlos Bernal.
Chromogenic print; 23 x 23 cm.
Collection of the Center for Creative Photography, University of Arizona, Gift of the Mexican American Legal Defense and Educational Fund, 82.77.75.

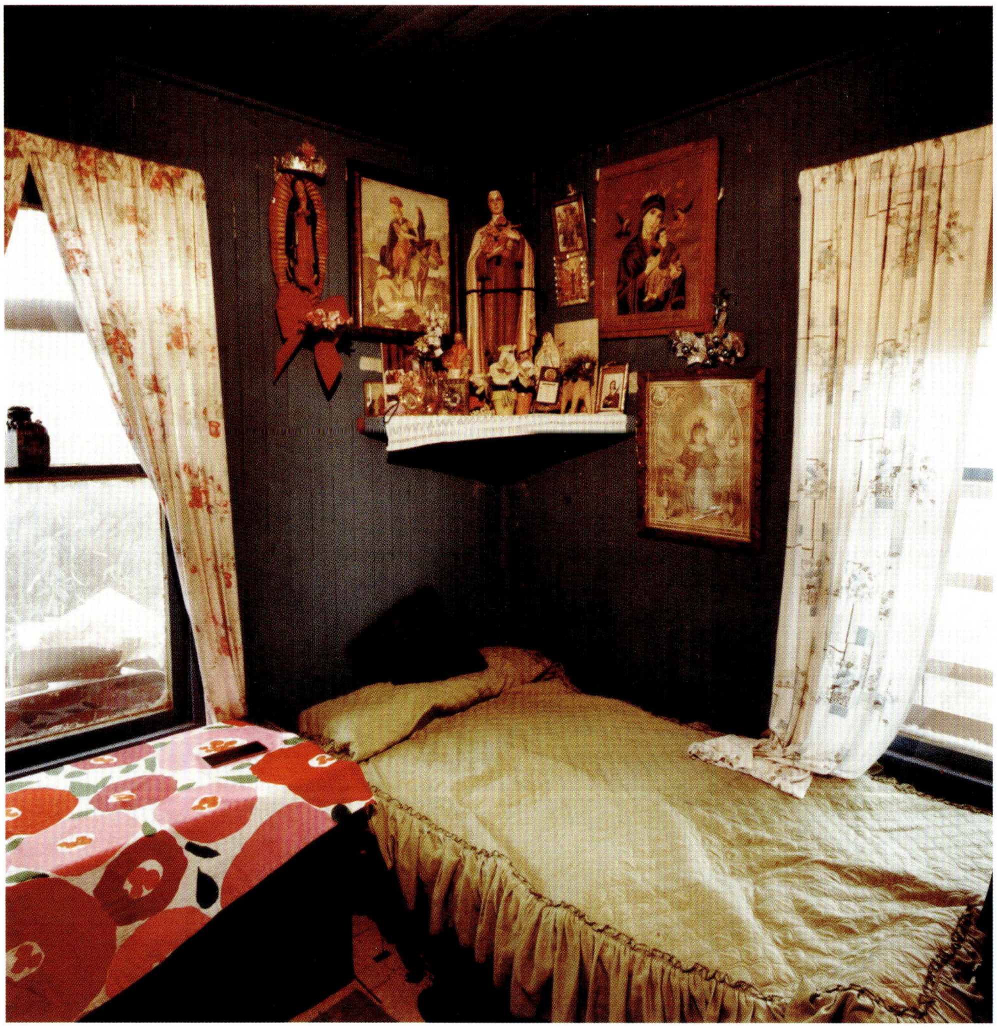

Figure 20. *An Ofrenda for Dolores del Rio*, 1984, revised 1991. Amalia Mesa-Bains (American, born 1943). Mixed-media installation including plywood, mirrors, fabric, framed photographs, found objects, dried flowers, and glitter; 243.8 x 182.9 x 121.9 cm. Smithsonian American Art Museum, Museum purchase through the Smithsonian Institution Collections Acquisition Program, 1998.161. © 1991 Amalia Mesa-Bains

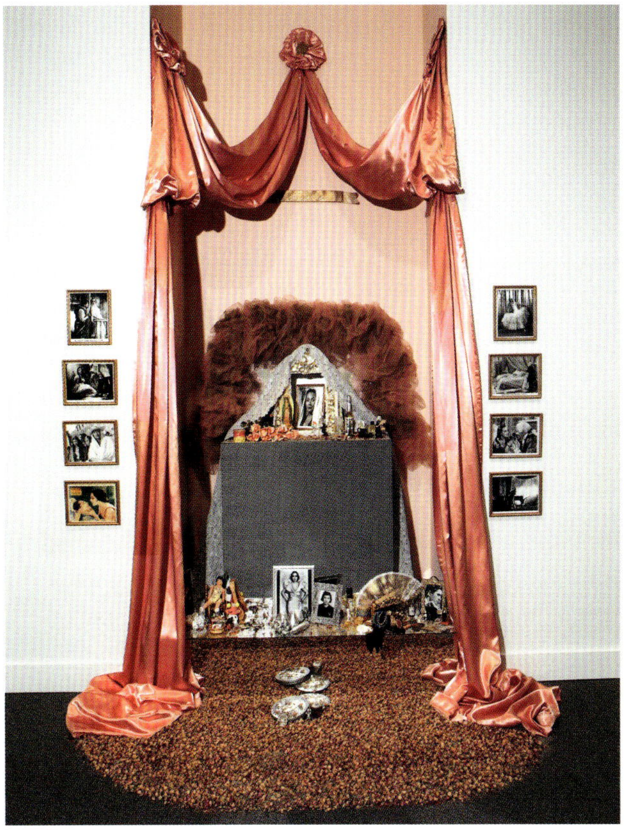

of the surroundings as well as the woman's ingenuity in creating a meaningful display space with limited resources. By positioning the woman in front of the self-made space she crafted, Bernal highlights her role as an artist and a cultural producer. As part of his larger photographic practice, this image embodies his concern with highlighting domestic spaces that challenge normative ideas of American identity.

The inclusion of home altars of one type or another, often with the woman of the household posing in front of them, is a recurring theme in Bernal's photographs [26, 27]. Introduced by Spanish Franciscan missionaries, the home altar flourished in the state of Jalisco in the sixteenth century, migrating to other regions of Mexico, Central and South America, the Caribbean, and eventually the United States along with migrant laborers and their families.[10] The syncretic practice combines Catholic iconography, folk crafts, and regional customs to create a place for private, domestic worship, the focus of prayers for miracles and devotional offerings. Historically, the women of a household have been in charge of constructing the altars, a role that "asserts the woman as an active producer of culture for the first time in Mexican art history."[11]

In subsequent iterations in the United States, the home altar acquired additional layers of meaning for the working-class Chicano community and became a form that artists such as Amalia Mesa-Bains (born 1943) appropriated in the 1980s as a vehicle for investigating resistant and hybrid identities within the community. Drawing on the genealogies of the tradition's integration within domestic, feminized spaces, Mesa-Bains created over-the-top altars as installation art, such as *Ofrenda for Dolores del Rio* (1984), which blends elements of the home-altar tradition with Latinx popular culture in the United States (fig. 20). Mesa-Bains sees her work as opposing *la familia de la raza*, "a way of calling into question the patriarchal control of the domestic sphere and subverting its representation through visual practices."[12]

Aesthetically, Mesa-Bains's altars, and home altars in general, feature the baroque embellishments that have often been identified as "kitsch," or what the Chicano author Tomás Ybarra-Frausto terms *rasquachismo*, meaning vernacular, vulgar, inferior, or in poor taste.[13] More recently, Mesa-Bains has directly engaged with the border through her installation *Emblems of the Decade: Borders* (2015). Using furniture, photographs, and objects to evoke a home interior, the work asks, "How does one create Home while existing within temporary constructs?"[14] The altar's various components and its layered meanings reference the present-day experience of those who call the border home as well as histories of familial separation and displacement.

Family altars enable everyday working-class women to present their life stories in artful and monumental ways within the private spaces of their homes. The keepers and guardians of familial and cultural archives, these women-as-matriarchs cross racial, national, class, and generational boundaries. Through Bernal's and Mesa-Bains's work, we become witness to the creative forces of ordinary women who transform social ritual and personal memories into carefully curated arrangements of pictures, paintings, textures, and even smells [28] and [45] (see Scenters-Zapico's essay in this volume).

The migratory roots of the home altar, and the themes of matriarchal governance they came to embody at this time,

[**28**] *Yrenia Cervantes*, 1990. Laura Aguilar. Gelatin silver print; 22.9 x 30.5 cm. The Cleveland Museum of Art, Karl B. Goldfield Trust, 2023.10. © The Laura Aguilar Trust

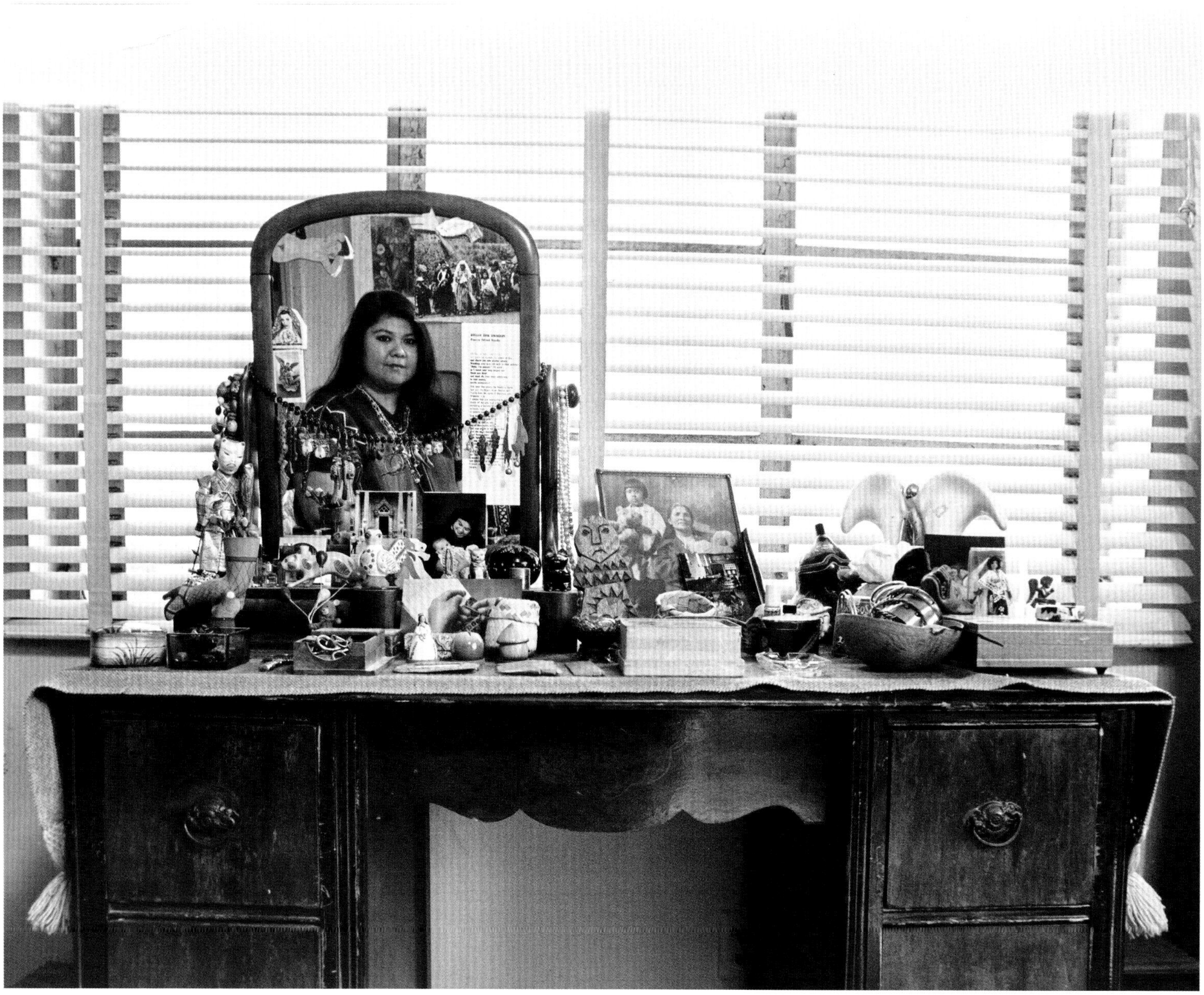

are particularly visible in a series Bernal made in Texas in 1987. One day, while photographing barrio residents in the city of Lubbock, several of Bernal's subjects mentioned an Afro-Cuban immigrant who lived in the area, a *curandera* (healer) named Caridad Sanchez. Bernal recounted that over the course of several days, and through word-of-mouth messages sent among local residents, he was able to arrange a visit to the woman's home. When he arrived, early on a Saturday morning, Sanchez showed him the alcove in her living room built to hold her elaborate home altar of Catholic, African, and Caribbean statues.[15] She pointed out the doll at the center of the altar that was custom-made to look like her, a testament to the deeply personal nature of the objects and an acknowledgment of the lack of racialized representations in traditional religious iconography.

In Bernal's contact sheets from that day, Sanchez, wearing a printed dress and gold jewelry, poses beside her meticulously arranged altar [29]. The formal tone of her portrait captures Caridad's mythology and renown in the local community as a healer and spiritual guide. Bernal also photographed Caridad's daughters in more casual portraits, attesting to the significant degree of access and trust he was able to gain in a short time [30]. Each daughter poses on her bed in a different room, beneath the family photographs, religious imagery, and colorful posters that adorn the rest of their home. The contact sheets of the family's portraits, each representing a different generation, form a lineage of women living in a female-headed household. In this series, matriarchal genealogy is mapped onto the spaces of the home, a transnational space that traces the customs of the Cuban immigrant mother through to her daughters. The portraits also counter the relative invisibility of Afro-Latinxs from imagery associated with the Chicano movement.

La familia de la raza also provided fertile ground for Ricardo Valverde's early photographic investigations. In his interior-family photographs—which include not only his wife and son but also his sister, Maya, and her partner, Sue Ella—Valverde radically upends the notion of the home as a site of feminine virtue and obedience [31]. The power, sexuality, and defiance conveyed by his portraits challenge the prescribed social and familial roles within the Chicano community while illustrating a crucial shift in societal roles.

After graduating from UCLA with an MFA in 1976, Valverde was employed as a meter reader for the Department of Water and Power (DPW) in Los Angeles, a job that took him to different neighborhoods all over South and East LA, as well as into people's homes. Often bringing his lightweight 35mm camera with him, he had a distinct talent for making people feel comfortable around him, which led to several impromptu portrait sessions. Like Bernal, Valverde was afforded an ease of access to the homes of immigrant and Latinx families stemming from his ability to speak Spanish and his cultural familiarity with the community. These sessions resulted in many intimate single and family portraits, such as *Tres Mujeres*, taken in a Los Angeles barrio situated near Interstate 110 (Arroyo Seco Parkway/Harbor Freeway) [32].

Esperanza Valverde, Ricardo's wife, recalls that *Tres Mujeres* was part of her husband's *Walking Series*, made during the late 1970s and early 1980s, a time when neighborhoods in South Central were becoming more populated by Latinx families who began as renters but increasingly became homeowners.[16] Valverde took the photographs in *Walking Series* while navigating the city on foot in his capacity as a meter reader for the DPW.[17] The series can be contextualized within broader, conceptual photographic practices featuring

[**29**] Lubbock, Texas, 1987. Louis Carlos Bernal. Color contact sheet; 27.9 x 21.6 cm. Collection of the Center for Creative Photography, University of Arizona, Louis Carlos Bernal Archive.

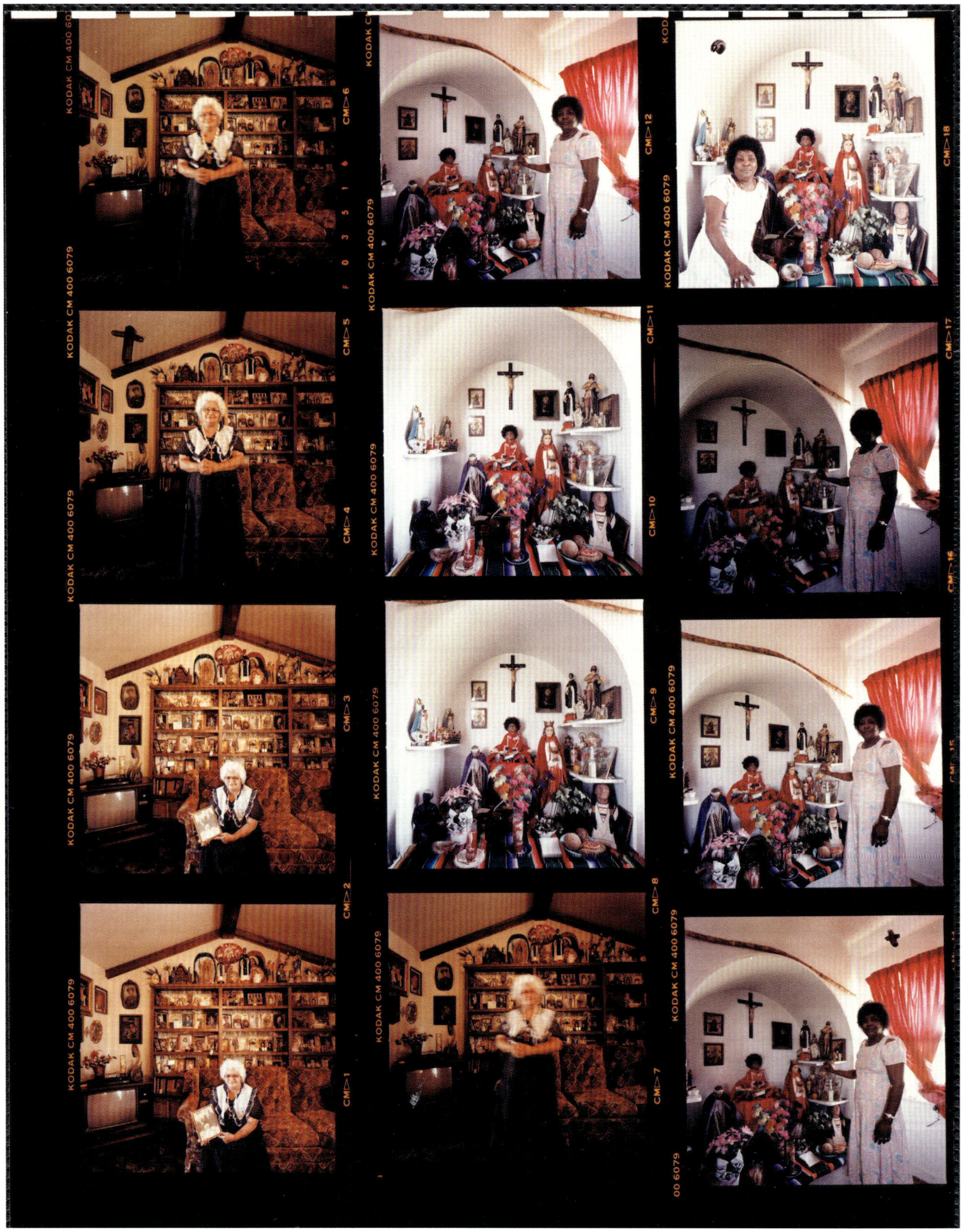

[**30**] Lubbock, Texas, 1987. Louis Carlos Bernal. Color contact sheet; 27.9 x 21.6 cm. Collection of the Center for Creative Photography, University of Arizona, Louis Carlos Bernal Archive.
© Lisa Bernal Brethour and Katrina Ann Bernal

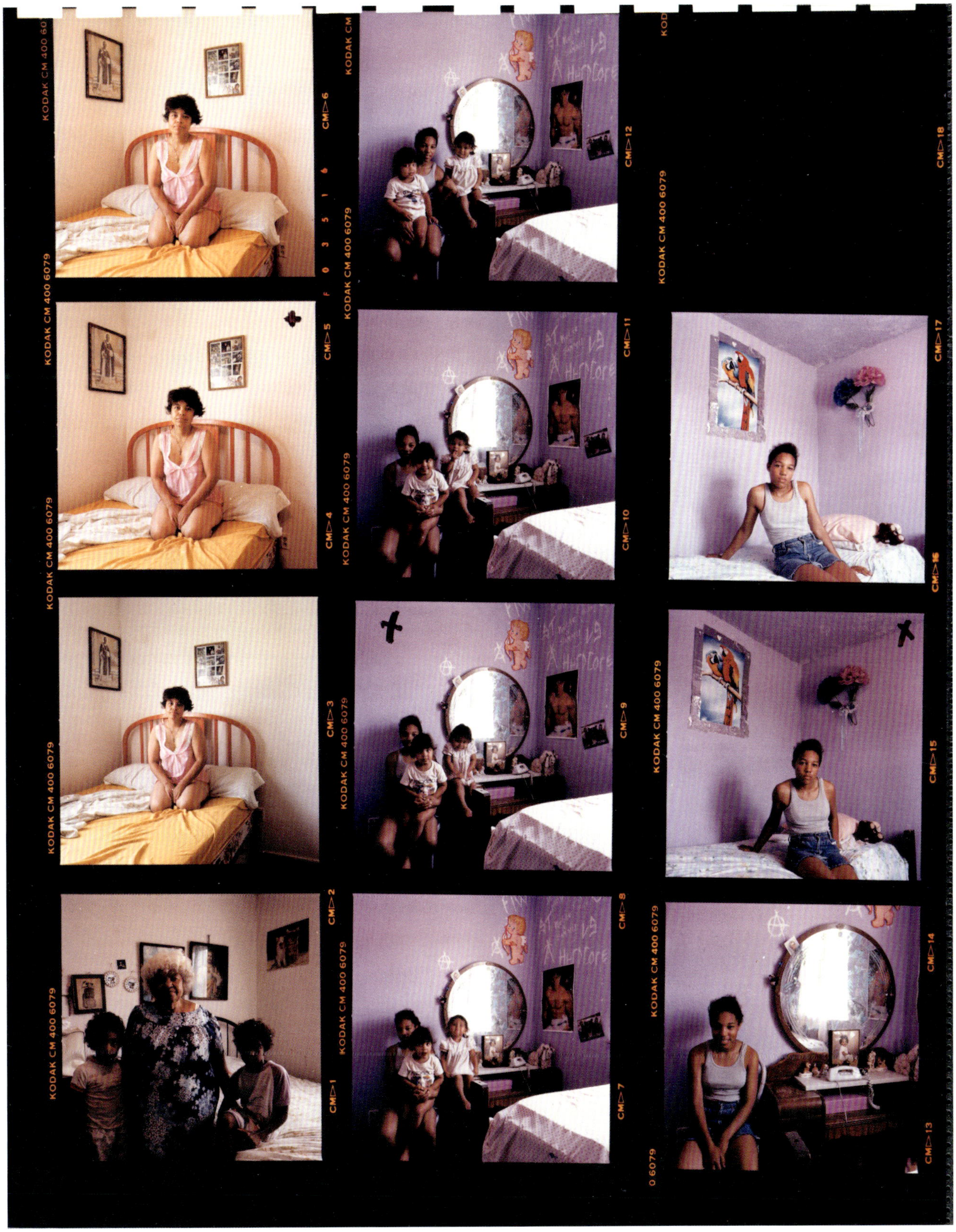

[**31**] *Jude and Espie at Home*, 1977. Ricardo Valverde. Gelatin silver print; 27.9 x 35.6 cm. Collection of Esperanza Valverde and Christopher J. Valverde, Ricardo Valverde Estate. © Esperanza Valverde and Christopher Jude Valverde

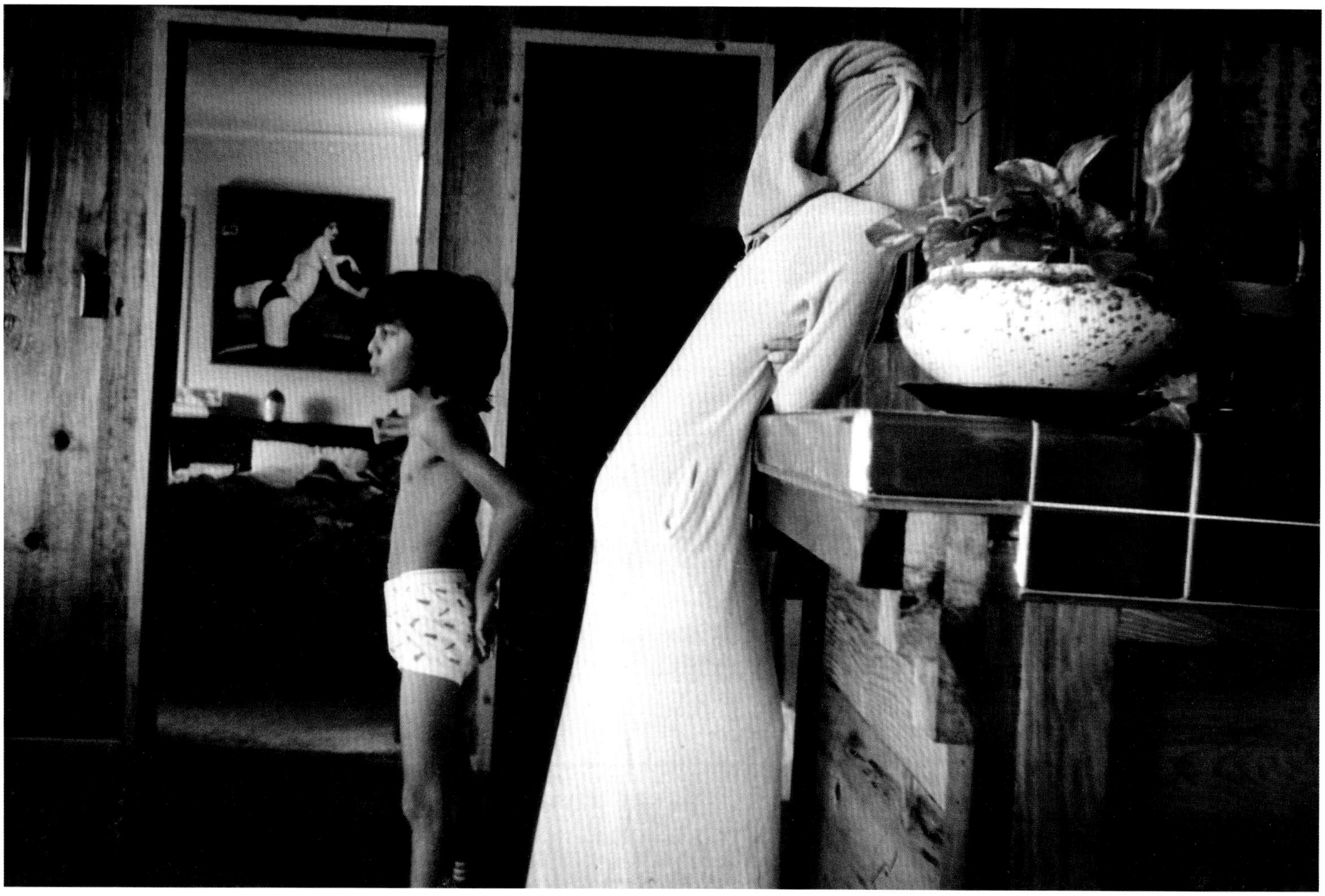

[**32**] *Tres Mujeres*, from the *Walking Series*, 1982. Ricardo Valverde. Gelatin silver print; 27.9 x 35.6 cm. Collection of Esperanza Valverde and Christopher J. Valverde, Ricardo Valverde Estate. © Esperanza Valverde and Christopher Jude Valverde

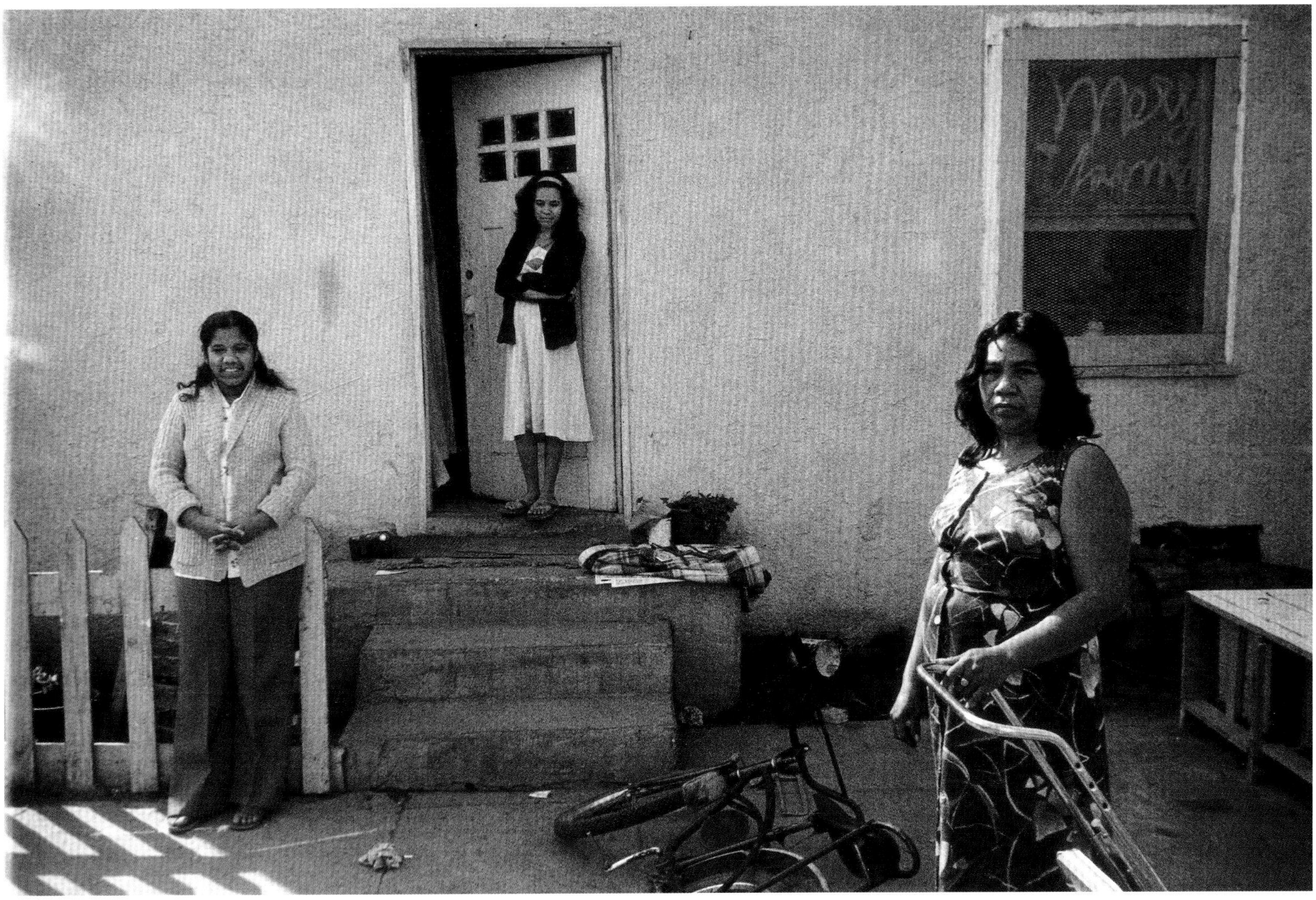

[**33**] *#8*, from the *Walking Series*, 1981. Ricardo Valverde. Gelatin silver print; 20.3 x 25.4 cm. Collection of Esperanza Valverde and Christopher J. Valverde, Ricardo Valverde Estate. © Esperanza Valverde and Christopher Jude Valverde

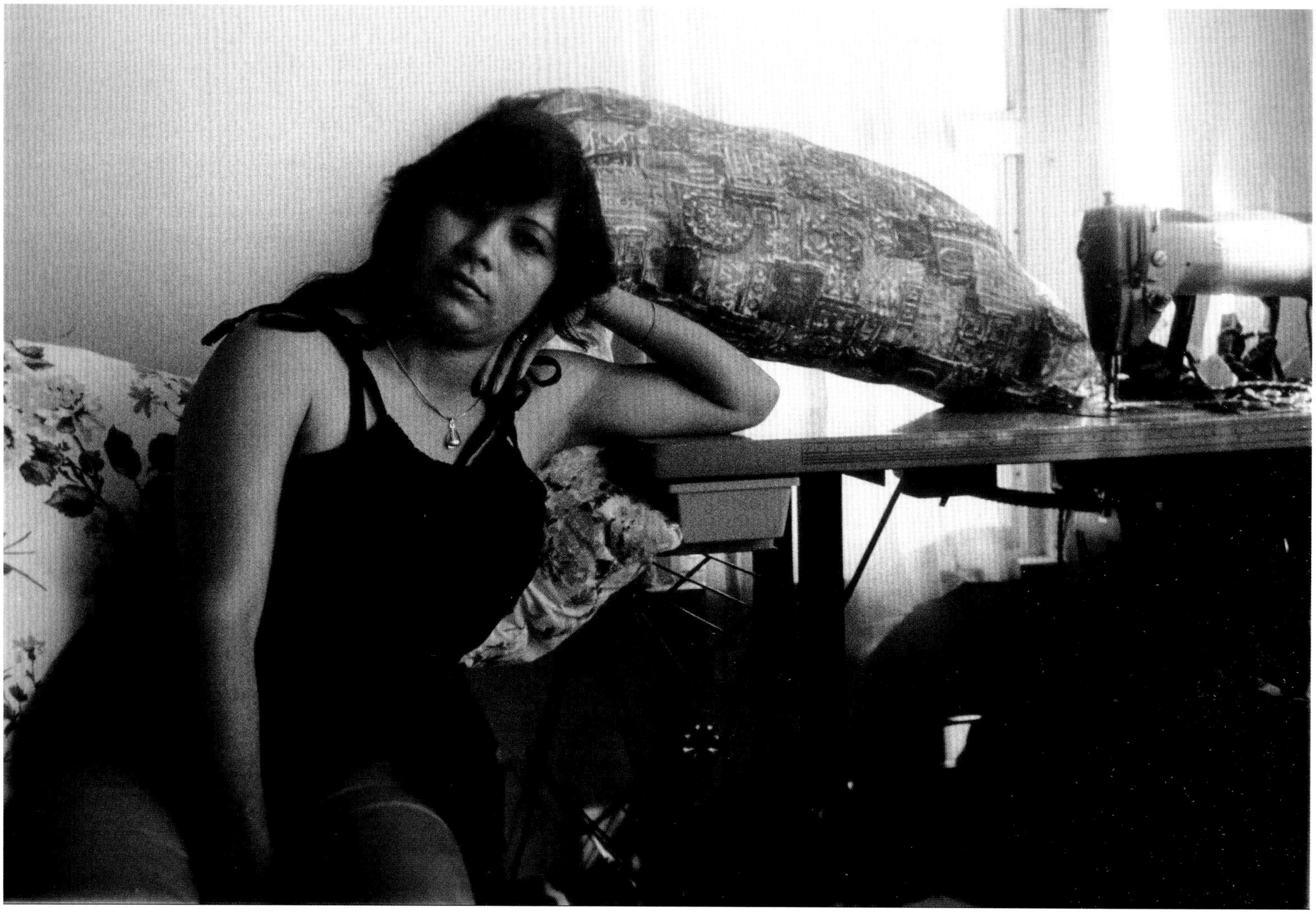

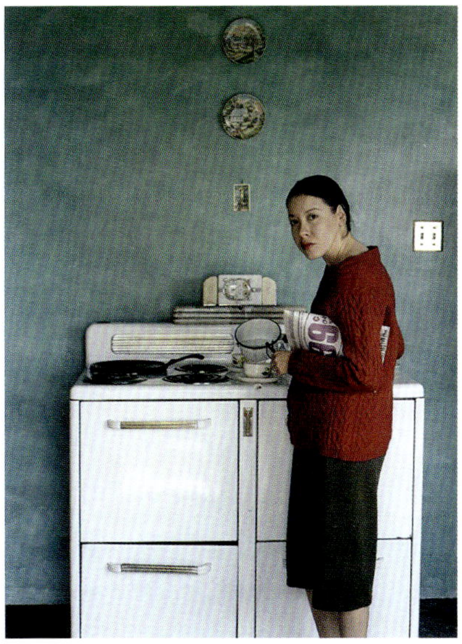

Figure 21. *María's Great Expedition* (detail of María in the kitchen), 1995–96. Christina Fernandez (American, born 1965). © Christina Fernandez. Photo: New York Public Library, nypl.org

non-white subjects. Similar to Carrie Mae Weems's *Kitchen Table Series* (1990), Valverde's cycle features working-class immigrant families as protagonists, focusing on the domestic sphere of their homes and providing a glimpse into their small but deeply cared-for spaces [33].

In addition to photographing his own and other biological families, Valverde also documented the "chosen family" of his fellow artists in East LA, among them his friends in the performance art collective Asco. Throughout the 1970s and 1980s, Valverde often photographed the members of Asco and documented their performances, in many of which Asco artists "shot back" at mainstream Hollywood productions, offering alternative imagery of familial dynamics, sexual identity, and gender roles. In Asco's works from this period, artist and writer Coco Fusco identifies their goal of contesting cultural stereotypes, "explor[ing] the alienating underside of conventional social relations, which are usually seen as linchpins of Latino community stability."[18] By depicting this chosen family and their unconventional lifestyle, Valverde explicitly challenged normative tropes concerning the family, sexuality, and gender.

In Christina Fernandez's *María's Great Expedition* (1995–96), the artist focuses on her great-grandmother María Gonzalez, who originally migrated from Mexico and, like Caridad Sanchez in the Bernal series discussed above, had achieved a legendary status in the family's oral history, stories the artist grew up listening to. As its title indicates, Fernandez's (born 1965) multimedia installation, which includes photographs, maps, and texts, reimagines María's migratory journey as an expedition, imbuing it with a sense of discovery and exploration. Fernandez poses as María in a series of six photographs, each representing a different time period throughout the first half of the twentieth century. The images oscillate between moments of domesticity, transition, and labor in and outside of her homes throughout her journey (fig. 21). Countering the historical emphasis on the male migrant, or bracero, that is most often associated with migration during this period, each image emphasizes María's role as protagonist of her own narrative and in control of her surroundings. In this way, the project gives voice to the lesser-told story of a family's matriarch leading the path of migration.[19]

While conducting family interviews about María, Fernandez learned that there were only two extant photographs of her great-grandmother.[20] By standing in as María herself in each portrait and using photographic processes corresponding to the eras they were intended to represent, the artist created a photographic record of maternal leadership where one did not previously exist. With *María's Great Expedition*, Fernandez seemingly responds to Chicana feminist Cherríe Moraga's fear that "when our storytellers go, taking their unrecorded memory with them, we their descendants go too."[21]

Another contemporary artist who makes conceptual use of the family archive with regard to migration and memory is Muriel Hasbun (born 1961), who immigrated to the US from El Salvador but whose family has roots from locales across the globe. In an extended project titled *Santos y sombras / Saints and Shadows* (1991–97), Hasbun explores the complex history of the Palestinian-Salvadoran Christian and Polish-French Jewish sides of her family, a family history of "people in exile." Traveling back to the places where her parents and grandparents had lived, her project gives texture to the stories of their lives. Here, as elsewhere, she uses a process of layering items from the family archives over her own photographs, combining negatives of contemporary and historical

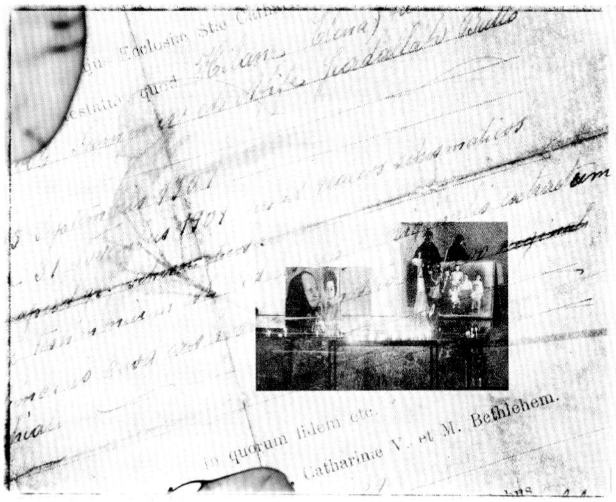

Figure 22. *Todos los santos (Graecos schismaticos) / All the Saints (Greek Schismatics)*, from the series *Santos y sombras / Saints and Shadows*, 1991–97. Muriel Hasbun (American, born El Salvador, 1961). Toned gelatin silver print; 35.6 x 45.7 cm. © Muriel Hasbun. Image courtesy of the artist

records in the darkroom to create a composite image that spans time and space.

In one work from the series, *Todos los santos (Graecos schismaticos) / All the Saints (Greek Schismatics)*, Hasbun superimposes an image of a home altar made by her grandmother Elena over a document verifying Elena's baptism in El Salvador in 1907 (fig. 22). The small, private altar was one of three home altars Hasbun found in her family's intergenerational home when she traveled to El Salvador in 1996. Along with this discovery, she learned that the altars were attended to even after her grandparents had passed, demonstrating how memories of loved ones are kept close despite geographic dispersal. The series is marked by a dialectic between absence and presence, movement and stasis, and the fragile tensions between them. Imbued with a sense of the uncanny, the haunting images challenge the notion of the home as a site of linear continuity and patriarchal control. They also play on one of the integral qualities of photography articulated by Roland Barthes—its connection to the specter of death—by commemorating someone who has passed or by implying their imminent passing.[22]

An artist who features the abstract framing of her home is Guadalupe Rosales (born 1980). For a series conceived during the COVID-19 lockdown, she photographed sites in her city of Los Angeles devoid of human presence. Instead of inhabitants posing inside their home, as in many of the photographs discussed in this chapter, one image from the series, titled *home* (2022), is a view of an inhabitant looking out at their neighborhood from the interior of their own space. In this image, Rosales offers us a view of her neighborhood through a metal door screen, a ubiquitous sight in the East LA cityscape, when many were required to shelter in place [34]. While evoking the particular memory of the pandemic, Rosales also prompts viewers to reflect on the subjective qualities of the place one calls home and the complicated emotions it can evoke for family members with histories of migration, displacement, and layered or conflicting identities.

For the artists in this chapter, the concept of the home and family variously becomes a means to challenge and put forth their own practices, a vehicle for political engagement, and a way to oppose stereotypical notions of the family in their communities and within dominant culture. In line with contemporaneous critiques of the Chicano movement advanced by feminist and queer theorists, these artists subvert the trope of home as a site of patriarchal oppression. Furthermore, they highlight how—given common histories of displacement among migrants—traditional family structures acquire different meanings when families are dispersed, reimagining transnational social spaces not defined by national borders.

[**34**] *home*, 2022. Guadalupe Rosales (American, born 1980). Archival pigment print, aluminum frame; 65.4 x 95.9 x 3.8 cm. © Guadalupe Rosales. Image courtesy of the artist and Commonwealth and Council, Los Angeles, Mexico City. Photo of artwork: Paul Salveson

1. Bernal notes the relationship between the sitters in his field notes and contact sheets. Louis Carlos Bernal Collection, Center for Creative Photography, Box 20, University of Arizona, Tucson (CCP).

2. *Dos Mujeres* circulated in exhibitions, catalogues, art magazines, and related press, including the exhibitions *Hecho en Latinoamérica* (Mexico City, 1978); *Espejo: Reflections of the Mexican American* (Oakland, 1978); *LATHEMES* (Los Angeles, 1979); and *Foto latina en el suroeste de los Estados Unidos* (Mexico City, 1981); and the art journal *Artes Visuales* (Mexico City, 1981).

3. Catherine S. Ramírez, *The Woman in the Zoot Suit: Gender, Nationalism, and the Cultural Politics of Memory* (Durham, NC: Duke University Press, 2009), 113. See also Reies López Tijerina, *They Call Me "King Tiger": My Struggle for the Land and Our Rights*, trans. Jose Angel Gutierrez (Houston: Arte Público, 2000); and José Armas, "Preface to the Third Edition," *De Colores: Journal of Emerging Raza Philosophies* 3, no. 2 (1976): 4–10.

4. Richard T. Rodríguez, *The Family in Chicano/a Cultural Politics* (Durham, NC: Duke University Press, 2009), 2.

5. For detailed discussions of *la familia de la raza*, see Rodríguez, 2–4; and Ramírez, *The Woman in the Zoot Suit*, 7–13.

6. For critical writing on the concept of machismo, see Ray González, *Muy Macho: Latino Men Confront Their Manhood* (New York: Anchor Books, 1996); and Stan Steiner, *La Raza: The Mexican Americans* (New York: Harper and Row, 1979).

7. Press release for *LATHEMES*, May 1979, LACE Archives, Los Angeles.

8. Quoted in James Enyeart's untitled essay in Louis Carlos Bernal and Ann Simmons-Myers, *Louis Carlos Bernal: Barrios* (Tucson: Pima Community College and the University of Arizona Library, 2002), 13.

9. Transcript of Bernal's interview with Ben Rider, 1982, 4, Bernal Collection, Box AG182, CCP.

10. While the colonists violently repressed the religious beliefs of the Indigenous populations, introducing the home altars into churches was a practice that blended with Native rituals, and people began erecting the altars in their homes. Celeste Donovan, "Icons behind Altars: María Izquierdo's Devotional Imagery and the Modern Mexican Catholic Woman," *Journal of Decorative and Propaganda Arts* 26 (April 2010): 162. See also Dana Salvo, *Home Altars of Mexico* (Albuquerque: University of New Mexico Press, 1997).

11. Donovan, 161, 168.

12. Amalia Mesa-Bains, "Domesticana," in *Chicana Feminisms: A Critical Reader*, ed. Gabriela F. Arredondo et al. (Durham, NC: Duke University Press, 2009), 299.

13. Ybarra-Frausto elaborates, "An underdog perspective . . . presupposes a world view of the have not, but it is a quality exemplified in objects and places and social comportment. . . . It has evolved as a bicultural sensibility." Tomás Ybarra-Frausto, "*Rasquachismo*: A Chicano Sensibility," in *Chicano Aesthetics: Rasquachismo* (Phoenix: MARS, Movimiento Artístico del Río Salado, 1989), 7.

14. This quote appears on the artist's website: amaliamesabains.com/exhibit/borders-emblems-of-the-decade-home-memory-and-future/.

15. Simmons-Myers, *Louis Carlos Bernal*, 32; Bernal's interview with Rider, 4, Box AG182, Bernal Collection, CCP.

16. Author's conversation with Esperanza Valverde, February 21, 2018.

17. Ramón García, *Ricardo Valverde* (Los Angeles: UCLA Chicano Studies Research Center Press, 2013), 27.

18. Coco Fusco, "Ethnicity, Politics, and Poetics: Latinos and Media Art," in *Illuminating Video: An Essential Guide to Video Art*, ed. Doug Hall and Sally Jo Fifer (New York: Aperture, 1990), 314.

19. The Spanish word *braceros* literally means "strong-armed workers," but it came to refer to migrant farm laborers throughout the United States. The term also makes reference to the World War II–era Bracero Program (1942–64), a bilateral agreement between the US and Mexico to fill wartime labor shortages in the US. More recently, the program has been criticized as a system of labor exploitation, a colonial construct of the US empire, and a gendered modernization project since contracts were available only to healthy male laborers. See, for example, Kitty Calavita, *Inside the State: The Bracero Program, Immigration, and the I.N.S.* (New Orleans: Quid Pro, 2010); and Gilbert G. Gonzalez, *Guest Workers or Colonized Labor? Mexican Labor Migration to the United States* (Boulder, CO: Paradigm, 2006).

20. Lucy Gallun and Christina Fernandez, "Christina Fernandez's *María's Great Expedition*," moma.org/magazine/articles/75.

21. Cherríe Moraga, *Native Country of the Heart* (New York: Farrar, Straus and Giroux, 2019), 3.

22. "Whether or not the subject is already dead, every photograph is this catastrophe." Roland Barthes, *Camera Lucida: Reflections on Photography*, trans. Richard Howard (New York: Hill and Wang, 1981), 96.

4 IMAGES OF CROSS-BORDER IDENTITIES

[**35**] *Cholos, White Fence, East Los Angeles*, 1986. Graciela Iturbide (Mexican, born 1942). Gelatin silver print; 32 x 21.9 cm. The J. Paul Getty Museum, Los Angeles, Gift of Leslie and Judith Schreyer and Gabri Schreyer-Hoffman in honor of Virginia Heckert, 2017.41. © Graciela Iturbide

In Graciela Iturbide's photograph *Cholos, White Fence, East Los Angeles*, four women pose in front of a wall in their East Los Angeles neighborhood bearing the painted portraits of three male Mexican icons: the revolutionaries Emiliano Zapata (1879–1919) and Pancho Villa (1878–1923), and the nineteenth-century president Benito Juárez (1806–1872) [35].[1] The women are dressed in signature 1980s chola attire, wearing tight jeans or men's chino pants, tank tops, and heavy makeup.[2] They pose with attitudes of strength, assuredness, and solidarity. The two women to the left embrace one another with their right hands and display gang signs to the camera with their left. The other two women also hold hands, and one holds up a single finger, a gesture that could alternately be read as "number one" or a sign emphasizing the Mexican revolutionaries or the graffiti tags behind her. Three of the women do not smile, posing with stoic expressions, even as one, Rosario, affectionately cradles her child, Boo Boo. The image is a group portrait of female kinship, a matriarchal union of first-generation Mexican American women in the East LA neighborhood of Boyle Heights, with subsequent generations signaled by the presence of the baby.

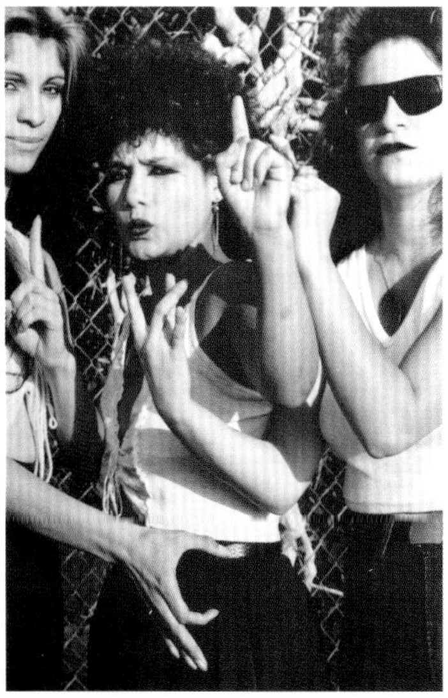

Figure 23. *Rosario, Cristina y Liza, White Fence*, 1986. Graciela Iturbide. Gelatin silver print; dimensions variable. © Graciela Iturbide. Image courtesy of the artist

From Iturbide's description of the *Cholos/as* (1986) series, to which this photograph belongs, we know that the women are hearing-impaired, a factor that complicates the meaning of their hand gestures, reading as both sign language and gang signs (fig. 23). In posturing for the camera as such, the women are staking a claim to their urban environment. Their method of communication is also foregrounded, as is the slippage between the sign language they use as hearing-impaired individuals and the gang signs that are more universally employed throughout the White Fence group, of which they are a part.

The complexity of citizenship and political or national identity within the US-Mexico borderlands comprises one thematic focus of *Picturing the Border*. Photographs featuring Latinx residents that speak to this complexity include images by Graciela Iturbide (born 1942), Louis Carlos Bernal, John Valadez (born 1951), Guadalupe Rosales, and Thalía Gochez (born 1992). The subjects in these photographs have a complicated relationship to both the United States and Mexico stemming from the constructed nature of the border in general—a symbolic (and relatively recent) division between nations that does not represent lived reality or any true divide between identities and cultures.[3] The cross-cultural references that permeate these images are key to understanding the interstitial identities of their subjects, all of whom are borderlands residents. In each case, photographers investigate an assumed cultural identity that is neither "Mexican" nor traditionally "American" but retains qualities of both.

In 1986, Mexican photographer Graciela Iturbide traveled to Los Angeles to embark on a series that would focus on cholo/as, in particular the female members of a gang in East Los Angeles, with help from her network of Angeleno

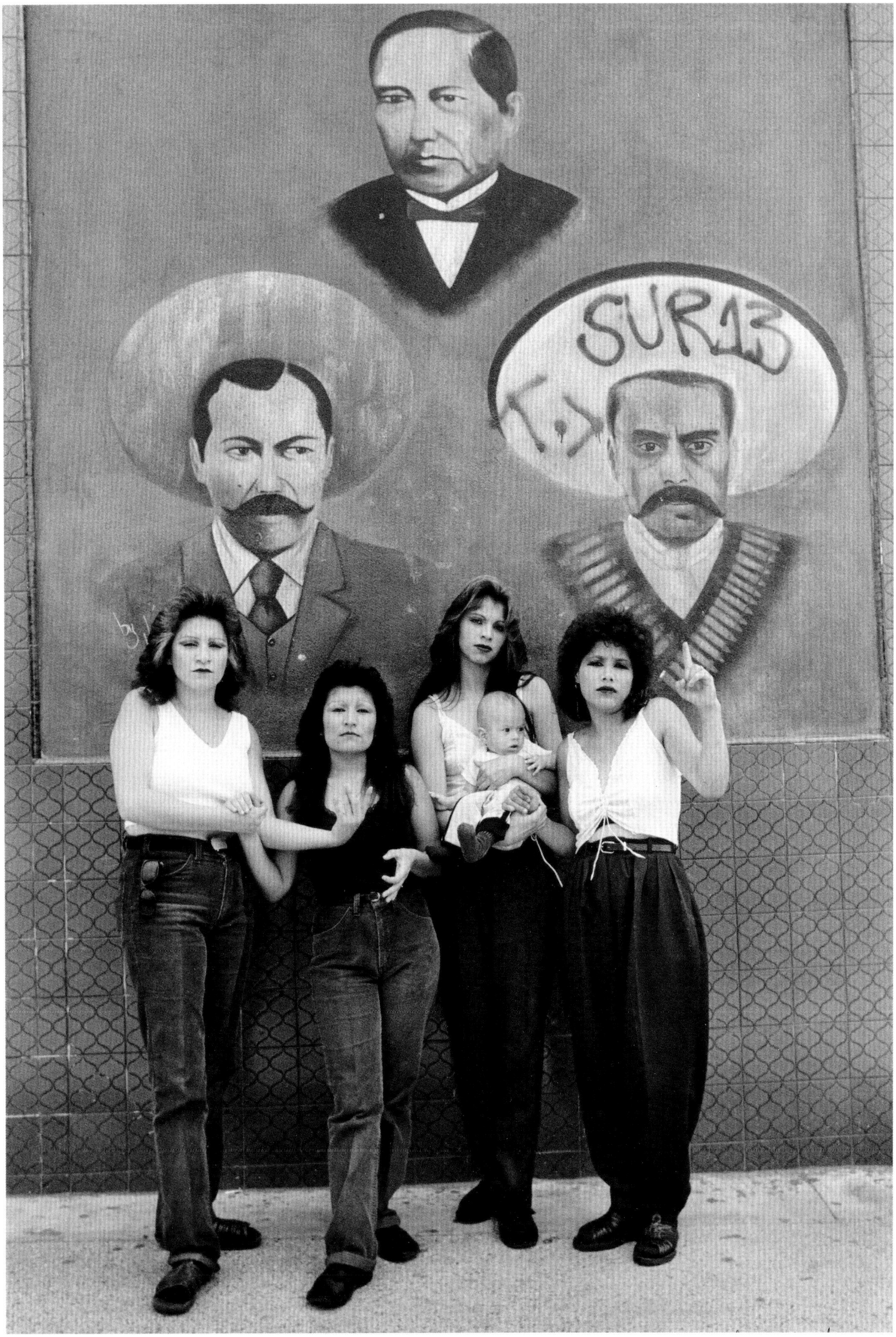
SUR13

[**36**] *East Los Angeles*, negative 1960s, printed 2021. George Rodriguez. Gelatin silver print; 21.7 x 32.2 cm. The J. Paul Getty Museum, Los Angeles, 2021.31.1. © George Rodriguez

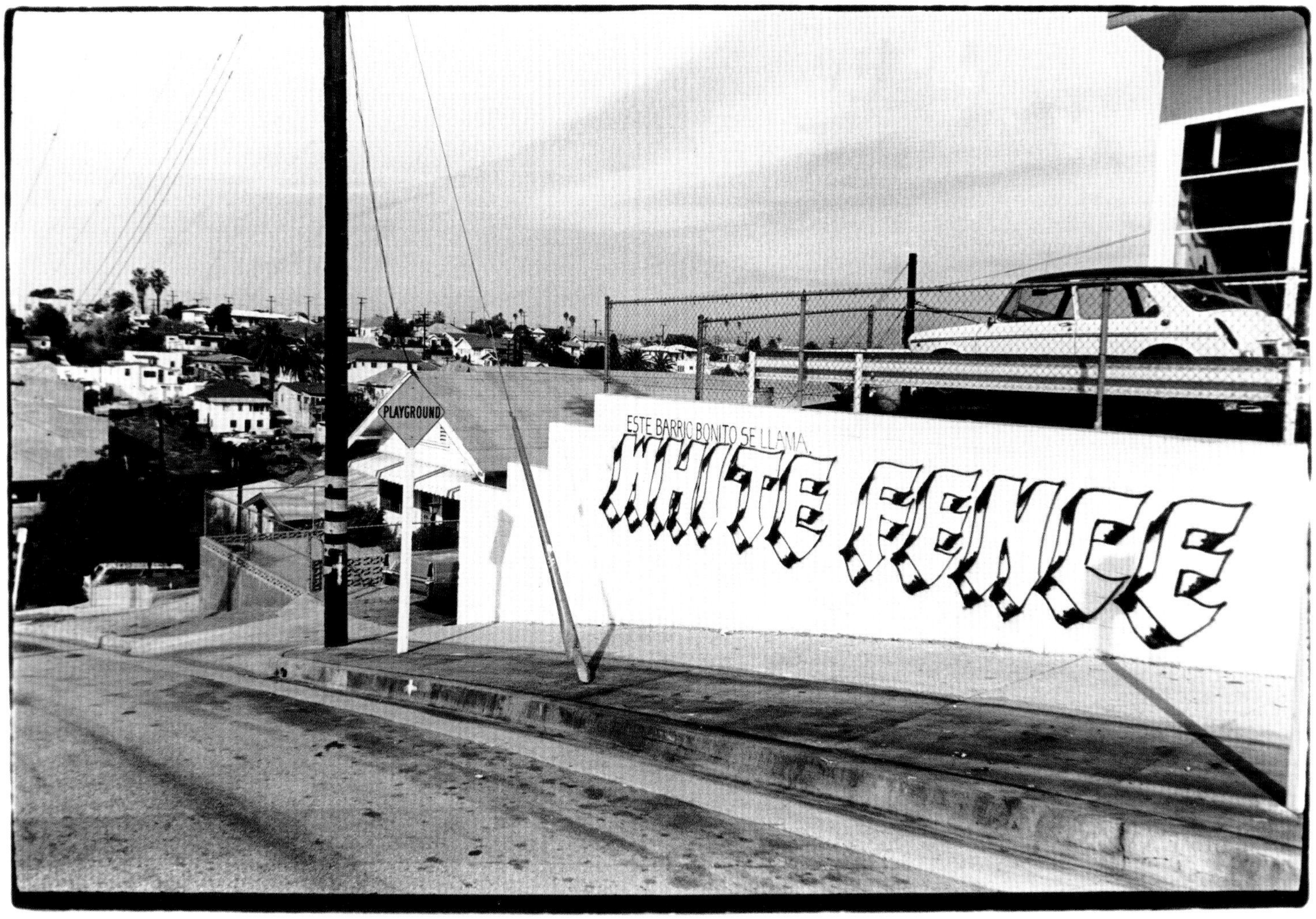

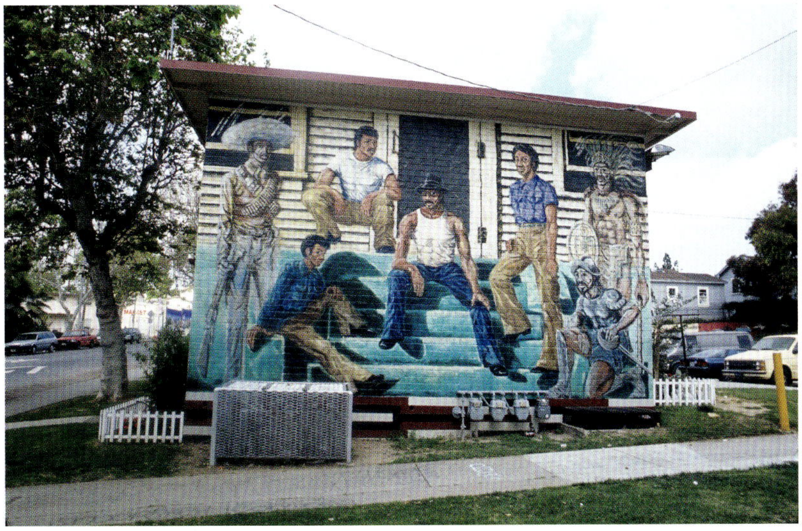

Figure 24. *Ghosts of the Barrio, Ramona Gardens*, 1974. Wayne Healy. Mural, 2731–37 Lancaster Avenue near Murchison Street, Los Angeles. Photo: Robin J. Dunitz, courtesy of the USC Digital Library, Robin Dunitz Slides of Los Angeles Murals Collection.

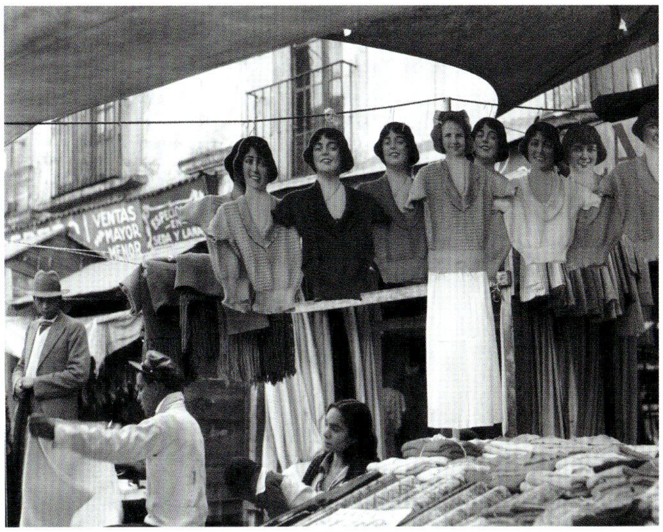

Figure 25. *Maniquis riendo (Laughing Mannequins)*, 1930. Manuel Álvarez Bravo (Mexican, 1902–2002). Gelatin silver print; 18.6 x 23.8 cm. © Archivo Manuel Álvarez Bravo, S.C.

photographer friends.[4] The women were members of White Fence, a Mexican-heritage gang based in East Los Angeles that was formed in the 1920s and whose history is highly politicized [36]. The project took shape as an intimate series of photographs documenting the White Fence women as mothers with their children, posing throughout their East LA neighborhood and in their homes, sometimes in sensual nude poses.

Iturbide's photographs of the border depart from many of those discussed elsewhere in this volume in that she is not a border resident and does not document her own communities. Rather, she is picturing a group of which she herself is not a part, having embedded herself among them and gotten to know them intimately. As an outsider and a Mexican, she consciously inserts visual cues throughout the series that tie the cholo/as' lifestyle to its Mexican roots and historical legacies, drawing attention to the issues surrounding *mexicanidad*, or Mexican identity, in the borderlands. Although they are of Mexican lineage, many of her subjects have never traveled to Mexico, which has led to fraught relationships with their heritage.[5]

The artist recounts, "This group of *cholos* were all deaf-mute [*sordomudos*], who lived together and belonged to a gang called White Fence. Lisa [Liza], Arturo, Cristina, Rosario and her baby Boo Boo (the only one who was not deaf) accepted that I would work with them on this project. I stayed and lived with them in their home, following them with my camera in their daily life."[6] Although initially drawn to her subjects for their dually marginalized status—as both gang members, stereotyped as criminals and outcasts, and hearing-impaired—she came to admire the women for their strength as individuals as well as members of a close-knit community.

According to Iturbide, the women in *Cholos, White Fence, East Los Angeles* claimed not to know the identity of the painted figures, telling her that Zapata, Villa, and Juárez were "mariachi singers."[7] Nonetheless, the women's defiant stance in front of the mural resists the male militarized culture of the East LA visual landscape as also seen, for example, in Wayne Healy's Ramona Gardens mural, *Ghosts of the Barrio* (1974), depicting assertive, muscular Chicano male youths alongside a revolutionary conquistador and an Aztec warrior (fig. 24). Iturbide visually emphasizes the women's contrast to the male portraits to signify their complex relationship to their Mexican heritage and their performance of strong femininity against the machismo of the male icons, White Fence gang culture, and the patriarchy of US culture.

As a photographer who has built a career photographing a range of Mexican subjects and scenes, Iturbide recognized in the cholas a familiarity with her own country, displaced and transformed within the East LA urban environment. And while she had by this point distinguished her photographs from the Surrealism-inflected images of her former teacher, Manuel Álvarez Bravo (1902–2002), there is an aspect of the allusion to Mexican icons that is made strange and uncanny through their appropriation in an LA barrio. Like the floating heads of smiling white women who appear strikingly out of place in a Mexican market in Álvarez Bravo's *Maniquis riendo (Laughing Mannequins)* (1930; fig. 25), the disembodied heads of the Mexican heroes must have been an unusual motif for Iturbide to encounter.

The chain-link fence that seems to line the wall on which the mural appears and that is behind the group as they stand on the pavement symbolizes the separation between the women in California and the Mexican origins of the mural's subjects.

A ubiquitous sight in inner cities, fences and barriers are a common backdrop to the photographs in Iturbide's *Cholos/as* series [37–39]. They pattern the background of a tightly cropped portrait of three of the women and make up the surface against which a group of cholos' shadows are cast in another image.

The fence motif in "border art" is common, given its visual similarity to the "Tortilla Curtain" border fence that divided the United States and Mexico at this time.[8] Literary theorist Claire Fox has analyzed the chain-link fence in border art as a device to reinforce the division between national and corporate territories, given the growing urbanization and industrialization of the border throughout the 1980s. She also describes the multiple symbolic binaries the fence tends to reinforce: Anglo/Mexican, public/private, citizen/noncitizen, and privileged access/barred exclusion.[9] Most of the photographs Fox discusses are of the actual border fence, and although Iturbide photographed images of this fence, they do not feature prominently in her series [40]. Rather than directly pictured, the fence is evoked in scenes like *Cholos, White Fence, East Los Angeles* and thus becomes a metaphorical representation of the border between the two nations. The motif also plays on the name of the gang itself, White Fence.[10]

While Iturbide's *Cholos/as* series features imagery of gang members brandishing weapons, displaying gang signs and tattoos, and posing boldly in their urban environment, it also features intimate portraits of them in their homes [41]. In this way, Iturbide upends the typical imagery of cholo/as as criminals and further highlights the "borders" her subjects transgress by purposefully blurring the lines between their public, expected behavior and their private selves. The combination of disparate images in a single series upsets conventional oppositions between "bad" and "good" youths and lends richness and nuance to the subjects' characters and identities.

The bedroom, a space of transition between public and private selves and thus a liminal space, is the site of all the domestic-interior photographs that feature Rosario; her son, Joe (Boo Boo); and the other members of the household. In one frame, Rosario is photographed sitting on the bed with Boo Boo at her side [42]. She turns and gestures to someone beyond the frame. Both mother and son are bathed in natural daylight coming from a window to the right of the frame, an effect that provides strong tonal contrast. The candid scene captures the striking youth of the mother and a moment of vulnerability that belies the tough-girl persona she manifests on the streets elsewhere in the series.

The raking light also adds an element of drama to the scene, not unlike the chiaroscuro of a Baroque painting. The scene's reference to the Virgin and Child is reinforced by a crucifix that hangs on the wall behind the pair, which Rosario unwittingly emphasizes through her placement and the gesture of her arms, and which is positioned directly over the baby's head. In conjuring the Baroque, Iturbide references a long tradition of colonial influence in Latin American art, along with the style's recent revitalization as a tool to subvert colonialist and patriarchal legacies.[11] Rosario embodies this subversion by directing her gaze away from, rather than toward, the Christ statue, a Christian symbol of familial devotion and female modesty.

Other domestic-interior portraits in Iturbide's series depict various combinations of household members in the bedroom. In several of them, Cristina poses nude—images that attest to the remarkable amount of trust and access the photographer was able to gain in a short time [43]. Iturbide's inclusion

[**37**] *Cholos, Harpys, East L.A.*, negative 1986, printed 1990. Graciela Iturbide. Gelatin silver print; 30 x 41.9 cm. The J. Paul Getty Museum, Los Angeles, Gift of Susan Steinhauser and Daniel Greenberg, 2007.65.4. © Graciela Iturbide

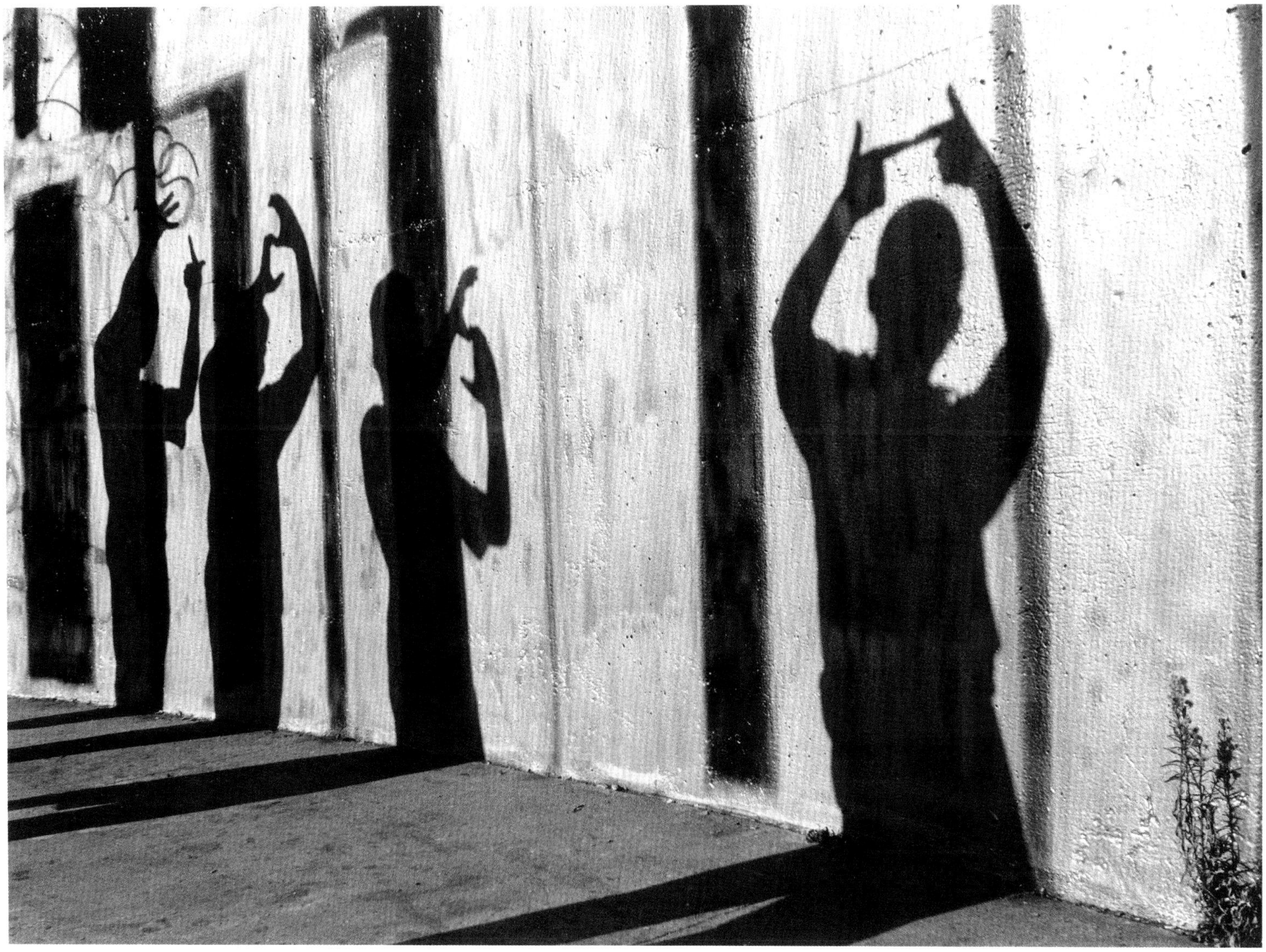

[**38**] *Cholo, East L.A.*, 1986. Graciela Iturbide. Gelatin silver print; 32 x 21.5 cm. The J. Paul Getty Museum, Los Angeles, 2007.11.22. © Graciela Iturbide

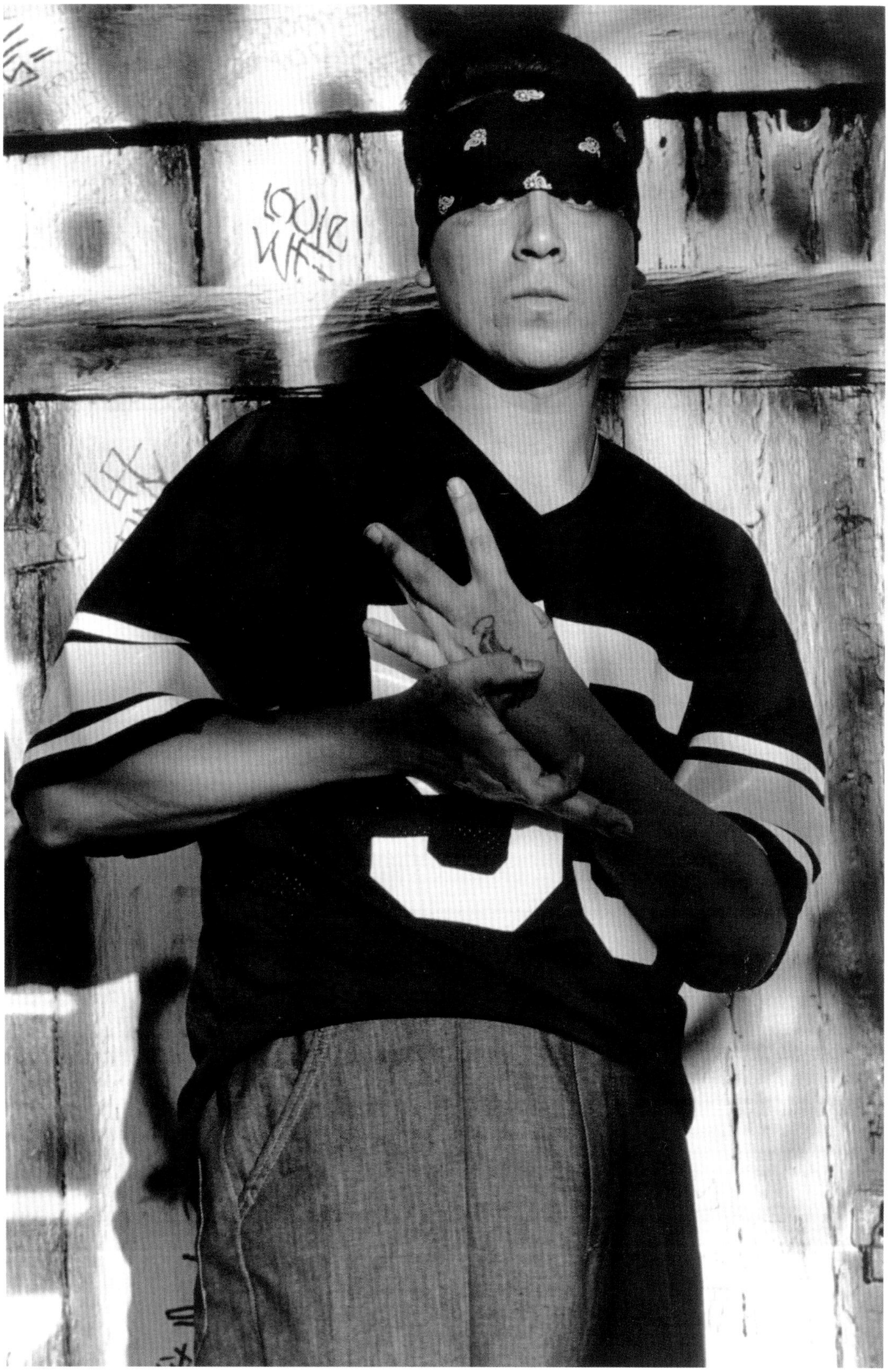

[**39**] *Maravilla, parque en East L.A.*, 1986.
Graciela Iturbide. Gelatin silver print;
30.9 x 20.6 cm. The J. Paul Getty Museum,
Los Angeles, 2007.11.23. © Graciela Iturbide

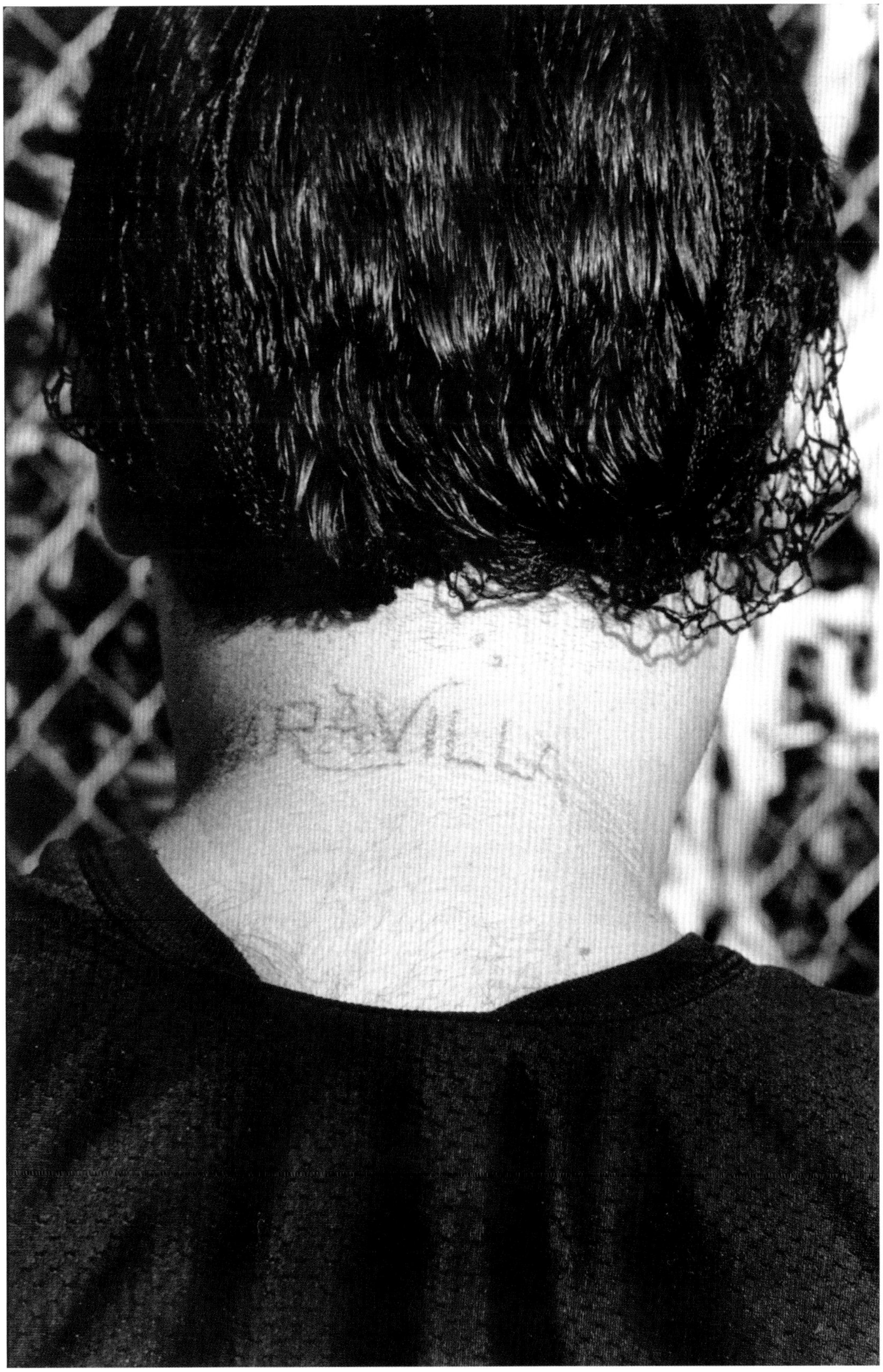

[**40**] *Cholos in Tijuana*, negative 1990, printed 2007. Graciela Iturbide. Gelatin silver print; 32.1 x 21.6 cm. The J. Paul Getty Museum, Los Angeles, Gift of the artist and Rose Gallery, 2007.24.1. © Graciela Iturbide

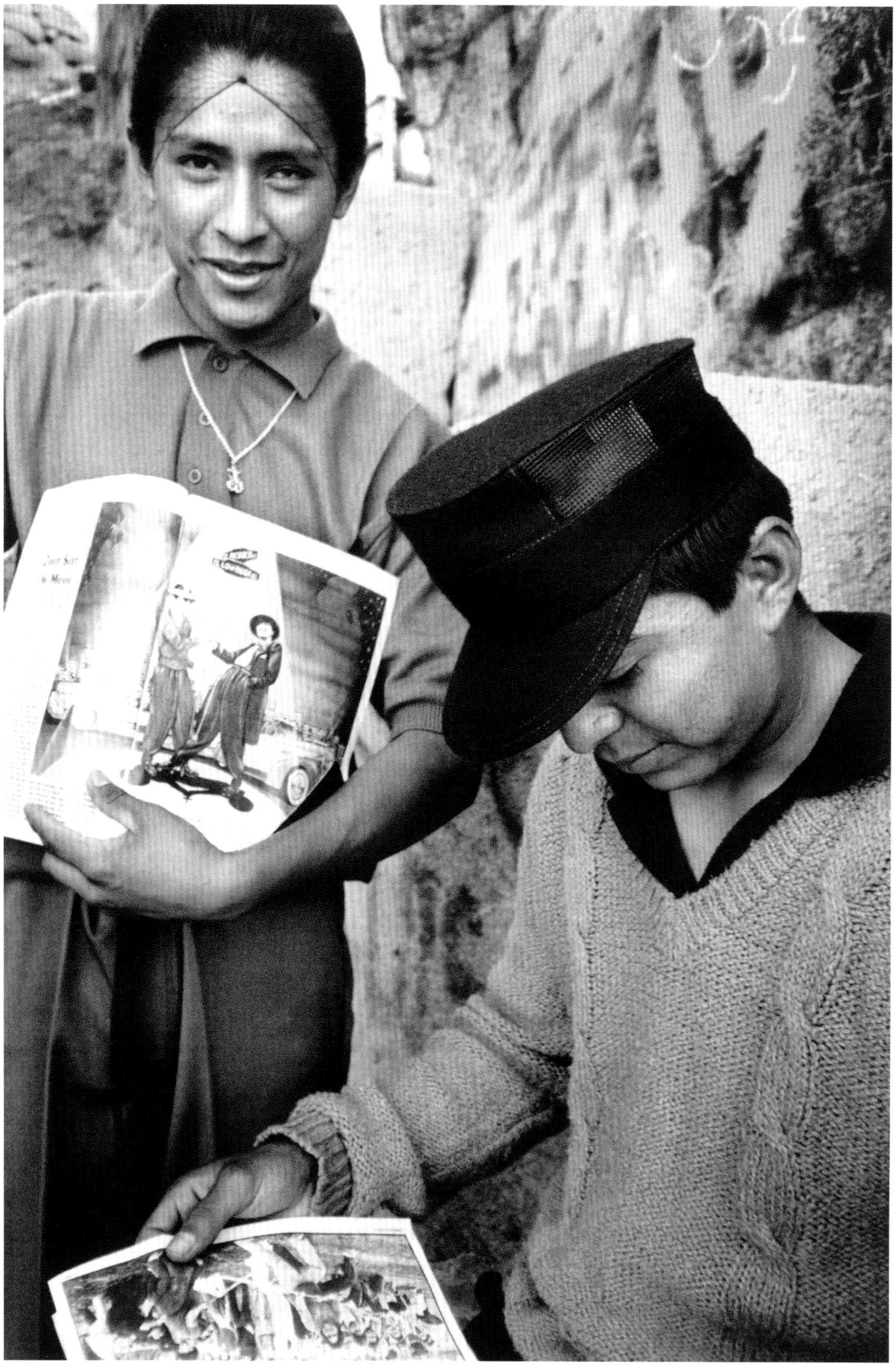

[**41**] *Cholos, White Fence, East L.A.*, negative 1986, printed 1990s. Graciela Iturbide. Gelatin silver print; 30.5 x 45.8 cm. The J. Paul Getty Museum, Los Angeles, Gift of Susan Steinhauser and Daniel Greenberg, 2007.65.5. © Graciela Iturbide

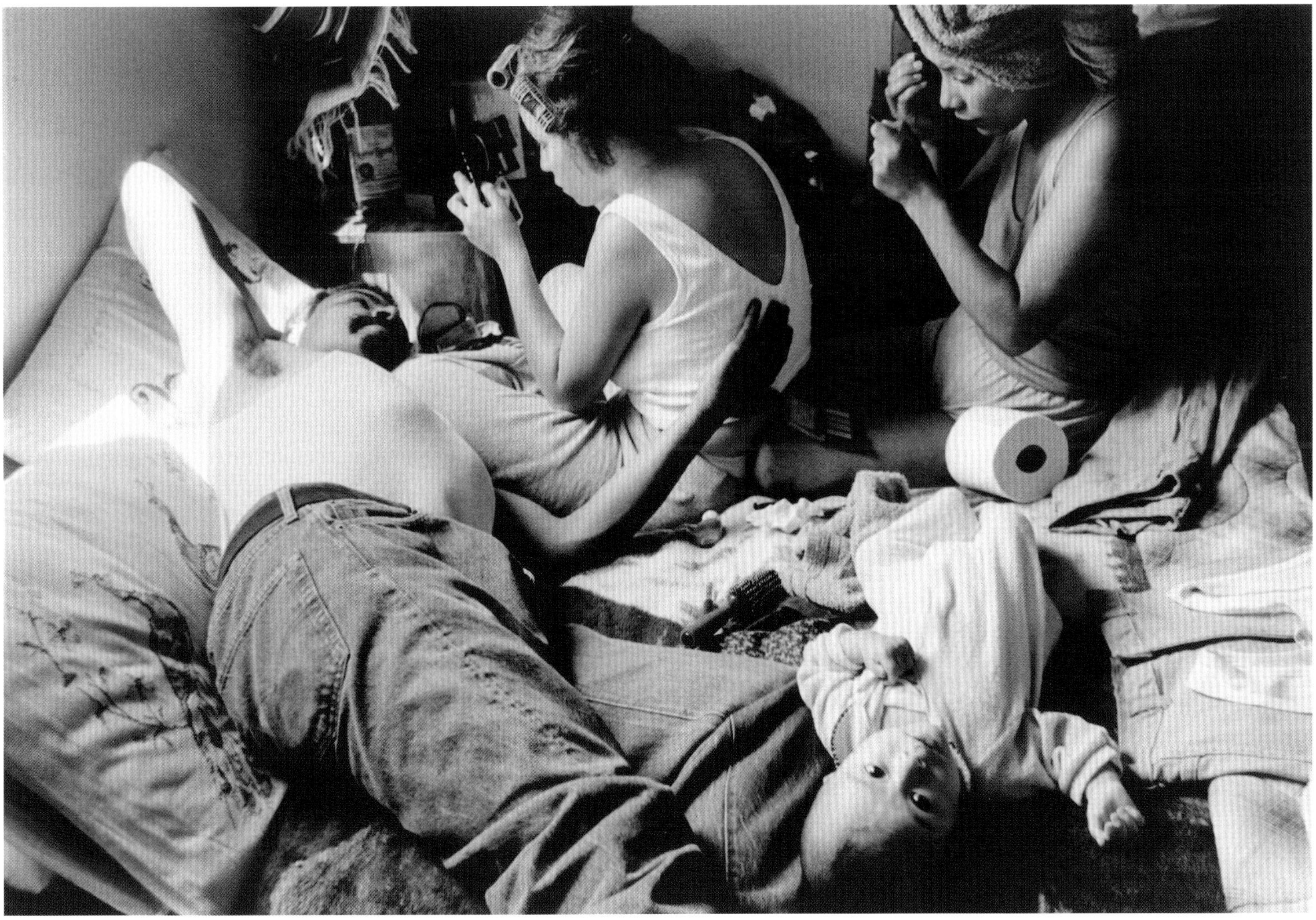

[**42**] *Rosario y Boo Boo en su casa, East L.A.*, negative 1986, printed 2006. Graciela Iturbide. Gelatin silver print; 32.7 x 22 cm. The J. Paul Getty Museum, Los Angeles, 2007.38.1. © Graciela Iturbide

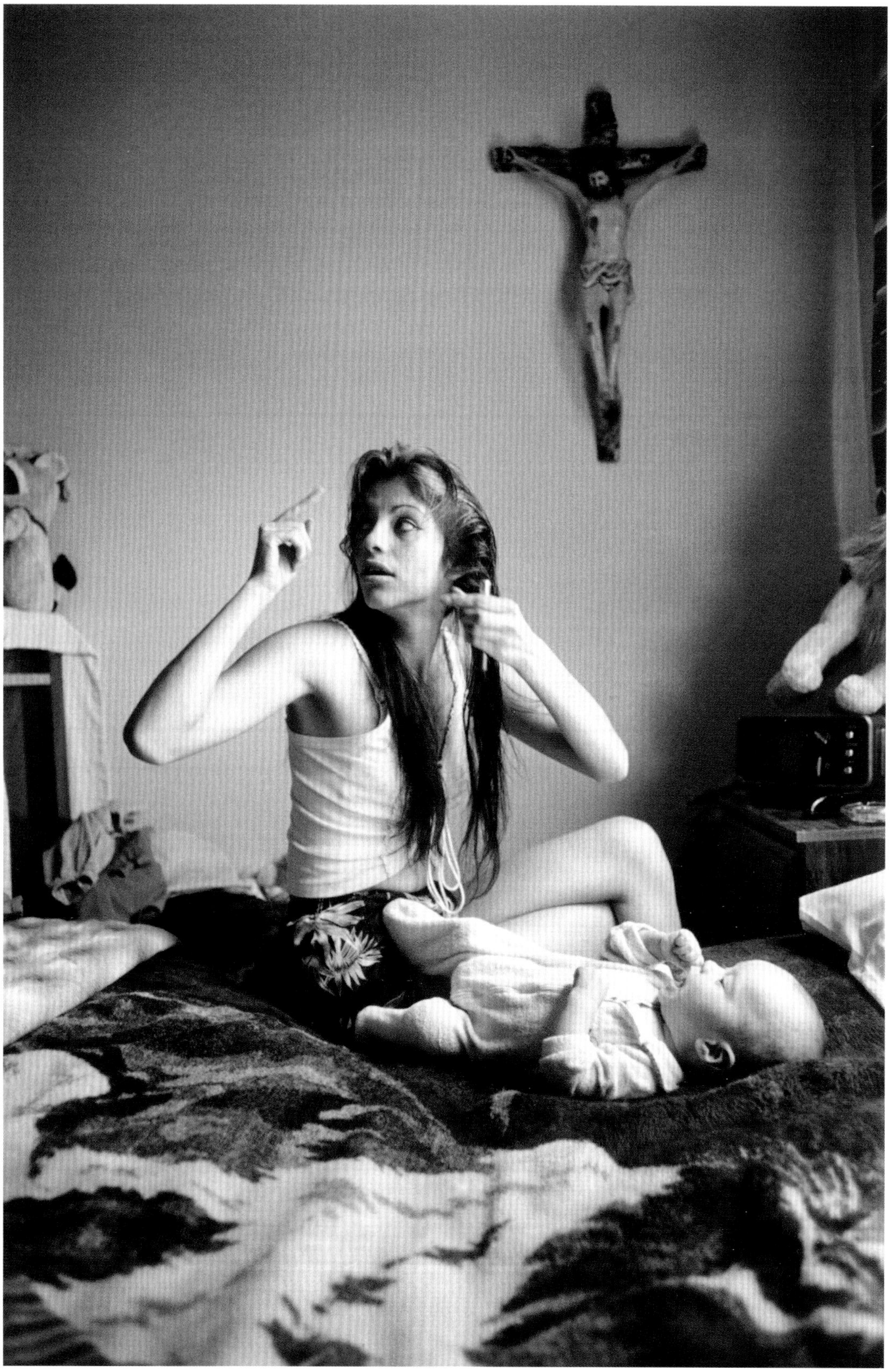

[**43**] *Cristina, White Fence, East L.A.*, negative 1986, printed 1990s. Graciela Iturbide. Gelatin silver print; 31.8 x 46.6 cm. The J. Paul Getty Museum, Los Angeles, Gift of Susan Steinhauser and Daniel Greenberg, 2007.65.8. © Graciela Iturbide

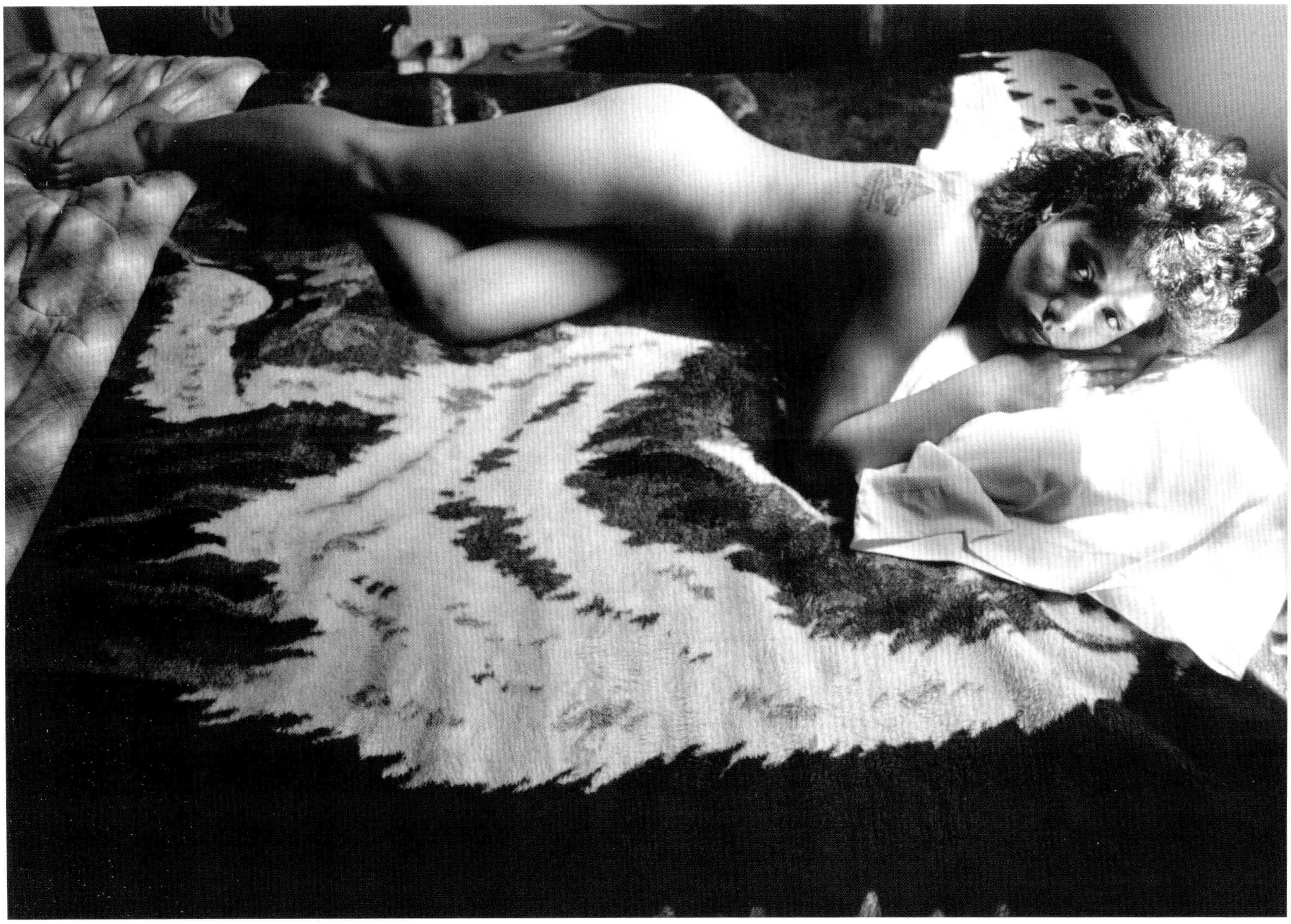

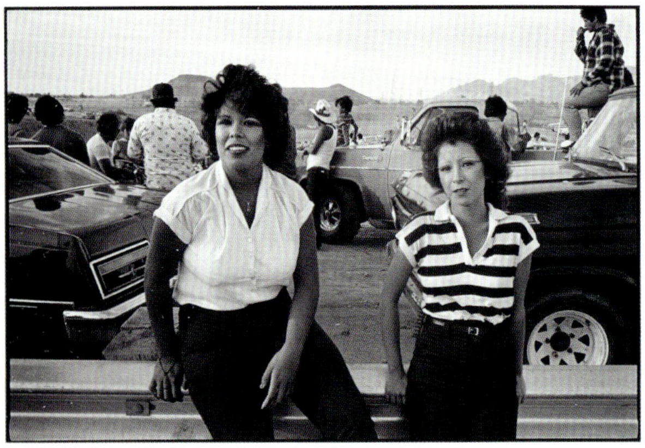

Figure 26. *Dos Cholas, Tucson, Arizona*, 1982. Louis Carlos Bernal. Gelatin silver print; 20.3 x 30.5 cm. Collection of the Center for Creative Photography, University of Arizona, Louis Carlos Bernal Archive,, 2018.38.1. © Lisa Bernal Brethour and Katrina Ann Bernal

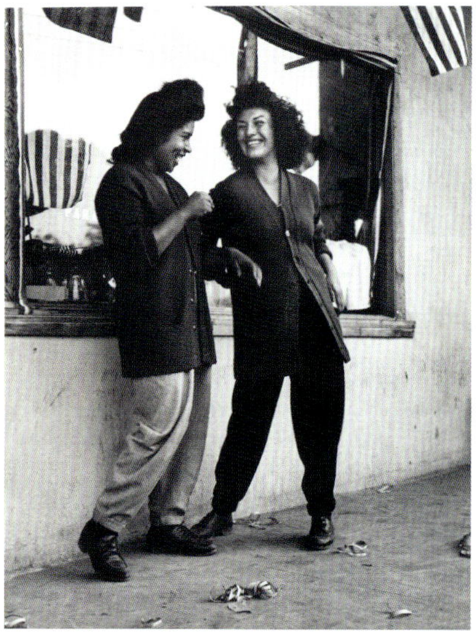

Figure 27. *Two Women*, 1946. Max Yavno (American, 1911–1985). Gelatin silver print; 32.9 x 26.6 cm. The Cleveland Museum of Art, John L. Severance Fund, 1991.279. © Center for Creative Photography, The University of Arizona Foundation.

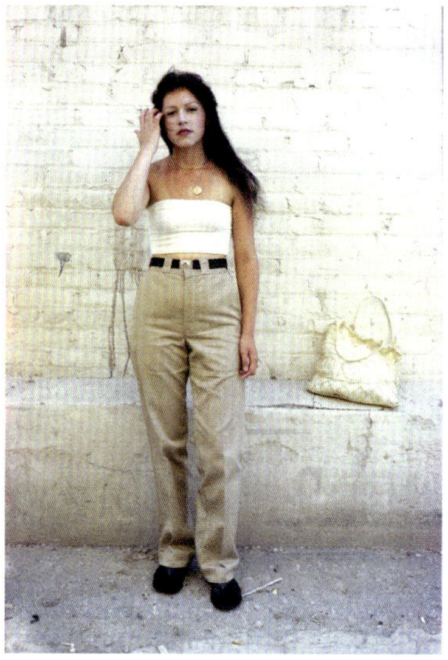

Figure 28. *Alice*, 1978–80. John Valadez (American, born 1951). Archival inkjet print; 63.5 x 41.9 cm. © John Valadez. Image courtesy of the artist

of both indoor domestic scenes and outdoor street scenes within a single series blurs the line between public and private spheres, and highlights the cholas' abilities to effortlessly code switch based on their environment, a skill befitting their binational identities. This power to inhabit "extranational" group identities is vital to the cross-border identities the *Cholo/as* photographic series documents and foregrounds the cross-border identities of residents in the US-Mexico borderlands. Viewed as a totality, the photographs also present a complex portrait of a community at a particular moment in time, the legacy of which I will return to.

Iturbide's interest in cholo/as was inspired in part by Louis Carlos Bernal's photographs (fig. 26). As discussed in the previous chapter, Bernal's expansive photographic practice evolved in the 1970s to encompass portraits of Latinx communities throughout the Southwest. Bernal's work is part of a longer lineage of photographers, such as Max Yavno (1911–1985), John Valadez (born 1951), and Miguel Gandert (born 1956), who documented both cholo/as and their predecessors, pachuco/as, as early as the 1940s (figs. 27, 28).

Bernal began photographing cholo/as in US-Mexico border cities in the late 1970s, and by the time Iturbide undertook her project in 1986, his work in this subject area had received widespread critical acclaim. His black-and-white photographs from the 1970s and 1980s are examples from a larger, extensive series on cholo/as in the Southwest, a series ahead of its time in documenting the spread of cholo/a culture in the US borderlands beyond Los Angeles. They include *La Reina de Mi Vida* (1983) [44]. Taken in the borderlands of Arizona, the photograph shows a male figure from behind with his shirts lifted and back exposed to display a large tattoo of the Virgin of Guadalupe. The man's tattoo is particularly detailed and vivid, perhaps indicating its newness, and he strains with both hands to provide a full view of the design. Across the bottom of the tattoo, an angel at the Virgin's feet hovers over a banner that reads, "La Reina de mi Vida" (The queen of my life).[12] The man's identity is at once concealed by the photograph's rear viewpoint and affirmed by the cultural icon he bears, tying him to the larger collective identity of Mexicans and Mexican Americans in the United States.

The Virgin of Guadalupe is an important symbol of *mexicanidad* that migrated across the border and into Chicano culture, embodying a cultural identity directly linked with the spaces of the US-Mexico border. Chicana feminist Gloria Anzaldúa emphasizes the figure's power to represent Indigenous traditions as an emblem of colonial resistance. "Today, *la Virgen de Guadalupe* is the single most potent religious, political, and cultural image of the Chicano/*mexicano*. She, like my race, is a synthesis of the old world and the new, of the religion and culture of the two races in our psyche. . . . To Mexicans on both sides of the border, *Guadalupe* is the symbol of our rebellion. . . . She mediates between Chicanos and the white world."[13] Appearing in the photograph in the form of a tattoo, the Virgin of Guadalupe embodies the "imprint" of Mexican culture on the communities of the borderlands while resisting static conceptions of national identity—elements that gesture to the "openness" of border culture for both residents and their photographic communities.

More recently, the contemporary artist Guadalupe Rosales created a now-popular Instagram account, *Veteranas and Rucas*. Rosales started the account in 2015, and it has become a crowdsourced archive honoring Latinx youth

[**44**] *La Reina de Mi Vida,* 1983. Louis Carlos Bernal. Gelatin silver print; 30.3 x 20.4 cm. Collection of the Center for Creative Photography, University of Arizona, Gift of Helen Unruh, 2010.20.4.

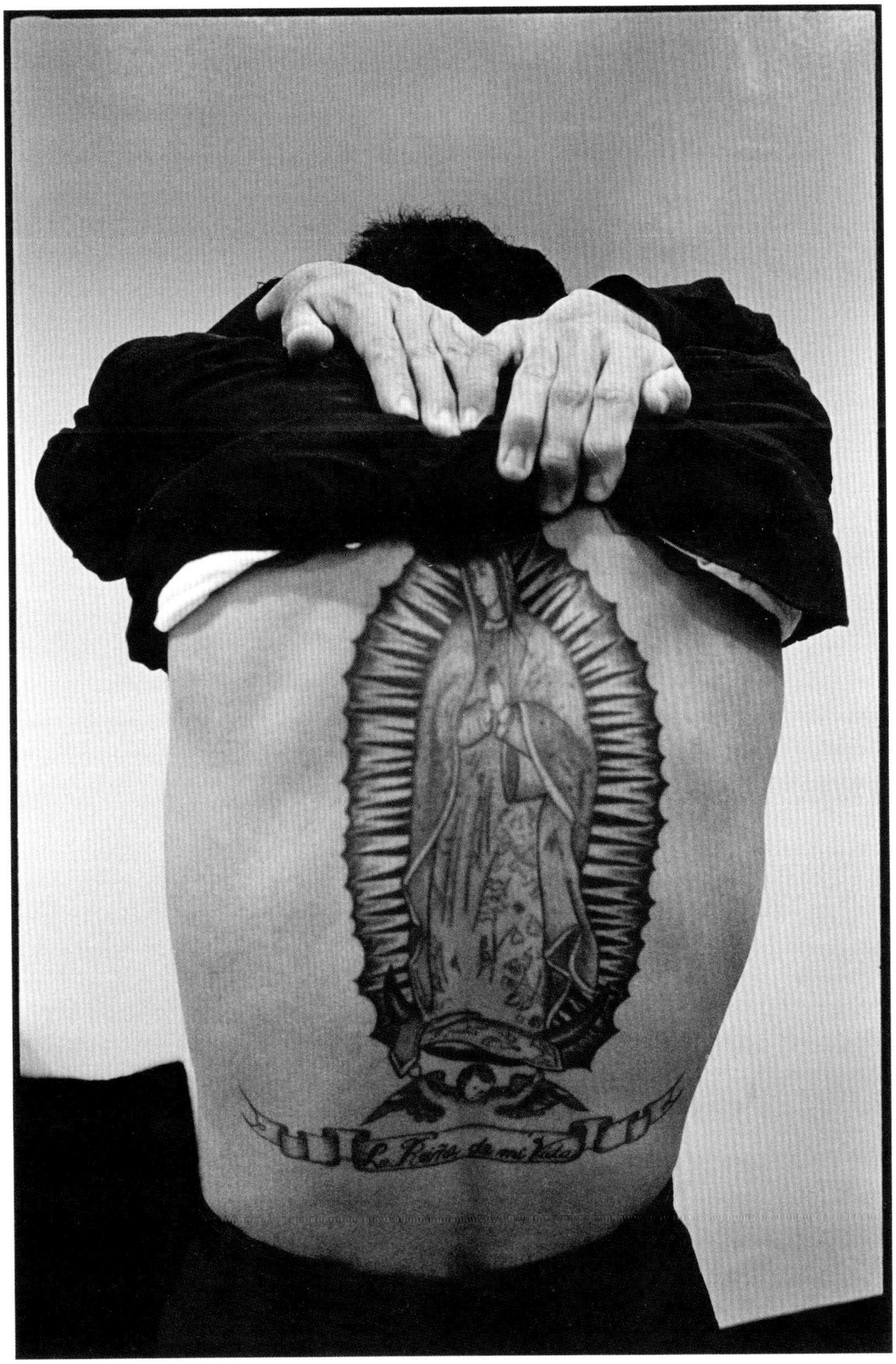

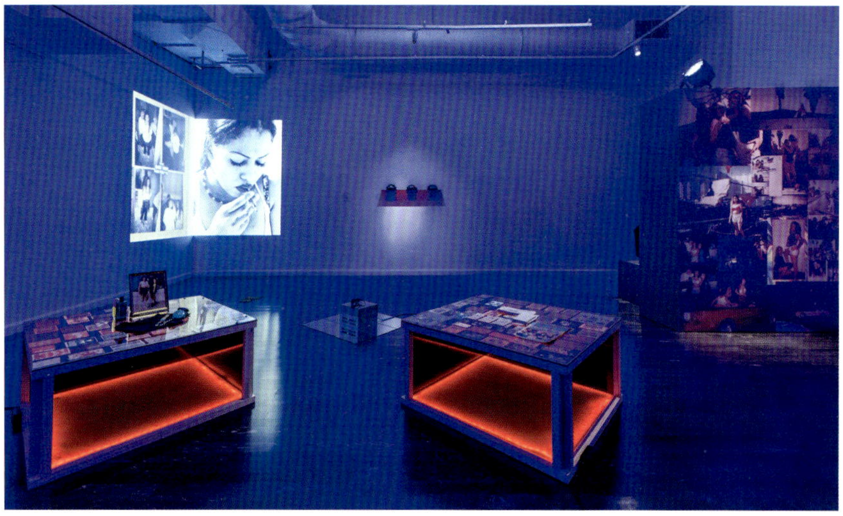

Figure 29. Installation view of *Echoes of a Collective Memory* featuring Guadalupe Rosales's *Veterans and Rucas* (2015–), 2018–19, Vincent Price Art Museum, Monterey Park. © Guadalupe Rosales. Image courtesy of the artist and Commonwealth and Council, Los Angeles, Mexico City. Photo: Monica Orozco

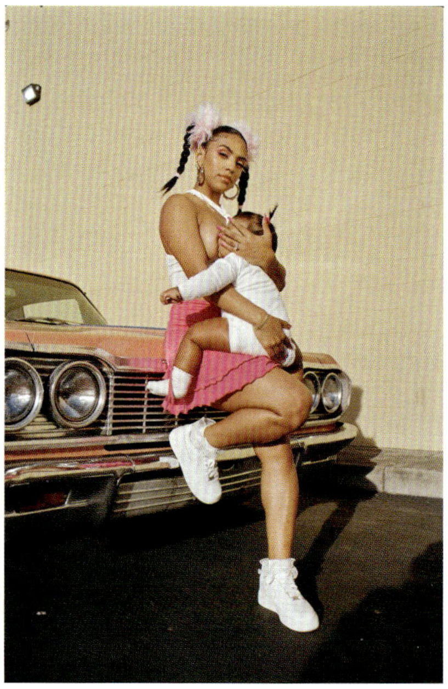

Figure 30. *Mama and Mija*, 2022. Thalía Gochez (American, born 1992). © Thalía Gochez

culture in 1990s East LA and farther south. The artists explains that the archive "humanizes and reflects the positive and honest attributes of our shared culture. It creates a space for collective healing and storytelling and finds ways for new dialogue to emerge about youth culture in Southern California that would not exist otherwise."[14] She was motivated to begin collecting material to counter the underrepresentation, misrepresentation, and historical erasure of Latinx communities. Scrolling through the @veteranas_and_rucas Instagram feed, now 273,000 followers strong, you encounter snapshots and home videos from celebrations, parties, and friend groups, all meticulously captioned by Rosales with detailed information regarding identifiable subjects, places, and times. Comments on each post range from messages of solidarity and gratitude to humorous anecdotes of viewers' own experiences that intersect with the ones shown on the page. As custodian of the archive, Rosales remains active in responding to and reaffirming participants' comments and posting requested or submitted content honoring family members or past events. This archive as living document has morphed into a public, shared history of experiences as well as collective affirmation of life in Southern California. When it is included in museum or gallery settings, Rosales often constructs arrangements of the archive that incorporate ephemera such as clothing, dried flowers, and magazines, sometimes displaying the photographs over mirrors so that the handwritten notations on their versos can be seen (fig. 29).

The work of Los Angeles–based Latinx photographer Thalía Gochez, the child of immigrants from Mexico and El Salvador, is also marked by an affirmative pride of place. Her color photographs feature subjects with heritage from Mexico, Central America, and farther south on the streets of LA, with an eye to the unique attire they confidently don. She particularly focuses on Latinx women, with an emphasis on empowerment. Working intuitively with her subjects, Gochez often depicts them with a solemn gaze, looking directly at the camera, posing in the streets or in domestic settings in California cities. She states, "I'm so grateful because I usually have the privilege of capturing folks in environments that mirror their identity and that they feel connected to and rooted in. Sometimes that's their home, other times it's childhood restaurants, stores or street corners. The environment deeply and authentically informs their identity because it's a part of their personal history. . . . There's a level of comfort that naturally forms when you're home, and that's what I hope to capture in every photograph I take" (fig. 30).[15]

Returning to Iturbide's *Cholo/as* series, the artist resumed contact with her subjects years later, returning on subsequent occasions to photograph them in 2018 and 2019. Iturbide recounts, "On the penultimate trip, one of the Cholas, Liza [*sic*], was in the hospital with cancer and she invited me to visit her and there I took photos at the hospital. The next day there was a party and I was able to go photograph them too. In the end, Liza passed away and I couldn't go to the funeral, but I went back to accompany her friends to the cemetery and there I took more photos with the community."[16] In one of Iturbide's images of Lisa at the hospital, her subject sits propped up in her bed under a sign that designates her "Sensory Impairment" (fig. 31). She communicates with someone over Facetime on an iPhone while her daughter looks on attentively. A tray of food sits beside Lisa, and beyond that, a large bouquet of flowers can be seen in the corner. Although ill, Lisa is pictured surrounded by evidence of care and her community. Iturbide's images from the following year, after Lisa's passing, illustrate a continuation

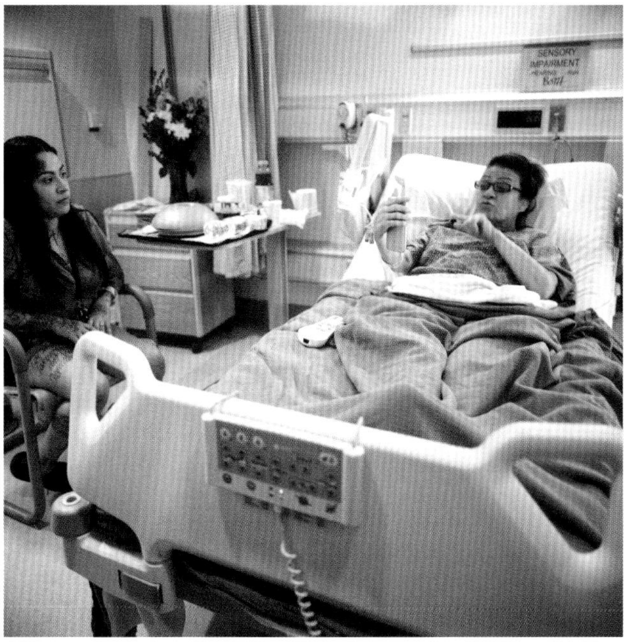

Figure 31. *Liza with her daughter at the hospital*, 2018. Graciela Iturbide. Gelatin silver print; dimensions variable. © Graciela Iturbide. Image courtesy of the artist

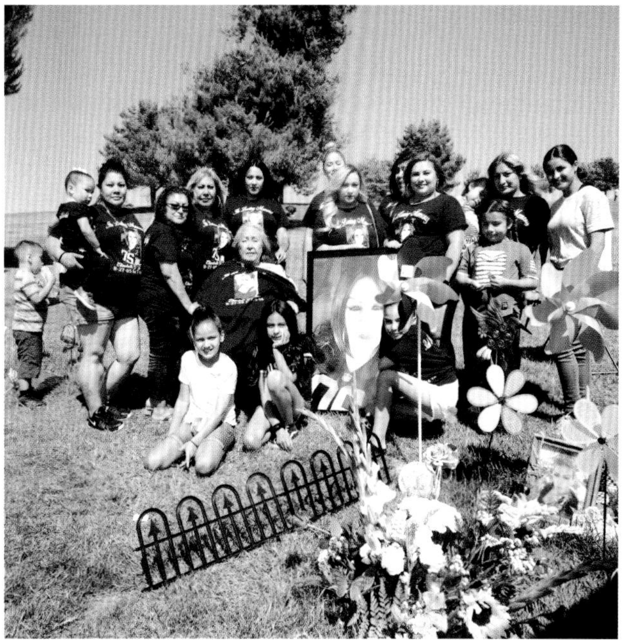

Figure 32. *Everyone at the graveyard*, 2019. Graciela Iturbide. Gelatin silver print; dimensions variable. © Graciela Iturbide. Image courtesy of the artist

of this legacy (fig. 32). Numerous family members and loved ones, consisting almost entirely of women and girls, are pictured next to Lisa's burial site, decorated with photographs, flowers, and pinwheels. The members of the group wear T-shirts that read, "In Loving Memory," with Lisa's photograph and life dates across their chests. Like Iturbide's photographs from 1986, these later images construct a space where her subjects are not circumscribed by discriminatory perceptions or marginalization, but instead occupy a multigenerational space of solidarity and female empowerment.

In 2020, Rosales posted an image from Iturbide's 1986 series on the *Veteranas and Rucas* Instagram in memoriam of Lisa "La Sleepy": a color Polaroid test print of Iturbide's *Cholos, White Fence, East Los Angeles*, along with a Google Maps image of the original location where it was taken.[17] As the last image in the post indicates, the mural with the three male Mexican portraits no longer exists. Below the Polaroid, one woman commented that Lisa was her mother and described the gratitude she felt toward Iturbide for taking the photographs of her mother in her final days, photographs the artist sent to the family after Lisa's passing and that, the woman noted, she added to her family album. The works of Iturbide and Rosales across decades, intermingling in the same communities, comprise a touching cycle in which family snapshots are elevated to art and "fine art" prints are cherished in family photo albums.

Mexican sociologist José Manuel Valenzuela Arce has argued that the cholo/as and their precursors are important because they demarcate the rise of a new form of collective group identity. Arce sees visionary potential in youth culture, along with hopes for a better future stemming from their resistance to, and rejection of, existing societal norms.[18] In the tradition of artworks documenting the emergence of new identities in the borderlands, Iturbide's, Bernal's, Rosales's, and Gochez's projects exemplify the transformative power of those identities and honor their histories. These photographers explore the imaginative possibilities of their subjects as catalysts for changing social dynamics and challenging the dominant perceptions of Latinx communities in the borderlands.

The artists mentioned in this chapter draw on cross-border photographic communities to create images of cross-border identities beyond the confines of what defines citizenship, borders, or national sovereignty. Artist and writer Guillermo Gómez-Peña aptly summarizes the cross-border permutations these artists, their subjects, and their audiences in the borderlands continually navigate: "In my fractured reality, but reality nonetheless, live two histories, languages, cosmogonies, artistic traditions, and political systems dramatically opposed—the border is the continuous confrontation of two or more referential codes."[19]

1. Portions of this chapter previously appeared in Nadiah Rivera Fellah, "Graciela Iturbide's *Cholos/as* Series: Images of Cross-Border Identities," *History of Photography* 43, no. 3 (2019): 308–30, https://www.tandfonline .com/.

2. James Diego Vigil describes the history and cross-cultural implications of the term "cholo": "*Cholo* is a label that Americans and Mexican Americans have used to refer to . . . poor, marginalized Mexican immigrants. The term is several hundred years old and was used in various areas of Latin America where Indian populations are concentrated. The label describes an indigenous person who is halfway acculturated to Spanish ways—in short, a person marginal to both the original and the more recent European culture. In the contemporary U.S. cultural context, it is used to denote individuals who are marginally associated with both Anglo and Mexican culture. Thus, cholo is a term . . . associated with culture change and people caught between two cultures. . . . Chicano street populations who have undergone intense culture change embrace and use this label with pride to denote their speech, dress, and other customs and habits as well as themselves." James Diego Vigil, "Cholo! The Migratory Origins of Chicano Gangs in Los Angeles," in *Global Gangs*, ed. Jennifer M. Hazan and Dennis Rodgers (Minneapolis: University of Minnesota Press, 2014), 57.

3. See the introduction for a detailed history of the US-Mexico border.

4. In 1986, artist Isabel Castro connected Iturbide with a local community center in Los Angeles, El Centro de la Raza, and with the painter Margarita García (born 1951). Iturbide had been invited to contribute to a large photo-book project titled *A Day in the Life of America*, in which HarperCollins commissioned two hundred photographers from around the world to take a photograph on the same day, May 2, 1986, as part of the larger *Day in the Life* book series.

5. Elizabeth Ferrer, "*Manos Poderosas*: The Photography of Graciela Iturbide," *Review: Latin American Literature and Arts* 47 (Fall 1993): 78.

6. Graciela Iturbide, from *White Fence*, Consejo Mexicano de Fotografía (CMF, 1988), brochure text; reprinted as "Viajes al centro de la imagen II," *Luna Córnea* 34 (2013): 410 (my translation), Centro de la Imagen Archives, Mexico City.

7. *Graciela Iturbide: External Encounters, Internal Imaginings*, San Francisco Museum of Modern Art (January 12–March 11, 1990), brochure text by Diana du Pont, n.p., Museum of Modern Art Archives, New York.

8. In October 1978, the Immigration and Naturalization Service (INS) announced the forthcoming installation of new twelve-foot-high fences topped with barbed wire in El Paso and San Ysidro, along the boundary line between San Diego and Tijuana. Although various fences had already existed along the border, the US press sensationalized the story, criticizing the military-style constructions, meant to keep unlawful immigrants and smugglers out, and calling the new addition the "Tortilla Curtain." The negative press that the fence generated brought national attention to the border at this moment, prompting Mexican government officials to quickly oppose the fence, especially the dangers they were intended to pose to border crossers. Criticism from human rights and immigration advocacy groups soon followed, with William Clemens, the governor of Texas, likening the fence to the Berlin Wall. Protests held in El Paso in December 1978 resulted in intensified criticism of the growing militarization of the border. Timothy Dunn discusses the coverage of this development in newspapers ranging from the *Washington Post* and the *New York Times* to the *El Paso Herald Post*. Timothy J. Dunn, *The Militarization of the U.S.-Mexico Border, 1978–1992: Low-Intensity Conflict Doctrine Comes Home* (Austin: CMAS Books, University of Texas at Austin, 1997), 66–67.

9. Claire Fox, *The Fence and the River: Culture and Politics at the U.S.-Mexico Border* (Minneapolis: University of Minnesota Press, 1999), 45.

10. The name was inspired by the white picket fence surrounding La Purísima Catholic Church in eastern Los Angeles where a group of young men formed a church-affiliated sports team in the 1910s. Gradually, the moniker acquired a symbolic and even ironic overtone, signaling the divide between the highly segregated Anglo/white and Latinx communities in Los Angeles.

11. The concept of *rasquache*, invented and theorized in the late 1980s, refers to an over-the-top appropriation of Baroque aesthetic traditions that restores agency to the visual language of Latinx popular culture and working-class immigrant communities in the United States. While appropriative uses of the Baroque appear most often in sculpture, installation art, painting, and architecture, Iturbide subtly inserts the practice into her photographs. See chapter 3 and Tomás Ybarra-Frausto, "*Rasquachismo*: A Chicano Sensibility," in *Chicano Aesthetics: Rasquachismo* (Phoenix: MARS, Movimiento Artístico del Río Salado, 1989), 5–8.

12. This black-and-white photograph circulated widely in Bernal's lifetime, and he was particularly proud of the image. When gifting a print of it to a friend, Bernal wrote in an enclosed note that he believed the photograph "will one day be an important part of my work." Bernal, handwritten note, c. 1983, Louis Carlos Bernal Collection, Center of Creative Photography, Box AG233, University of Arizona, Tucson.

13. Gloria Anzaldúa, *Borderlands / La Frontera: The New Mestiza* (San Francisco: Aunt Lute, 1987), 30.

14. Guadalupe Rosales's website: veteranasandrucas.com

15. "Latinx Photographer Thalia Gochez on Why Real Life Is Having to Wait," hypebae.com /2023/8/latinx-photographer-thalia -gochez-polaroid-collaboration-interview.

16. Graciela Iturbide, email to the author, December 15, 2021.

17. Post on *Veteranas and Rucas* Instagram, August 24, 2020. I am grateful to writer Caroline Tracey for pointing out this post in her article "The Instagram Counter-Archive: Guadalupe Rosales, Graciela Iturbide and Chicana Representation across Borders," *Burlington Magazine* (June 2021), contemporary.burlington.org.uk/journal /journal/the-instagram-counter-archive -guadalupe-rosales-graciela-iturbide-and -chicana-representation-across-borders.

18. José Manuel Valenzuela Arce, "Modernidad, postmodernidad y juventud," *Revista Mexicana de Sociología* 53, no. 1 (1991): 202.

19. Guillermo Gómez-Peña, "Wacha esa border son," *Jornada Semanal* (Mexico City), October 25, 1987, 3.

Natalie Scenters-Zapico

LAID TO REST IN CONCORDIA

1. On my way to school every day, my mother, siblings, and I would drive through towering overhead freeway passes in central El Paso, Texas. From these lifted concrete bridges, which locals call the "Spaghetti Bowl," you can see Juárez, the Bridge of the Americas into Mexico, Loretto Academy and the convent's curved yellow building, and you can look down into one of the oldest cemeteries in the area: Concordia.

Established in 1856, Concordia is home to more than 66,000 dead Paseños. Concordia is both a very real marker of the dead for many families who visit and leave flowers for their deceased as well as home to hundreds of unmarked graves. One of the major points of interest in Concordia is that of researchers and families looking to identify where, exactly, their relatives or famous historical figures are buried. "Looking for a lost loved one? Our researchers will help you find their grave," boasts their website. Concordia is also home to a ghost tour, where for $25 you can learn about Lady Flo, "the lady in white"; gunslinger John Wesley Hardin; and Mexican Revolutionary President Victoriano Huerta. For close to two centuries, this cemetery, trapped on all sides by urban development, has stood as a reminder of what happens to the dead in border communities all too often—they are forgotten, nameless, and held only by an unforgiving desert that shows its love by returning all to rock.

Every day on my way to school, framed by the square of my car window, I would look at the graves that from the soaring freeway bridges seemed haphazardly placed and tenuous, with not a tree in sight save for some palo verdes and cactus. Growing up in a Catholic household and attending the Catholic school where my mother worked, I was made to volunteer cleaning graves in Concordia Cemetery during Lent. "Service as penance," the nuns would say. I would scrub headstones and fix fallen grave markers, pricking my fingers on scrub plants that protect the dead from strangers, both kind and unkind. "Service as penance," I'd say to myself at thirteen years old, as I shielded my face from dirt kicked up by desert spring winds. What exactly I was serving penance for was never clear but always present. I would touch the graves with the hard palms of my hands and scrape their names with my nails to get the dirt out. "One day, we'll all be buried here together," my mother would say. As a girl I used to dread the thought of being buried

[**45**] *Sr. Ernesto Villa, Barrio Hollywood*, 1978. Louis Carlos Bernal. Chromogenic print; 22.9 x 22.9 cm. Collection of the Center for Creative Photography, University of Arizona, Gift of the artist, 80.45.3. © Lisa Bernal Brethour and Katrina Ann Bernal

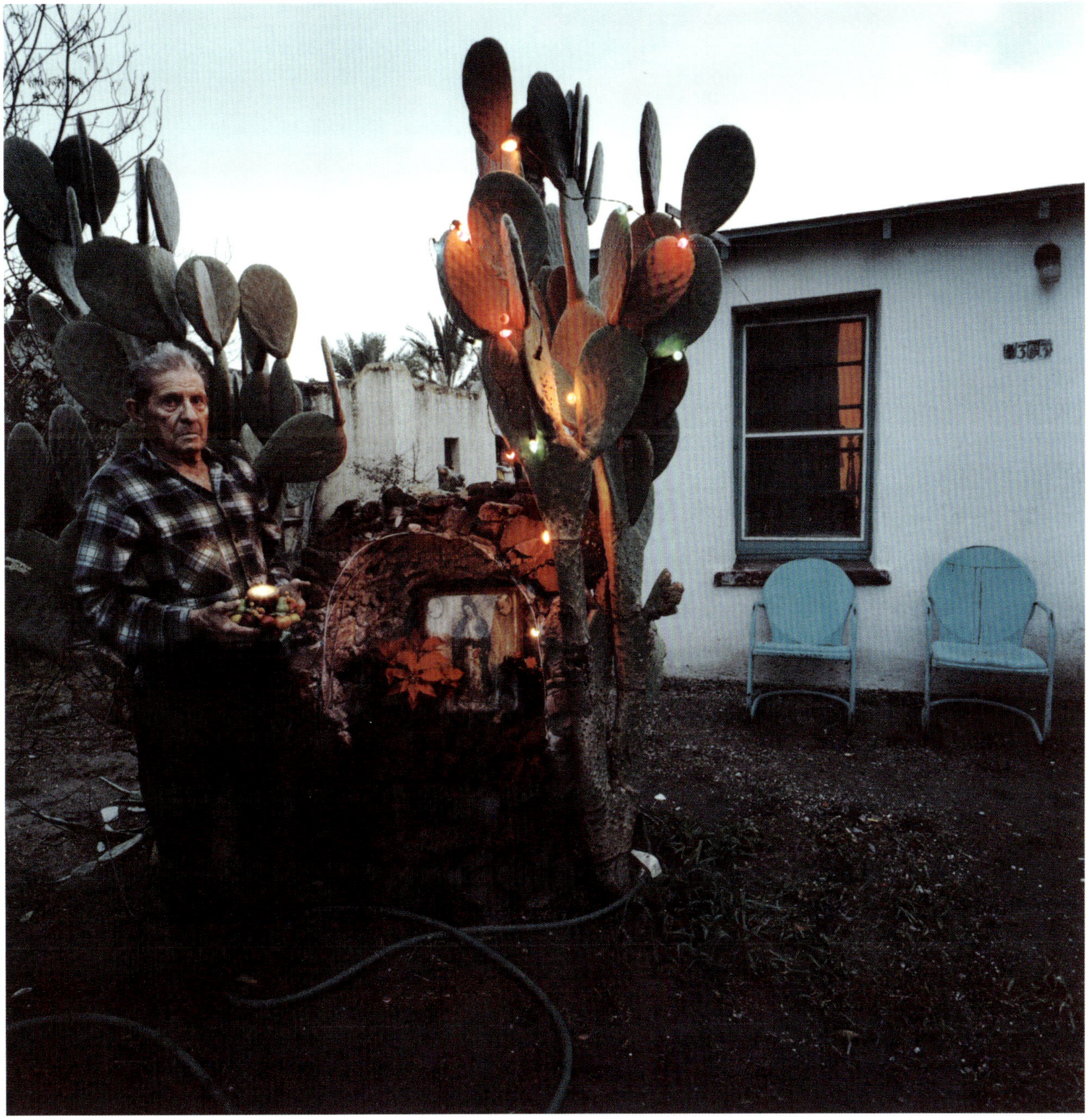

in Concordia. I would see in books and movies the lush, green-grass-covered plots of other people's graves in the United States and would think, "Why can't I be buried in a gentle place like that? Why does everything around us have to be so hard, so harsh, even in death?" We'd all be buried together in Concordia, or so I thought until my siblings and I moved away, until my mother was also forced to move away to complete cancer treatment.

Merely a few miles away, across an international bridge to Ciudad Juárez, while I was a teenage girl cleaning headstones, there were other teenage girls who were working in maquiladoras at all hours of the day and night putting together the toxic metal pieces of Dell computers that were sold all over the United States. "Your family is so broke, your dinner is a cup of water," my classmates would insult one another. This is not a joke that is particular to the border, but when used in that space it carried a different set of implications. The joke would sting for us because the implication was not just that your family couldn't afford dinner, but that your mother was working the nightshift and couldn't make your family dinner. Never mind why men couldn't make dinner in a joke like this, the real pain was in the implication that your mother is out at night, where sexual dangers lurk and missing women are found mutilated or in mass graves in the desert. The "your mother" in the joke maybe isn't your mother, but could also be replaced by "your sister," or even "you."

2. On Saturday mornings, we'd go to Juárez. We'd drive across in our car and didn't need a passport or visa. We'd drive across without worry to shop and eat and pay visits. We'd enter without problems and leave complaining that the lines to enter the US were getting longer and longer. There were women going missing, but this was before the "War on Drugs," before the militarization of Juárez, before all the places we would go to became vacant from shootings. We went less often than some of my classmates whose families lived in El Paso but worked in Juárez, but more often than some of my classmates whose families were terrified to step foot across the border. We moved freely, a sign of our privilege, and thought nothing of it until confronted by a missing flyer. Another girl, another girl, another girl,

another girl—maybe none of them drank a cup of water for dinner, maybe all they needed was a cup of water and a wire from a neighbor to keep the lights on. And we would go home to our house and fill our pantry with meats and cheeses and pastries we bought cheap with American dollars.

Everywhere in Concordia Cemetery, and with each step closer to the border, we'd find crumpled, dirtied missing flyers for girls our age gone missing. Their photographic stills of who their parents or guardians thought them to be, never who they actually were, never who they weren't allowed to be or allowed to ever become. I started keeping the missing flyers of women I'd find when I was sixteen years old and started sneaking out to go to Juárez with friends to drink in bars and clubs and go to my classmates' mansions in Campestre and brush the hair of their horses. I started keeping missing flyers of girls that had gone missing because I hated seeing these girls' pictures stepped on, crumpled up, tossed into gutters. No one cared about these flyers because they figured the girl was probably dead. What did it matter if you held on to her picture? But I couldn't let these girls go. I started keeping a book of flyers for missing people, mostly girls, and I couldn't tell you why I held on to them. I wasn't actively looking for them. I wasn't memorizing their faces to see if I saw them in a crowd or at an Oxxo. I kept them because I wanted to hold on to proof that they had lived once and that if found they might live again. The photograph, not picked by the missing or the deceased, became proof that they meant something to someone somewhere at one time even if it was the person who stopped to take the photograph, even if that person was themselves missing. "Aren't you lucky," the nuns would say, "to be cleaning headstones and not dead in a ditch somewhere." By dead in a ditch, they meant dead in Juárez. "Lucky lucky," I'd say, and wonder which photo of me my mom would pick if I went missing.

3. At the hotel bar there are TV screens hung up high in all corners the eye can see. The blue light from CNN tinges everyone's faces blue so that we all look like ghosts gathering in a cemetery. It's 2016. Trump has just been elected president, and I am at a writers' conference in Washington, DC. That night, I felt like a ghost unable to mobilize myself for a protest of the Trump presidency staged by a group of writers

in front of the White House. I couldn't get myself out of the hotel bar because I was caught in a cycle of fright by the TV screens that were showing on a loop my hometown of El Paso, Texas, as ground zero for the border crisis. I might not have been the only one watching the TV that night at the hotel bar, but I felt like the only one who was transfixed.

There, suspended above me, was drone footage of the border wall, of El Paso and Juárez from the US side and there, for a few quick stills, Concordia Cemetery flashed like a phantom landscape. Just a few miles from there, they showed the impenetrable bollards constructed to make a wall that I had protested as an undergraduate student at the University of Texas at El Paso. The impenetrable rust-colored rods piercing what will always be to me the most beautiful blue sky in the world. They showed the steel bollards like toothpicks climbing up and down mountains across a desert that I could feel was meant to seem exotic to the viewer, even if it was home to me. What always impresses me about these cold and sterile images of the border is that the images feel foreign to me. I catch myself saying things like, "Oh look, they're downtown. It *looks* like the Santa Fe Bridge," or "Is that El Paso or Santa Teresa? They keep saying El Paso, *but I don't think it is*." The eye with which these news outlets document the border is as if that of an outsider, with the intention of making all viewers feel as though they too are outsiders looking in. I could feel that they showed Concordia Cemetery because they were from places where their cemeteries are green and gentle; they want to show how rough a place the border can be. I cringed because I remembered those thoughts as a girl, ashamed of where I was from, afraid to end up in a place the world had taught me was ugly. What I wouldn't give now to buy a plot in Concordia, but poetry had taken me far away into this America, these United States.

There is a violence to this kind of depiction of the border with a particular rhetorical purpose to justify the inhumane treatment of people and the destruction of land that is often considered vacant and worthless. The rise of drone footage of the border is to make viewers feel as far away from the border and its "crises" as possible. In the imagination of outsiders, the border's deserts can then become an empty vessel to hold all their fear and anxiety, and act as a site to carry out the violence of their anger at a rapidly changing, globalized world.

The difficulty with the twenty-four-hour news cycle and its attempts to capture the humanity of the border crisis, even when well intentioned, is that they view the border as a static place that exists physically as a line or a periphery and in legal documents that dictate the violence we see play out in the form of detention centers and DHS checkpoints. What these images fail to recognize is the metaphorical, imaginative, and psychic power that the border plays on its inhabitants. Immigration across the US-Mexico border is a trauma, however great or small. Whether it be crossing multiple borders and landscapes, overstaying a visa, applying for permanent status, surrendering oneself through biometrics, or even if "The border crossed you"—these are the stories that deeply mark the narrative of Latinx identity. This liminal space, this broken and incomplete cycle, this removal from the society—while always present in the society—is the trauma, the scar, that fascinates Latinx artists with the border.

4. She is laying her body to rest in Concordia Cemetery. She has picked out her headstone, it is paid for. She wants to become a part of the desert that raised her. She wants to become a part of the place and hopes one day her headstone will be lost and not matter much to anyone. Before she dies, she wants to lay her body down to rest for a bit and take a photograph that can be used in case she goes missing. If she goes missing, she hopes that people will resist the urge to assume she's dead. Maybe the right photograph will help. Maybe a photograph of a wall across her face, of palo verde down her spine, will show the viewer that she is more than her disappearance. She is a woman in touch with the psychic wounds caused by the verge she lives on—the beginning of one thing and the end of another in constant rotation. She wants the photograph to do more than show what is true. She wants the photograph to do more than show she has a name. She wants the photograph to show she is alive and that even in her absence and even in her dying she is alive, alive, alive, and flourishing like the palo verde that provides little shade but is still a child of the sun.

BIBLIOGRAPHY

Aguilera-Hellweg, Max. *Max Aguilera-Hellweg: La Frontera Sin Sonrisa*. El Paso, TX: El Paso Museum of Art, 1995.

Alvarez, C. J. *Border Land, Border Water: A History of Construction on the US-Mexico Divide*. Austin: University of Texas Press, 2019.

Anzaldúa, Gloria. *Borderlands / La Frontera: The New Mestiza*. San Francisco: Aunt Lute, 1987.

Armas, José. "Preface to the Third Edition." *De Colores: Journal of Emerging Raza Philosophies* 3, no. 2 (1976): 4–10.

Arredondo, Gabriela F., et al., eds. *Chicana Feminisms: A Critical Reader*. Durham, NC: Duke University Press, 2009.

Avalos, David. "The Donkey Cart Caper: Some Thoughts on Socially Conscious Art in Anti-Social Public Space," *Community Murals: An International Visual Arts Magazine* 11 (Fall 1986): 14–15.

Avila, Eric. *The Folklore of the Freeway: Race and Revolt in the Modernist City*. Minneapolis: University of Minnesota Press, 2014.

———. *Popular Culture in the Age of White Flight: Fear and Fantasy in Suburban Los Angeles*. Berkeley: University of California Press, 2006.

Barthes, Roland. *Camera Lucida: Reflections on Photography*. Translated by Richard Howard. New York: Hill and Wang, 1981.

Bartletti, Don. *Between Two Worlds: The People of the Border*. Oakland, CA: Oakland Museum, 1992.

Bernal, Louis Carlos, Morrie Camhi, Abigail Heyman, Roger Minick, Neal Slavin, and Bert N. Corona. *Espejo: Reflections of the Mexican American*. Oakland, CA: Oakland Museum, 1978.

Bernal, Louis Carlos, and Ann Simmons-Myers. *Louis Carlos Bernal: Barrios*. Tucson: Pima Community College and the University of Arizona Library, 2002.

Calavita, Kitty. *Inside the State: The Bracero Program, Immigration, and the I.N.S.* New Orleans: Quid Pro, 2010.

Canclini, Néstor García. *Hybrid Cultures: Strategies for Entering and Leaving Modernity*. Minneapolis: University of Minnesota Press, 1989.

Castellote, Alejandro. *Mapas abiertos: Fotografía latinoamericana, 1991–2002*. Barcelona: Lunwerg Editores, 2003.

Chavoya, C. Ondine. "Orphans of Modernism: The Performance Art of Asco." In *Corpus Delecti: Performance Art of the Americas*, edited by Coco Fusco, 240–63. London and New York: Routledge, 2003.

Chavoya, C. Ondine, Mundo Meza, David Evans Frantz, and Macarena Gómez-Barris. *Axis Mundo: Queer Networks in Chicano L.A.* Los Angeles: DelMonico Books-Prestel, 2017.

Cowie, Jefferson. *Capital Moves: RCA's Seventy-Year Quest for Cheap Labor*. Ithaca, NY: Cornell University Press, 1999.

Crewdson, John. *The Tarnished Door: The New Immigrants and the Transformation of America*. New York: Times Books, 1983.

Davis, Mike. *Magical Urbanism: Latinos Reinvent the U.S. City*. London and New York: Verso, 2001.

Debroise, Olivier, et al. *La era de la discrepancia: Arte y cultura visual en México, 1968–1997*. Madrid: Turner, 2007.

———. *Mexican Suite: A History of Photography in Mexico*. Austin: University of Texas Press, 2001.

Donovan, Celeste. "Icons behind Altars: María Izquierdo's Devotional Imagery and the Modern Mexican Catholic Woman." *Journal of Decorative and Propaganda Arts* 26 (April 2010): 160–79.

Dunn, Timothy J. *The Militarization of the U.S.-Mexico Border, 1978–1992: Low-Intensity Conflict Doctrine Comes Home*. Austin: CMAS Books, University of Texas at Austin, 1996.

Epstein, Rebecca, Sybil Venegas, Pilar Tompkins Rivas, et al. *Laura Aguilar: Show and Tell.* Los Angeles: UCLA Chicano Studies Research Center Press, 2017.

Fajardo-Hill, Cecilia, et al. *Ricardo Valverde: Experimental Sights, 1971–1996.* Los Angeles: Vincent Price Art Museum, Chicano Studies Research Center, University of California Los Angeles, 2015.

Famighetti, Michael, and Pilar Tompkins Rivas. *Latinx*. New York: Aperture Foundation, 2021.

Fellah, Nadiah Rivera. “Graciela Iturbide’s *Cholos/as* Series: Images of Cross-Border Identities,” *History of Photography* 43, no. 3 (2019): 308–30.

Fernández, Celestino, and Lawrence Pedroza, “The Border Patrol and News Media Coverage of Undocumented Mexican Immigrants during the 1970s: A Quantitative Content Analysis in the Sociology of Knowledge.” *Mexican American Studies and Research Center* 2 (1981): 1–29.

Fernández, Horacio. *The Latin American Photobook*. New York: Aperture, 2011.

Fernández de Castro, Miguel, and Daisy Nam. “Ballroom Marfa: Interview with Miguel Fernández de Castro,” 2020. Translated by Gabriela Carballo. ballroommarfa.org/wp-content/uploads/MFC_INTERVIEW-1.pdf.

Fernández-Kelly, María Patricia. *For We Are Sold, I and My People: Women and Industry in Mexico’s Frontier.* Albany: State University of New York Press, 1983.

Ferrer, Elizabeth. *Latinx Photography in the United States: A Visual History.* Seattle: University of Washington Press, 2020.

———. “*Manos Poderosas*: The Photography of Graciela Iturbide.” *Review: Latin American Literature and Arts* 47 (Fall 1993): 69–78.

Fox, Claire. *The Fence and the River: Culture and Politics at the U.S.-Mexico Border.* Minneapolis: University of Minnesota Press, 1999.

———. “The Portable Border: Site-Specificity, Art, and the U.S.-Mexico Frontier.” *Social Text*, no. 41 (1994): 61–82.

Fox, Jonathan. “Indigenous Mexican Migrants.” In *Beyond La Frontera: The History of Mexico-U.S. Migration*, edited by Mark Overmyer-Velázquez, 161–78. New York: Oxford University Press, 2011.

Fusco, Coco. *English Is Broken Here: Notes on Cultural Fusion in the Americas.* New York: New Press, 1997.

———. “Ethnicity, Politics, and Poetics: Latinos and Media Art.” In *Illuminating Video: An Essential Guide to Video Art*, edited by Doug Hall and Sally Jo Fifer, 304–16. New York: Aperture, 1990.

Gallun, Lucy, and Christina Fernandez. “Christina Fernandez’s *María’s Great Expedition.*” moma.org/magazine/articles/75.

Gamboa, Fernando, Carla Stellweg, and María Josefa Ortega. *Artes visuales: Una selección facsimilar; En homenaje a Fernando Gamboa.* Mexico City: Museo de Arte Moderno, 2010.

Gamboa Jr., Harry. *Urban Exile: Collected Writings of Harry Gamboa Jr.,* edited by Chon A. Noriega. Minneapolis: University of Minnesota Press, 1998.

García, Ramón. *Ricardo Valverde.* Los Angeles: UCLA Chicano Studies Research Center Press, 2013.

Goin, Peter. *Tracing the Line: A Photographic Survey of the Mexican-American Border.* Reno: Library, University of Nevada–Reno, 1987.

Goldman, Shifra M. *Dimensions of the Americas: Art and Social Change in Latin America and the United States.* Chicago: University of Chicago Press, 1994.

Gómez-Peña, Guillermo. “Wacha esa border son,” *Jornada Semanal* (Mexico City), October 25, 1987, 3.

Gonzalez, Gilbert G. *Guest Workers or Colonized Labor? Mexican Labor Migration to the United States.* Boulder, CO: Paradigm, 2006.

González, Juan. *Harvest of Empire: A History of Latinos in America*. New York: Penguin, 2011.

González, Ray. *Muy Macho: Latino Men Confront Their Manhood*. New York: Anchor Books, 1996.

Goodman, Adam. *The Deportation Machine: America's Long History of Expelling Immigrants*. Princeton, NJ: Princeton University Press, 2020.

Grobet, Lourdes. *Lourdes Grobet*. Madrid: Turner, 2005.

Grobet, Lourdes, and Néstor García Canclini. *Tijuana: La casa de toda la gente*. Tijuana: Instituto Nacional de Antropología e Historia, 1989.

Hall, Douglas Kent. *The Border: Life on the Line*. New York: Abbeville, 1988.

Harvey, David A. *Social Justice and the City*. London: Edward Arnold, 1973.

Hecho en Latinoamérica: Primero coloquio latinoamericano de fotografía. Mexico City: Consejo Mexicano de Fotografía, 1978.

Hecho en Latinoamérica: Secondo coloquio latinoamericano de fotografía. Mexico City: Consejo Mexicano de Fotografía, 1981.

Hernández, Kelly Lytle. *Bad Mexicans: Race, Empire, and Revolution in the Borderlands*. New York: W. W. Norton, 2022.

———. *Migra! A History of the U.S. Border Patrol*. Berkeley: University of California Press, 2010.

Indych-López, Anna. *Judith F. Baca*. Minneapolis: University of Minnesota Press, 2018.

Iturbide, Graciela. "White Fence." In *White Fence*. Exhibition brochure. Mexico City: Consejo Mexicano de Fotografía (CMF), 1988. Reprinted as "Viajes al centro de la imagen II." *Luna Córnea* 34 (2013): 409–13.

Johnson, Tim, ed. *Zoe Leonard: Al río / To the River*. Texts by C. J. Alvarez, Ariella Azoulay, Cecilia Ballí et al. Luxembourg: Mudam Luxembourg-Musée d'Art Moderne Grand-Duc Jean; Berlin: Hatje Cantz, 2022.

"Latinx Photographer Thalia Gochez on Why Real Life Is Having to Wait." hypebae.com/2023/8/latinx-photographer-thalia-gochez-polaroid-collaboration-interview.

Latorre, Guisela. *Walls of Empowerment: Chicana/o Indigenist Murals of California*. Austin: University of Texas Press, 2008.

Lefebvre, Henri. *The Urban Revolution*. Paris: Gallimard, 1970.

Martin, Patricia Preciado, and Louis Carlos Bernal. *Images and Conversations: Mexican Americans Recall a Southwestern Past*. Tucson: University of Arizona Press, 1983.

Martínez, Eniac, and Eduardo Vázquez Martín. *Mixtecos: Norte Sur*. Mexico City: Editor Grupo Desea, 1994.

Martínez, Oscar J. *Border People: Life and Society in the U.S.-Mexico Borderlands*. Tucson: University of Arizona Press, 1994.

McDonnell, Patrick. "All-Out Border War to Stem Alien Flow Is High-Tech Affair." *Los Angeles Times*, April 13, 1986.

Meiselas, Susan, and Kristen Lubben. *Susan Meiselas: In History*. New York: International Center of Photography, 2008.

Minian, Ana Raquel. *Undocumented Lives: The Untold Story of Mexican Migration*. Cambridge, MA: Harvard University Press, 2018.

Moraga, Cherríe. *Native Country of the Heart*. New York: Farrar, Straus and Giroux, 2019.

Mraz, John. *Looking for Mexico: Modern Visual Culture and National Identity*. Durham, NC: Duke University Press, 2009.

Ortiz Monasterio, Pablo, and Marisa Giménez Cacho. *Testigos y complices*. Mexico City: Martín Casillas, 1982.

Overmyer-Velázquez, Mark, ed. *Beyond La Frontera: The History of Mexico-U.S. Migration*. New York: Oxford University Press, 2011.

Parada, Esther. "C/Overt Ideology: Two Images of Revolution." *Afterimage* 11, no. 8 (March 1984): 7–16.

du Pont, Diana. *Graciela Iturbide: External Encounters, Internal Imaginings.* Exhibition brochure. San Francisco: San Francisco Museum of Modern Art, 1990.

Rael, Ronald. *Borderwall as Architecture: A Manifesto for the US-Mexico Boundary.* Oakland: University of California Press, 2017.

Ramírez, Catherine S. *The Woman in the Zoot Suit: Gender, Nationalism, and the Cultural Politics of Memory.* Durham, NC: Duke University Press, 2009.

Read, Bridget. "Where the Border Ends." *Vogue* (December 7, 2018). vogue.com/projects/13547630/asylum-seekers-waiting-to-enter-the-united-states-in-tijuana.

Rendon, Armendo B. "El Plan Espiritual de Aztlán" (The Spiritual Plan of Aztlán), 1969. In *Takin' It to the Streets: A Sixties Reader,* edited by Alexander Bloom and Wini Breines, 177–80. New York: Oxford University Press, 1995.

Rhodan, Maya, and Emma Talkoff. "We Are Americans, Revisited: The Dreamers, Five Years Later." *Time* (September 4, 2017). time.com/daca-dream-act-jose-antonio-vargas-time-cover-revisited/.

Ribalta, Jorge. *Not Yet: On the Reinvention of Documentary and the Critique of Modernism: Essays and Documents, 1972–1991.* Madrid: Museo Nacional Centro de Arte Reina Sofía, 2015.

Rosas, Alejandro. *Chicano and Latino Artists of Los Angeles.* Los Angeles: Los Angeles Department of Cultural Affairs, 1993.

Rodríguez, Richard T. *Next of Kin: The Family in Chicano/a Cultural Politics.* Durham, NC: Duke University Press, 2009.

Russell, George, et al. "The Policy Dilemma: Trying to Stem the Illegal Tide Congress, Once Again, Prepares to Tackle Reform Proposals." *Time* (July 8, 1985): 50–54.

Salvo, Dana. *Home Altars of Mexico.* Albuquerque: University of New Mexico Press, 1997.

Sekula, Allan. "The Body and the Archive." *October* 39 (1986): 3–64.

———. "Dismantling Modernism, Reinventing Documentary (Notes on the Politics of Representation)." *Massachusetts Review* 19, no. 4 (1978): 859–83.

Sheren, Ila N. *Portable Borders: Performance Art and Politics on the U.S. Frontera since 1984.* Austin: University of Texas Press, 2015.

Sontag, Susan. *On Photography.* New York: Anchor, 1977.

Steiner, Stan. *La Raza: The Mexican Americans.* New York: Harper and Row, 1979.

Tejada, Roberto. *National Camera: Photography and Mexico's Image Environment.* Minneapolis and London: University of Minnesota Press, 2009.

Tibol, Raquel. *Episodios fotográficos.* Mexico City: Libros de Proceso, 1989.

Tichenor, Daniel J. *Dividing Lines: The Politics of Immigration Control in America.* Princeton, NJ: Princeton University Press, 2009.

Tijerina, Reies López. *They Call Me "King Tiger": My Struggle for the Land and Our Rights.* Translated by Jose Angel Gutierrez. Houston: Arte Público, 2000.

Tracey, Caroline. "The Instagram Counter-Archive: Guadalupe Rosales, Graciela Iturbide and Chicana Representation across Borders." *Burlington Magazine* (June 2021). contemporary.burlington.org.uk/journal/journal/the-instagram-counter-archive-guadalupe-rosales-graciela-iturbide-and-chicana-representation-across-borders.

Trillo, Ada. *La Caravana del Diablo: On the Run from the Northern Triangle to America*. The Hague: Komma No Ordinary, 2021.

Valenzuela Arce, José Manuel. "Identidades culturales: Comunidades imaginarias y contingentes." In *Decadencia y auge de las identidades: Cultura nacional, identidad cultural y modernización*, edited by José Manuel Valenzuela Arce, 97–120. 2nd ed. Tijuana: Colegio de la Frontera Norte; Mexico City: Plaza y Valdés, 2000.

———. "Modernidad, postmodernidad y juventud." *Revista Mexicana de Sociología* 53, no. 1 (1991): 167–202.

Vallejo, Linda, et al. *Día de los Muertos: A Cultural Legacy, Past, Present & Future*. Los Angeles: Self-Help Graphics and Art, 2017.

Valverde, Ricardo. "First Communication Meeting Held." *CLP/USA Newsletter* 2 (January 1980).

Vigil, James Diego. "Cholo! The Migratory Origins of Chicano Gangs in Los Angeles." In *Global Gangs*, edited by Jennifer M. Hazan and Dennis Rodgers, 49–64. Minneapolis: University of Minnesota Press, 2014.

Waller, Marguerite. "Border Boda or Divorce Fronterizo?" In *Negotiating Performance: Gender, Sexuality, and Theatricality in Latin/o America*, edited by Diana Taylor and Juan Villegas, 67–87. Durham, NC: Duke University Press, 1994.

Webb, Alex. *Crossings: Photographs from the U.S.-Mexico Border*. New York: Monacelli, 2003.

Weisman, Alan, and Jay Dusard. *La Frontera: The United States Border with Mexico*. Tucson: University of Arizona Press, 1991.

Ybarra-Frausto, Tomás. "*Rasquachismo*: A Chicano Sensibility." In *Chicano Aesthetics: Rasquachismo*, 5–8. Phoenix: MARS, Movimiento Artístico del Río Salado, 1989.

LIST OF PLATES

Laura Aguilar
(American, 1959–2018)

[20] *Three Eagles Flying*, 1990
Gelatin silver print; triptych;
each 61 x 50.8 cm
The Laura Aguilar Trust, Los Angeles

[28] *Yrenia Cervantes*, 1990
Gelatin silver print; 22.9 x 30.5 cm
The Cleveland Museum of Art,
Karl B. Goldfield Trust, 2023.10

Louis Carlos Bernal
(American, 1941–1993)

[1] *Albert y Lynn Morales, Silver City, N.M.*, 1978
Chromogenic print; 23 x 23 cm
Collection of the Center for Creative Photography, University of Arizona,
Gift of the artist, 80.45.1

[23] *Dos Mujeres, Douglas, Arizona*, 1978
Chromogenic print; 22.9 x 22.9 cm
Collection of the Center for Creative Photography, University of Arizona,
Gift of the artist, 80.45.2

[25] *Nanita Mendibles, Barrio Anita*, 1978
Chromogenic print; 23 x 23 cm
Collection of the Center for Creative Photography, University of Arizona,
Gift of the Mexican American Legal Defense and Educational Fund, 82.77.67

[27] *Recamara de Catalina Olomos, Phoenix, Arizona*, 1978
Chromogenic print; 23 x 23 cm
Collection of the Center for Creative Photography, University of Arizona,
Gift of the Mexican American Legal Defense and Educational Fund, 82.77.75

[45] *Sr. Ernesto Villa, Barrio Hollywood*, 1978
Chromogenic print; 22.9 x 22.9 cm
Collection of the Center for Creative Photography, University of Arizona,
Gift of the artist, 80.45.3

[2] *Untitled [Undocumented worker holding Huelga flag at United Farm Workers Demonstration, El Mirage, Arizona]*, negative 1978, printed 2016
Digital Injket Print; 40.6 x 40.6 cm
Collection of the Center for Creative Photography, University of Arizona,
The Louis Carlos Bernal Archive.

[26] *Untitled*, 1979
Chromogenic print; 22.9 x 22.9 cm
Collection of the Center for Creative Photography, University of Arizona, Gift of Morrie Camhi, 97.46.36

[44] *La Reina de Mi Vida*, 1983
Gelatin silver print; 30.3 x 20.4 cm
Collection of the Center for Creative Photography, University of Arizona,
Gift of Helen Unruh, 2010.20.4

[24, 29, 30] Lubbock, Texas, 1987
Color contact sheets; 27.9 x 21.6 cm
Collection of the Center for Creative Photography, University of Arizona,
The Louis Carlos Bernal Archive.

Estudio Teddy Cruz + Fonna Forman

Teddy Cruz
(American, born Guatemala, 1962)

Fonna Forman
(American, born 1968)

[5] *Radicalizing the Local: 60 Miles of Trans-Border Urban Conflict*, 2008
Print from a digital file; dimensions variable
Courtesy of the artists

Miguel Fernández de Castro
(Mexican, born 1986)

[4] *Grammar of Gates / Gramática de las puertas*, 2019
Single-channel video with sound; 20:31 minutes
Courtesy of the artist

Lourdes Grobet
(Mexican, 1940–2022)

[8] *Tijuana: La casa de toda la gente*, 1989
Book; 25 x 25 cm
Collection of Nadiah Rivera Fellah

Graciela Iturbide
(Mexican, born 1942)

[38] *Cholo, East L.A.*, 1986
Gelatin silver print; 32 x 21.5 cm
The J. Paul Getty Museum, Los Angeles, 2007.11.22

[37] *Cholos, Harpys, East L.A.*, negative 1986, printed 1990
Gelatin silver print; 30 x 41.9 cm
The J. Paul Getty Museum, Los Angeles, Gift of Susan Steinhauser and Daniel Greenberg, 2007.65.4

[35] *Cholos, White Fence, East Los Angeles*, 1986
Gelatin silver print; 32 x 21.9 cm
The J. Paul Getty Museum, Los Angeles, Gift of Leslie and Judith Schreyer and Gabri Schreyer-Hoffman in honor of Virginia Heckert, 2017.41

[41] *Cholos, White Fence, East L.A.*, negative 1986, printed 1990s
Gelatin silver print; 30.5 x 45.8 cm.
The J. Paul Getty Museum, Los Angeles, Gift of Susan Steinhauser and Daniel Greenberg, 2007.65.5

[43] *Cristina, White Fence, East L.A.*, negative 1986, printed 1990s
Gelatin silver print; 31.8 x 46.6 cm
The J. Paul Getty Museum, Los Angeles, Gift of Susan Steinhauser and Daniel Greenberg, 2007.65.8

[39] *Maravilla, parque en East L.A.*, 1986
Gelatin silver print; 30.9 x 20.6 cm
The J. Paul Getty Museum, Los Angeles, 2007.11.23

[42] *Rosario y Boo Boo en su casa, East L.A.*, negative 1986, printed 2006
Gelatin silver print; 32.7 x 22 cm
The J. Paul Getty Museum, Los Angeles, 2007.38.1

[40] *Cholos in Tijuana*, negative 1990, printed 2007
Gelatin silver print; 32.1 x 21.6 cm
The J. Paul Getty Museum, Los Angeles, Gift of the artist and Rose Gallery, 2007.24.1

Zoe Leonard
(American, born 1961)

[14] *Al río / To the River*, 2022
Book (two volumes); 23 x 29 cm
Private Collection

Eniac Martínez
(Mexican, 1959–2019),

[7] *Mixtecos: Norte Sur*, 1994
Book; 26 x 26 cm
The Cleveland Museum of Art, Ingalls Library

Susan Meiselas
(American, born 1948)

[13] *2:00 a.m. Arrest and documentation of twelve-year-old boy, Imperial Beach, California*, from the series *Crossings*, 1989
Gelatin silver print; 44.5 x 73.7 cm
Susan Meiselas / Magnum Photos

[12] *7:30 a.m. Arrest of undocumented worker by U.S. Border Patrol in downtown San Diego, CA*, from the series *Crossings*, 1989
Gelatin silver print; 44.5 x 73.7 cm
Susan Meiselas / Magnum Photos

Rael San Fratello

Ronald Rael
(American, born 1971)

Virginia San Fratello
(American, born 1971)

[6] *Teeter-Totter Wall*, 2019
Single-channel video with sound; 4:13 minutes
Courtesy of the artists

George Rodriguez
(American, born 1937)

[36] *East Los Angeles*, negative 1960s, printed 2021
Gelatin silver print; 21.7 x 32.2 cm
The J. Paul Getty Museum, Los Angeles, 2021.31.1

[3] *Delano*, negative 1969, printed 2021
Gelatin silver print; 22.9 x 33.9 cm
The J. Paul Getty Museum, Los Angeles, 2021.31.4

[21] *Chicano Moratorium, Boyle Heights*, negative 1970, printed 2021
Gelatin silver print; 22.3 x 33 cm
The J. Paul Getty Museum, Los Angeles, 2021.31.8

[22] *LAPD Arresting a Chicano Student Protester, Boyle Heights*, negative 1970, printed 2021
Gelatin silver print; 22.1 x 32.8 cm
The J. Paul Getty Museum, Los Angeles, 2021.31.6

Guadalupe Rosales
(American, born 1980)

[34] *home*, 2022
Archival pigment print, aluminum frame; 65.4 x 95.9 x 3.8 cm
Courtesy of the artist and Commonwealth and Council, Los Angeles, Mexico City

Ada Trillo
(Mexican American, born 1976)

[15] *Sleeping by the River, Tecun-Uman Guatemala*, 2020
Digital print; 50.8 x 76.2 cm
The Cleveland Museum of Art, Gift of the artist

Ricardo Valverde
(American, 1946–1998)

[18] *Asco Days of the Dead Performance, Termites y Guerrero*, 1975
Gelatin silver print; 40.6 x 50.8 cm
Collection of Esperanza Valverde and Christopher J. Valverde, Ricardo Valverde Estate

[17] *La Reina—16 de Septiembre*, 1976
Gelatin silver print; 27.9 x 35.6 cm
Collection of Esperanza Valverde and Christopher J. Valverde, Ricardo Valverde Estate

[31] *Jude and Espie at Home*, 1977
Gelatin silver print; 27.9 x 35.6 cm
Collection of Esperanza Valverde and Christopher J. Valverde, Ricardo Valverde Estate

[16] *Whittier Boulevard*, 1979
Gelatin silver print; 18.8 x 27.9 cm
The J. Paul Getty Museum, Los Angeles, 2016.31.2

[19] *Gronk: Día de los Muertos, East LA*, 1981
Gelatin silver print; 40.6 x 50.8 cm
Collection of Esperanza Valverde and Christopher J. Valverde, Ricardo Valverde Estate

[33] *#8*, from the *Walking Series*, 1981
Gelatin silver print; 20.3 x 25.4 cm
Collection of Esperanza Valverde and Christopher J. Valverde, Ricardo Valverde Estate

[32] *Tres Mujeres*, from the *Walking Series*, 1982
Gelatin silver print; 27.9 x 35.6 cm
Collection of Esperanza Valverde and Christopher J. Valverde, Ricardo Valverde Estate

Alex Webb
(American, born 1952)

[11] *Waiting to Cross, Tijuana*, 1992
Digital C-print mounted on 3mm Sintra; 47 x 71.1 cm
Courtesy of the artist

[10] *Nuevo Laredo, Tamaulipas*, 1996
Digital C-print mounted on 3mm Sintra; 63.5 x 96.5 cm
Courtesy of the artist

[9] *Crossings: Photographs from the U.S.-Mexico Border*, 2003
Book; 29.8 x 24.8 cm
The Cleveland Museum of Art, Ingalls Library

LIST OF LENDERS

The Laura Aguilar Trust

Center for Creative Photography, The University of Arizona, Tucson

The Cleveland Museum of Art

The Cleveland Museum of Art, Ingalls Library

Estudio Teddy Cruz + Fonna Forman

Nadiah Rivera Fellah

Miguel Fernández de Castro

The J. Paul Getty Museum

Susan Meiselas / Magnum Photos

Ronald Rael + Virginia San Fratello

Guadalupe Rosales and Commonwealth and Council, Los Angeles, Mexico City

Collection of Esperanza Valverde and Christopher J. Valverde, Ricardo Valverde Estate

Alex Webb

INDEX

Page numbers in *italics* refer to illustrations.

AUTHOR AND CONTRIBUTOR BIOS

AUTHOR

Nadiah Rivera Fellah is curator of contemporary art at the Cleveland Museum of Art.

CONTRIBUTOR

Natalie Scenters-Zapico is a *fronteriza* poet. She is assistant professor in the department of English at the University of South Florida.